Contents

(continued next page)

(continued from previous page)

✝ The New Evangelization

Gather and Go Forth pages at the end of each chapter support faith, knowledge, and the goals of discipleship.

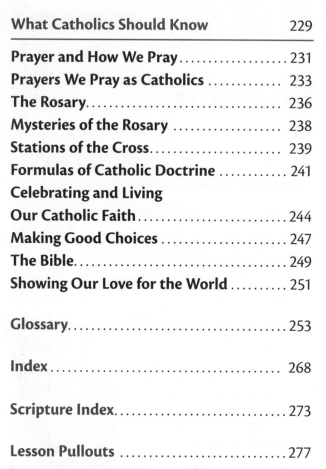

Note to Students

Dear Students,

You are entering the stage of life when you begin to ask some of the hard questions such as: Who am I? How do I know what is right? What is the meaning of life and death? Why do people suffer? These are questions that we can spend our lives trying to answer, especially if we try to do it alone. They are difficult questions, but good questions, because they can help us to arrive at a deeper faith and a deeper understanding of life.

Fortunately, we have Jesus who shows us how to live a life of faith, hope, and love. He is the center of our human existence. Jesus is what he calls himself, the Way, the Truth, and the Life.

Jesus is the Way. Through his words and actions, Jesus shows us what God is like. He shows us that God is always ready to reach out to the lost, to love the forgotten, and to forgive the sinner. Jesus shows us a God of unconditional love. Jesus is the way to his Father, and the way to peace and happiness. He is the way to help us fulfill the purpose of our lives.

Jesus is the Truth. Jesus reveals the Father to us. By his words and actions, he shows us the truth about God. It is a truth that all people seek. By the gift of the Holy Spirit, this truth is continuing to be revealed through the work, teachings, and worship of the Church.

Jesus is the Life. Throughout his life, Jesus promised to those who believe and follow him a share in his divine and eternal life. Jesus gives us this faith and continues to strengthen it through Scripture, prayer, the sacraments, the faith community, and the Church. It is faith that is alive and growing.

". . . I am the way and the truth and the life.
No one comes to the Father except through me.
If you know me, then you will also know my Father."

John 14:6–7

Note to Students

Jesus the Way, the Truth, and the Life is a tool to help you deepen your friendship with Jesus.

This course will help you learn more about how to live and nourish your faith. You will learn about what life was like in Palestine when Jesus lived. By studying the Scriptures, especially the Gospels, you will come to understand how the words and actions of Jesus apply to the lives of believers today. The course will focus on the mystery of our redemption through the death and Resurrection of Jesus. We will examine the Beatitudes as a code of life that can bring us happiness and peace.

An important part of living our faith is taking the time to pray and to celebrate the sacraments. You will learn different ways of praying, such as meditation and the Rosary. The sacraments are sacred moments when we encounter the risen Jesus. Through our participation in them, we are empowered to continue Jesus' mission of love in the world.

Each day may you respond with an open mind and an open heart to Jesus who is *the Way, the Truth, and the Life.*

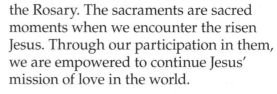
Erasmus.

Lord Jesus, the Way,
   the Truth,
   and the Life,
we pray,
do not let us stray
   from you,
   the Way,
nor distrust you,
   the Truth,
nor rest in anything else but you,
   the Life.
Teach us by the Holy Spirit
   what to do,
what to believe,
and where to take our rest.

Prayer of Erasmus,
16th-century scholar

Jesus Christ the Way

Jesus Shows Us the Way

JESUS WAS fully God and fully man. He wasn't play acting when he wept over the death of his friend Lazarus or lost his patience with the money changers in the Temple. Though subject to human trials and temptations, Jesus showed how to remain close to the Father no matter what befell him. Here are some habits that can help us follow Christ's way:

- *Jesus listened.* Time and again, groups of people came up to Jesus with a challenge. He listened calmly and completely before replying, even to those no one else would bother listening to—children, sinners, and enemies. We are called to do the same.

- *Jesus sought time alone.* Jesus often retreated from the crowds and his disciples to be alone. Purpose and patience come from being able to center ourselves, whether it means taking 10 minutes to meditate at the end of our workday or stepping away for a quick time out whenever our impulse is to rant at someone.

- *Jesus prayed.* Jesus prayed alone and with others, but he prayed often. The prayer he taught us, the Lord's Prayer, is a wonderful prayer to guide us through our day. But Jesus also taught us to pray from the depths of our experience—as he did during his time of agony in the garden of Gethsemane.

- *Jesus had priorities.* Jesus put first things first by taking to heart the words of the ancient prophets: God cares about the poor. He taught us to seek first the Kingdom of God, especially in service to those in most need.

Visit **www.christourlife.com** for more family resources.

God of Love

God says:
It is I, the strength and goodness of fatherhood.
It is I, the wisdom of motherhood.
It is I, the light and grace of holy love.
It is I, the Trinity.
It is I, the unity.
I am the sovereign goodness in all things.
It is I who teach you to love.
It is I who teach you to desire.
It is I who am the lasting fulfillment of all true desires.

— *Julian of Norwich (1342–1420)*

ABOVE: Rembrandt van Rijn, *Ecce Homo*, 17th century, oil on canvas, Dutch.

The Impact of Jesus

Jesus the Son of God

Who Are You?

You are one of God's special gifts to the world. You are unique! You make the world sparkle as no one else ever will. Like a diamond, you have many facets. You have gifts to discover and develop: skills, talents, and qualities. Like a pebble thrown into a pond, your life creates a ripple. What you do affects those around you. You count!

Who you think you are has a lot to do with who you are now and who you will become. That is why it is important to have a true picture of yourself. There is no better time than the present for discovering the mystery and the miracle of *you*.

Check the characteristics found at each level of creation.

	Things	Plants	Animals	People
Exist				
Grow				
Eat/Drink				
Reproduce				
Breathe				
Move				
Have 5 senses				
Think				
Choose				

How do you differ from plants, animals, and the rest of creation? You have been created body and soul by God. God directly created your soul united to your body within your mother.

What makes you human are the powers of your soul: your God-given gifts of intellect (ability to think) and free will (ability to choose and love). These are divine powers. You are made in God's image. You can share God's truth, goodness, and beauty and can some day share God's glory forever. With your intellect you can make decisions and judgments, and you can laugh. With your free will you can love and sacrifice. Because you have this freedom, you are responsible for your acts.

The whole of the material world has been created for your good. That means you are to see that what God has given you as a gift is to be cared for and to be used wisely.

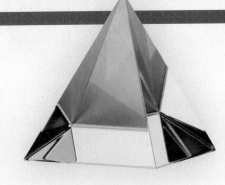

It Is in Your Hands

God has made you a member of a particular family. From your parents, you received certain traits. That is called heredity. You did not choose your inherited traits, such as curly hair or a quick temper. Psychologists think that even your place in the birth order of your family (first, middle, or last) shapes your personality traits. You also live in a particular area. It is your environment. You cannot control many things in your physical environment. However, you can control your personal environment: the friends you choose, the movies you see, the books you read, and the TV programs you watch. More importantly, you can control your reactions and attitudes. You can decide to develop good habits or bad habits.

You are growing in many ways: mentally, physically, spiritually, emotionally, socially, and culturally. You are responsible for what you do with your life. But Jesus is always with you, supporting you, calling you to further growth, and leading you to himself. The key to knowing yourself and becoming the best person you can be is to know Jesus.

Carpenter with Influence

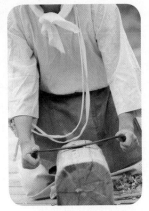

Have you ever heard of Rameses the Great? He was king of the Egyptian empire over 3,000 years ago. During the 67 years of his reign, Rameses was considered a god. He had many large monuments built as tributes to himself. Carved in these monuments were descriptions of his mighty deeds. Now Rameses is just a mummy in a museum and a name in a history book.

Jesus Christ lived about 2,000 years ago in Palestine. He was a Jewish craftsman who spent about the last three years of his life as a traveling preacher. He taught about the Kingdom of God and the laws of love. He healed the sick. To some religious leaders, though, he was a troublemaker. He attracted crowds and associated with everyone, even outcasts. The Romans executed Jesus as a criminal when he was in his early thirties. After his body vanished from his tomb, some of his followers saw him alive, risen from the dead. They began a movement called the Way, now known as Christianity. Today more than a billion people believe that Jesus is God and try to live by his teachings.

Jesus has a powerful and lasting influence because of who he is.

What are the signs of Jesus' influence in the world today?

Who Is Jesus?

A fish holds the answer to this question. During the persecutions of the first Christians, they used the sign of a fish as a secret means of identification. In Greek, each letter of the word *fish (ichthys)* begins a word in the phrase "Jesus Christ, Son of God, Savior."

The Christ

Jesus is the Christ, which means the Messiah, the great leader sent by God. He is the one the prophets foretold and the Jewish people awaited. Jesus, however, was much more than the Israelites expected.

Son of God

With the help of the Holy Spirit, the followers of Jesus came to realize that Jesus was the Son of God. Jesus had often referred to God as "my Father." He even called God *Abba,* a Hebrew word for "Dad."

As Son of God, Jesus was God too. Like the Jewish and Muslim people, Christians believe in one God. What makes us different is our belief in the Trinity. This main Catholic dogma (belief) states there are three Persons in one God: Father, Son, and Holy Spirit. These divine Persons are equal and work together. They have always existed together in a community of love, and they always will.

At a point in time, God the Father sent his only Son to give us **eternal life.** His Son, the Second Person of the Trinity, obeyed the Father and became man, Jesus. Jesus then is a person who has both a divine nature and a human nature. He is completely God and completely human. Jesus is not only Emmanuel, which means "God with us," but he is our brother. The mystery of God becoming human is called the **Incarnation** (*in + carn* = in the flesh). God shared in our humanity so that we could share in divinity.

Since Jesus is God, when we look at Jesus, we know what God is like. God had revealed himself to us before. Creation gives clues about his power and goodness. The Old Testament also tells of God's love through God's words and actions in history. With the Incarnation, God is revealed to us as fully divine and fully human. Jesus said, "The Father and I are one." (John 10:30) We call Jesus the Word from the Father. Despite God's Revelation, God remains a mystery beyond words.

Savior

Jesus is also the Savior. Even his name, Jesus, means "the Lord saves." By his life, especially through the Paschal (Easter) Mystery, Jesus rescued the human race. The Paschal Mystery is the work of salvation accomplished by Jesus Christ through his suffering, Death, Resurrection, and Ascension. By taking our sins upon himself, and dying and rising, Jesus ended the power of sin and death over us. He made it possible for us to have eternal life. At every Eucharist, we, the community of believers, proclaim and celebrate this great mystery of our faith.

❮ Fish, Symbol of Christianity.

Who Is Jesus for You?

Jesus is your personal Savior. He gives you an *identity*. You are not a "nobody." You are a beloved child of God. Jesus gives you a destiny—eternal happiness. He loved you enough to die a painful death for you. He is always ready to save you again from sin.

Our opinions of people change. For instance, Mark Twain said that when he was 14, he thought his father did not know anything. When he was 21, he was surprised how much his father had learned in 7 years! You will realize who Jesus is, gradually. Sometimes one aspect of him will be spotlighted and sometimes another.

Look at the Contents on page iii. What title of Jesus is your favorite now? Why? How did you first come to know about Jesus? Who helped you to know him? How can you come to know him better?

He is the image of the invisible God.
Colossians 1:15

Saint Augustine, retablo (Mexican folk art painting), 19th century.

How Others See Jesus

The Lord has turned all our sunsets into sunrises. (Clement of Alexandria)

We should rather choose to have the whole world against us than to offend Jesus. (Thomas à Kempis)

The Son is the face of the Father, for he who sees the Son sees the Father also. (Saint Ambrose)

Christ is never conquered. (Saint Augustine)

You are the Good Shepherd; look for me, a lamb, and do not overlook me in my wanderings. (Saint Andrew of Crete, eighth century)

Remember

Who is Jesus?

Jesus is the Son of God and the Savior. He is truly God and truly man.

What is the Trinity?

The Trinity is the mystery of one God in three divine Persons: Father, Son, and Holy Spirit.

What is the Incarnation?

The Incarnation is the mystery of God becoming man.

What does the Paschal Mystery include?

The Paschal Mystery includes the suffering, Death, Resurrection, and Ascension of Jesus.

Respond

"Lord Jesus Christ, Son of God, have mercy on me, a sinner." This is the Jesus Prayer, an ancient prayer popular in the Eastern Church. It is recited repeatedly. Try to pray it often.

Reach Out

1. Ask some friends and relatives what Jesus means to them. Invite them to share with you how knowing Jesus calls them to be the best they can be.

2. Create a poster or a flyer that calls attention to one of Jesus' titles. Put it somewhere in your home where it will cause people to reflect on who Jesus is.

3. Teach someone the Jesus Prayer. Commit yourself to pray it regularly.

4. Write an acrostic prayer to Jesus in which each letter in his name or one of his titles starts a line. Example:

Jesus, my God and Savior,

Each day you call me to love and

Serve others. Help me to

Understand what I must do

So that I might be with you forever.

Words to Know

eternal life
Incarnation

Know Yourself Fill in the blanks.

1. Powers that make you in the image of God and above the rest of creation are your

   _____ and _____.

2. Some things you can control in your life are the _____,

   _____, _____, and _____.

3. The key to knowing yourself is to know _____.

A Monogram If each statement is true, write **T**. If it is false, write **F**. Shade in the areas of the puzzle whose numbers correspond to the true statements. When you are finished, you should see a monogram for Christ.

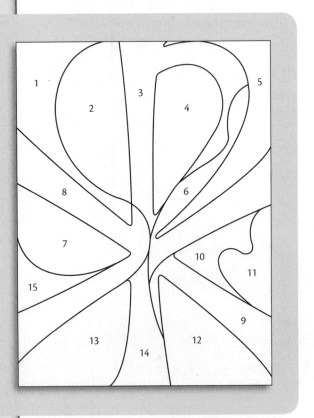

_____ 1. Everyone loved Jesus.

_____ 2. Abba means "holy one."

_____ 3. Christians believe in one God.

_____ 4. God the Father existed before God the Son.

_____ 5. We can fully understand the Trinity by studying Scripture.

_____ 6. The name Jesus means "the Lord saves."

_____ 7. Christians believe there are four Persons in God.

_____ 8. Jesus is both God and man.

_____ 9. The Incarnation is the mystery of God becoming human.

_____ 10. The man Jesus always existed.

_____ 11. God the Son only pretended to be a man.

_____ 12. Jesus' name means "the Word made flesh."

_____ 13. There are two persons in Jesus.

_____ 14. Jesus saved us from sin and death through the Paschal Mystery.

_____ 15. Jesus saved only Christians by his Death.

A Saving Mystery Number the events of the Paschal Mystery in the order they occurred.

_____ Death   _____ Ascension   _____ suffering   _____ Resurrection

When do we celebrate the Paschal Mystery? _____

Gather and Go Forth

Know and Proclaim

As Catholics we believe that Jesus, the Son of God, became incarnate of the Virgin Mary and assumed a human nature while never losing his divine nature. As such he perfectly expresses what it means for us to love God the Father and one another.

As Catholics we gather to celebrate the sacraments and listen to God's Word in the Scriptures.

"Go into the whole world and proclaim the gospel to every creature."

Mark 16:15

We Know Our Faith	We Proclaim Our Faith
God created us in his image in that he gave us a soul. The soul gives us the ability to think and choose and love.	Because everyone is made in God's image, Catholics strive to help people feel welcome and at home (individually and through the ministry of hospitality).
God the Father, Jesus, and the Holy Spirit form the Three Persons of the Trinity. They exist in a community of love.	When Catholics make the Sign of the Cross, they bless themselves in the name of the Father, and the Son, and the Holy Spirit. The Sign of the Cross is a prayer to the Holy Trinity.
Through the Paschal Mystery—the suffering, Death, Resurrection, and Ascension of Christ—Jesus made it possible for us to have eternal life.	When Catholics celebrate the Eucharist, they proclaim and celebrate the great mystery of faith: the suffering, Death, Resurrection, and Ascension of Jesus.

Test Your Catholic Knowledge

Fill in the circle that best completes the sentence.

The Three Persons in one God are:

◯ Jesus, Mary, and Joseph.

◯ priest, prophet, and king.

◯ Father, Son, and Holy Spirit.

◯ saints, angels, and apostles.

A Catholic to Know

The name *Lucy* means "light" and, as such, Saint Lucy is the patron saint of those who are blind or visually impaired. Despite her name, Lucy lived during the dark days of Christian persecution in the Roman Empire in the 300s. Few facts are known about Saint Lucy, except that she lived in Syracuse, a city on the eastern coast of the Italian island of Sicily. She vowed her life in service to Christ, and she lost it in defense of her faith. The fact that she is still mentioned in prayers during the Mass indicates the great respect the Church has for her. Saint Lucy is remembered each year on December 13 for shining a light of courage and inspiration for countless others to follow.

Saint Lucy

Witness and Share

These sentences describe what Catholics believe. Listen carefully as they are read. Ask yourself, "How strong are my Catholic beliefs?"

My Way to Faith

- I reflect God's image by respecting myself and others.

- I proclaim the mystery of faith reverently during the Mass.

- I pray the Sign of the Cross frequently as a prayer to the Holy Trinity.

- I believe Jesus is my personal Savior.

- I see the world as a gift from God, and I need to care for it and use it wisely.

- I believe that Jesus, the Son of God, assumed a human nature while never losing his divine nature. As a Divine Person, he is true God and true man.

Share Your Faith

Think about what you know about Jesus. What more would you like to know about him? Who is he? What does he mean to you? Write your ideas in your own words on the lines. Invite a trusted adult—relative, teacher, or priest—to talk with you more about his or her relationship with Jesus.

_____

_____

_____

_____

Friendship with Jesus

Jesus the Son of Man

Jesus, Fully Human

Suppose you are a brilliant scientist. In your laboratory, you are trying to design a robot that acts like a human being. What characteristics must your robot have to resemble a real person? (Hint: Think about what makes *you* human.)

Jesus sometimes referred to himself as the Son of Man. In one sense, this title means a human being. Jesus had all the traits in your list. He was like us in all things except sin. He breathed air, ate food, laughed, and got tired. He knew love, sadness, disappointment, and fear. He faced difficult decisions and had to live with the consequences of his choices. Like us, he learned and he suffered and died. He was not just pretending to be human. Amazing as it sounds, God the Son really became a man named Jesus.

Since Jesus is God, there is no evil in him. As a perfect person, Jesus reveals to us what we can be. He is our model for being human. Anyone who wants to lead a rich, full life has only to follow in his footsteps. To be like Jesus is not as impossible as it seems because God calls us to faith in him and empowers us through grace.

Someone You Can Trust!

When you are learning a new language, there are many words you do not recognize at first. You spend a lot of time looking them up in a dictionary until you become more familiar with the language. Faith is somewhat like being able to recognize those words. It is a supernatural power and a *gift*. Not everyone sees Jesus for who he is. Sometimes it requires a little help from others.

That Jesus lived is certain. Some early writings refer to him. That Jesus is God in the flesh, however, is a matter of faith. Faith is believing and trusting when you do not completely understand. Faith in Jesus is based on Scripture and Tradition. Those are two ways that God reveals himself, but they form a single "deposit of faith." Scripture is the Word of God, the written testimony of the faith of the early Church. Tradition is the truths handed down by the Church from generation to generation, from the time of the apostles. It includes teachings, liturgy, writings, and the lives of Christians.

Having faith in Jesus and being committed to him is a lifelong challenge. You can even expect to lose sight of Jesus at times. You can remain strong in the Christian faith by staying in touch with Scripture, Tradition, and faith-filled people. The sacraments are the special means Jesus has given to us to keep in touch. When we celebrate the sacraments, we receive the grace of the Holy Spirit that keeps us in a close relationship with Jesus. You and he will be special friends.

Friends, a Human Need

One of the most important things in your life right now is your friends. People need friends at every point in their lives. Having friends is a wonderful and necessary part of being human. You may have friendly relationships with many people, but have only a few deep and lasting relationships. A true friend is a gift from God.

What Is a Friend?

Read these definitions of a friend. Then write your own definition.

Friend

1. A person whom one knows well and is fond of. (dictionary definition)

2. A friend is someone who knows everything about you and still accepts you. (Saint Augustine)

3. A friend is someone who will always help you and stay with you no matter what happens. (junior high student)

4. A friend

   _____

   _____

   _____

   _____

The Real Thing

In true friendship, people help each other to become the best they can be. If you usually get into trouble when you are with certain people, they are not true friends. Friends do not lead each other to be selfish, unkind, disobedient, or dishonest. Instead they support each other in choosing good and avoiding evil, even when evil "looks like fun" and "everybody else is doing it." Friends help each other overcome temptation and habits of sin.

Friendship is not always easy. Sometimes you or your friends may be selfish or bossy. You or they may reveal a secret or not do a fair share of a job. You can be a bad influence on each other in a way that damages your relationship. When you fail to be real friends, you need to repair the damage in order to keep building your friendship. How?

Jesus' Friends

Jesus had friends. He was popular and attracted many people, young and old. Of

True Blue Friends

Discuss or role-play situations that challenge friendships such as these.

Jean's family has an extra ticket for the world premier of a movie. Jean invited Linda, her best friend. Linda has a gymnastics meet that same night. She has a commitment to her team, but Jean will be disappointed if she says no. What are Linda's options? Which choice do you think is better? How can Jean help Linda make her decision?

Miguel and Sam have been friends since third grade. They have always enjoyed playing tennis together. This year Miguel made the school track team. Whenever Sam wants to play tennis, Miguel is busy. Sam and Miguel still want to be friends. What can they do? Can friends be involved in different activities and still remain close?

these, several became his closest friends. From the twelve apostles, he singled out Peter, James, and John to share special events with him. He loved Lazarus and his sisters, Martha and Mary. When Lazarus died, Jesus felt so bad that he cried. Mary Magdalene was another friend. She stayed with Jesus through the Crucifixion, and she was the first one he appeared to after the Resurrection.

Invitation to Joy

Look, I am standing at the door, knocking. If one of you hears me calling and opens the door, I will come in to share a meal at that person's side.

Adapted from
Book of Revelation 3:20

Jesus invites you to friendship. He knocks at the door of your life, a door that you alone can open. You are free to open it or not. Jesus loves you and wants you to be happy. He wants you to know the joy that comes to those who walk through life with him. With Jesus at your side, you can be at peace even when you suffer.

You saw that Jesus' title Son of Man can refer to his being human. It can also refer to his Second Coming. In the Book of Daniel, the Son of Man is someone who comes in glory at the end of the world.

Jesus would like you, his friend, to share his glory, to spend an eternity of happiness with him, his Father, and the Holy Spirit. Will you enter into friendship with him? Will you feast with him at the banquet of heaven?

The Ultimate Test

Like all friendships, friendship with Jesus has its responsibilities. Jesus asks a great deal of you. Read John 15:12–17 in which Jesus speaks to you about being friends. Think about his words and complete these statements:

1. Jesus said that the greatest love a person can have for a friend is: _____

2. Jesus said we are his friends if we do what he commands, namely, _____

_____

3. When I act as Jesus' friend, I know I can count on his Father's help, for Jesus said

_____

_____

4. Add two endings to the following statement. Then rank all of them, using number 1 for the most difficult.

It is not always easy to carry out Jesus' command. I find it difficult to

_____ help with work at home.

_____ listen when adults talk.

_____ be kind when others do not play well in a game.

_____ be happy when someone gets what I want.

_____ _____

_____ _____

Growing in Friendship

Being Jesus' friend is more than knowing about him. It is knowing him personally. Luke 10:38–42 describes a visit Jesus made to Martha and Mary. While Martha prepared the meal, Mary spent time with Jesus. When Martha complained that Mary was not helping her, Jesus told her that Mary had chosen the better part.

As Jesus' friend, you are not only to serve him, but you are also to spend time with him. This is the only way you will get to know him. Do you see yourself more like Martha or Mary at this time?

> You are my friends if you do what I command you.
>
> John 15:14

A Moment with Jesus

Have you ever stopped to think what it really means to have Jesus as a friend? Take a moment and silently read the Scripture above. Pause and reflect on ways you can nurture your friendship with Jesus. Thank Jesus for his presence in your life.

Tips for Reflection Notebook Writers

1. Use the time you set aside for writing to do only reflective writing.

2. Be honest with the Lord and with yourself. Write how you really think and feel.

3. Be willing to share anything with the Lord. The Holy Spirit will help you choose what to write.

4. Listen to the Lord. He will speak to you through his Word, through other people, through events of your day, or through your own thoughts.

5. Keep your notebook private. Do not show it to others. Write to God alone. You may not feel totally free if you think someone else might read your reflections.

6. Make your notebook special and keep it neat, but do not worry too much about spelling and punctuation.

7. Reread your notebook every now and then to see how God has spoken to you and has been acting in your life.

Keeping in Touch: A Reflection Notebook

The time you spend with Jesus is prayer time. A good way to enrich your prayer time is to keep a reflection notebook. It is a book you use to write about yourself and your relationship with the Lord. You can write anything you want to say to God. You can tell God what you think and how you feel. You can share your joys and sorrows. You can thank God for gifts and graces. You can praise God and ask forgiveness. You can ask questions. What you write to God becomes your prayer. Sometimes you might even write a response God might make to you.

Your reflection notebook can be a real treasure. When you reread it, you will come to know yourself better. You will be reminded of God's great love for you and realize how God is working in your life. Best of all, a reflection notebook is a way to deepen your love for your friend Jesus.

2 Summary

Remember

What is faith?

Faith is a gift from God to believe and trust when we do not understand.

How does God reveal himself?

God reveals himself in Scripture and Tradition.

What is Scripture?

Scripture is the Word of God in the Bible. It is the written testimony of faith of the early Church.

What is Tradition?

Tradition is the Revelation of God through beliefs handed down by the Church from the time of the apostles.

What command of Jesus will you follow if you are his friend?

You will follow his command to "love one another as I love you." (John 15:12)

Jesus with Friends Mary and Martha, mosaic, Franciscan Church, Bethany, El-Azariya, Israel.

Respond

Find a blank book or a spiral notebook to use for your reflection notebook. Decorate it if you wish. Decide on a regular time when you will write in your reflection notebook.

Reach Out

1. Thank God for the true friends in your life. Do something special for one of them.

2. Write in your reflection notebook an explanation of why Jesus is a good best friend.

3. List reasons why you are a good friend. You might ask your friends for suggestions.

4. Make a list of five ways to make friends and five ways to lose friends.

5. Use one of the following prayer starters each day this week. Write your conversation in your reflection notebook.

- Tell Jesus about the beautiful things you saw today.

- Tell Jesus how you feel today and why.

- Talk to Jesus about something that you heard or saw today that made you sad.

- Talk to Jesus about gifts God has given you and how you can share them.

- Think about one wonderful person. Thank God for creating that person.

- Did you see a person who was lonely or hurting? Ask Jesus to show you how you could help.

Seeing Double   Complete these statements with the missing pair of words.

1. Jesus was both G _od_ and m _an_ .

2. Faith is b _elieve_ and t _rust_ when we do not understand.

3. God reveals himself in T _radition_ and S _cripture_ .

4. Two of Jesus' friends were the sisters M _ary_ and M _artha_ .

5. As Jesus' friends, we are to s _erve_ him and s _pend_ time with him.

The Right Choice   Circle the item that matches each description.

1. Title of Jesus that can refer to his Second Coming   God the Son   ⟨Son of Man⟩

2. The written testimony of the faith of the early Church   ⟨Scripture⟩   Tradition

3. One thing Jesus did not have in common with us   pain   ⟨sin⟩

4. The sign that we are friends with Jesus   ⟨love⟩   good luck

5. Truths handed down from the apostles by teachings, liturgy, writings, and example   Scripture   ⟨Tradition⟩

True or False   Write T if each statement is true or F if it is false.

_T_   1. True friends help each other choose good and avoid evil.

_F_   2. Jesus is not a good model for us because he was God.

_T_   3. Faith is a gift.

_F_   4. Jesus never cried.

_T_   5. You can know Jesus better through prayer and reflective writing.

Gather and Go Forth

Know and Proclaim

As Catholics, we believe that Jesus reveals to us the fullness of God's love at work in our world.

We Know Our Faith	We Proclaim Our Faith
Faith in Jesus is a gift from God. It is faith that allows us to believe that Jesus is God in the flesh.	As Catholics, we deepen our relationship with God by going to Mass on Sundays and going on retreats.
Scripture is the Word of God, the written testimony of the faith of the early Church.	Many Catholics read the Bible every day. The Church in the liturgy provides daily Scripture readings for Catholics to read and pray.
Tradition holds the truths of the Church that have been handed down from generation to generation, beginning with the apostles.	Catholics treasure many traditional prayers, such as the Lord's Prayer and the Hail Mary. Traditional prayers help unite the Church with a common way of talking to God.

Test Your Catholic Knowledge

Fill in the circle that best answers the question.

What two things form the single "deposit of faith" on which our faith in Jesus is built?

○ the Crucifixion and Resurrection

○ the sacraments and grace

○ Scripture and Tradition

○ prayer and liturgy

We are invited into friendship with the living God. As Jesus' disciples, he shares with us everything God the Father told him. With Jesus, we walk toward God.

"I have called you friends, because I have told you everything I have heard from my Father."

John 15:15

A Catholic to Know

Martin was a peacemaker as a boy, a soldier, and a bishop in the 300s. At age 15, he refused to fight in the Roman army and was taken away in chains. As a soldier, he cut his cloak to give half to a beggar suffering in the cold. That same night he dreamed of Jesus dressed in the beggar's portion of the cloak and, by the next morning, he chose to be baptized. Being both a Christian and a soldier did not appeal to Martin. He refused to fight and was thrown in prison but was soon released. Martin was free to give his life to follow Christ and in 372 he became bishop of Tours, France. As bishop, Martin opposed violence against heretics, despite being beaten for speaking the truth. We remember Saint Martin of Tours as a peacemaker for Christ on November 11.

Saint Martin of Tours

Witness and Share

These sentences describe what Catholics believe. Listen carefully as they are read. Ask yourself, "How strong are my Catholic beliefs?"

My Way to Faith

- I believe that God gives me the grace to be like Jesus.

- I support my friends by helping them make good choices.

- I pray using traditional Catholic prayers.

- I spend time alone with Jesus.

- I honor sacramental objects in my home, such as sacred statues, candles, medals, and rosaries.

Share Your Faith

Jesus asks you to be his disciple. How do you respond? What do you do that shows you are a disciple? Write your ideas in your own words on the lines. Invite a trusted family member or a friend to tell you about how he or she responds to Jesus' call to discipleship.

_____

_____

_____

_____

Scripture: A Portrait of Jesus

Jesus the Messiah

Sharing the Good News

About 30 years after Jesus' Death, this conversation might have taken place one day after the celebration of the Eucharist.

Mark: Peter was really moved while he was telling about Jesus forgiving that woman. I thought I saw tears in his eyes when he said, "She is forgiven much because she loved much."

Judith: I had never heard that story.

Stephen: I had. Jesus told everyone that, in memory of her, wherever the gospel would be preached, people would be told what she had done.

Mark: We are really lucky to hear about Jesus from the people who knew him. Our grand-children won't hear firsthand accounts.

Judith: Right. The apostles won't be with us forever. James has already been killed.

Stephen: I used to think that Jesus was return-ing to earth soon. Now I realize it might be years before his Second Coming. Someone should write down for future generations what he said and did.

Mark: I know a Christian who has written a collection of sayings of Jesus.

Stephen: Just think. If we had a record of Jesus' life, the Good News would spread through-out the empire.

Judith: And people interested in joining us could study what he has written.

Mark: I'd love to put together such a document. Excuse me. I'm going to talk to Peter.

Saint Mark Writing His Gospel. ❯

The New Testament

All of the books that form the New Testament were written by about A.D. 125. They testify to the life, Death, and Resurrection of Jesus. They tell us that Jesus, the Son of God, is the Messiah, the Savior that the people of the Old Testament longed for. Most exciting, they proclaim that Jesus is our risen Lord and is alive in our lives today.

By the Numbers

Use the list of the books in your Bible to complete this outline of the New Testament. Fill in the name and number of each type of book.

Number	Name
	G
	A of the A
	L (E)
	B of R
TOTAL #:	

Gospels: Knowing About Jesus

The word *gospel* means "good news." The Gospels are four accounts of the life and teachings of Jesus. They are documents of faith. According to John 20:31, they were written "that you may [come to] believe that Jesus is the Messiah, the Son of God, and that through this belief you may have life in his name." John's Gospel ends:

> There are also many other things that Jesus did, but if these were to be described individually, I do not think the whole world would contain the books that would be written.
>
> John 21:25

The Gospels were not meant to be biographies. They are more like portraits. Each Gospel writer chose incidents and shaped what he wrote to present what he considered was most important to know about Jesus. In addition, each writer directed his message about the risen Lord to members of his local Christian community. That is why some of the stories in the Gospels are told in a different way. The Gospels all proclaim the same news: *Jesus is the Messiah, the Son of God, who revealed the Father's love for us and saved us.*

Who Is This Jesus?

He said

- I am the way and the truth and the life. (John 14:6)
- I am with you always, . . . (Matthew 28:20)
- I am the bread of life. (John 6:48)
- Follow me. (Luke 5:27)
- [You] hypocrites . . . (Matthew 15:7)
- Young man, I tell you, arise! (Luke 7:14)
- This is my body, . . . (Luke 22:19)
- Whoever has seen me has seen the Father. (John 14:9)

He felt

- grief (John 11:35)
- love (Mark 10:21)
- anger (John 2:13–17)
- gentleness (Luke 19:5)

- sympathy (Matthew 9:18–19)
- affection (Mark 6:30–31)
- frustration (Luke 13:34)
- compassion (Matthew 15:32–38)

He did

- die on a cross (John 10:14–18)
- feed the hungry (Matthew 15:32–38)
- curse a fig tree (Matthew 21:18–22)
- make breakfast (John 21:1–14)
- change water into wine (John 2:1–11)
- go to a wedding (John 2:1–2)
- pray all night (Luke 6:12)
- eat with sinners (Mark 2:13–17)

What kind of person would say, feel, and do such things?

Although we are not certain who wrote the Gospels, Tradition gives the credit to Matthew, Mark, Luke, and John. These men are called the **Evangelists,** which means "proclaimers of the Good News." The Gospel of Mark was probably the first to be written. The writers of the Gospels of Matthew and Luke most likely drew their material from Mark and from another source that biblical scholars call "Q." Because the Gospels of Mark, Matthew, and Luke are so much alike, they are called **synoptic.** *Synoptic* means "same view." John's Gospel, the last to be written, has the style of a deep, religious poem and contains discourses (long speeches) and stories not found in the other Gospels.

The Gospels were written after Jesus sent the Holy Spirit. As Jesus had promised, the Spirit instructed the apostles and reminded them of all Jesus had taught. With the help of the Holy Spirit, the writers of the Gospels understood Jesus better than the people who knew him when he was living on earth. Through the help of the same Holy Spirit, Jesus is alive for us today. The Holy Spirit continues to be with the Church that Jesus founded, enlightening us so we may know the meaning of Scripture. Did you ever wish that you were alive when Jesus was so you could know him better? Actually, because of the Gospels, we probably understand Jesus more than his friends and neighbors did.

A Moment with Jesus

Each of the Evangelists—Mark, Matthew, Luke, and John—paint a unique portrait of Jesus in a way that their readers will understand him more easily.

Take a moment now to silently read the Portrait of Jesus in the table below. Then pause and think about which descriptions of Jesus are important to highlight for people today. Ask Jesus to help you proclaim the Good News through your words and actions.

	MARK A.D. 63–70	MATTHEW A.D. 80–100	LUKE A.D. 70–90	JOHN A.D. 90–100
Traditional Evangelist	Mark, companion of Peter	Matthew, apostle	Luke, Greek doctor, Gentile, companion of Paul	John, apostle
Symbol from the Opening	Lion (John's voice in the wilderness)	Man (the human ancestry of Christ)	Ox (Zechariah offering sacrifice)	Eagle (the Divine Word, thoughts soaring above Earth)
Main Audience	Persecuted Christians	Jewish converts	Gentile (non-Jewish) Christians	Christians defending their faith
Characteristics	Short, fast-moving	Quotations from Hebrew Scriptures Five sermons	Infancy stories Warm, human portraits	Poetic, symbols Reflective discourses
Portrait of Jesus	Man of action Man of suffering	Teacher New Moses	Savior and friend of all: sinners, the poor, women, Samaritans	Son of God Giver of life

Gospels: Knowing Jesus

God is the author of the Bible. However, he did not dictate the words to the Evangelists and other Scripture writers. God inspired all the books in the Bible. Inspiration is the action of God that moves people to communicate what God wants made known, using their own background, culture, language, and style. Inspiration makes the Gospels the Word of God. The Gospels, then, do not only help us know about Jesus. They help us know him personally because they are his all-powerful, living Word. Whenever we read Scripture, we meet God, and God speaks to us.

How are the Gospels honored at Mass?

_____

_____

_____

_____

_____

Other Inspired Books

In the Acts of the Apostles, Luke tells the story of the early Church. It begins with the

The Evangelists Luke and John.

Ascension of Jesus and continues with the coming of the Holy Spirit on Pentecost. The story tells how the first Christian communities were formed. Peter is the hero in the first part of the Acts of the Apostles. His first sermon results in the conversion of about 3,000 people. Through the intercession of Peter, some of the first miracles are performed. Peter recognizes that the Holy Spirit is calling the Church to move beyond the boundaries of the Jewish people and to proclaim the Gospel to the world.

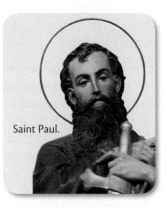

Saint Paul.

The apostle Paul is introduced as a persecutor of Christians. Through the direct intervention of Jesus, Paul is converted and becomes the greatest missionary in the early Church. While on his missionary journeys, Paul establishes Christian communities throughout the area around the northern Mediterranean Sea. In the final chapter of the Acts of the Apostles, although Paul is a prisoner in the city of Rome, he continues to proclaim the Gospel.

Next in the Bible are the letters, or epistles. Although they appear after the Acts of the Apostles in the New Testament, most of the letters were written before the Gospels. Most of the letters are from Paul, a man who never met Jesus, except as the risen Lord. There are also letters attributed to Peter, James, John, and Jude. Those letters tell us of the issues the early Church had to face as the people explored what it meant to be Christian in the Roman world.

The last book of the Bible is the Book of Revelation. It is a strange and difficult book to understand because the symbols it uses are generally unfamiliar to us. Written during a time of persecution, the Book of Revelation encourages Christians to accept the Cross for God who has already triumphed in Jesus.

Remember

What is the Gospel?

The Gospel is the Good News that Jesus' life, Death, and Resurrection have freed us from the power of sin and death.

What is inspiration?

Inspiration is the action of God that directs people to write what he wants made known through their own language and style.

What is the New Testament?

The New Testament consists of 27 books, arranged according to the kind of writing (Gospels, Acts of the Apostles, Letters, Book of Revelation).

Respond

Meet Jesus every day through his Word in the Bible. Assemble the Scripture booklet in the back of this book. Use it to know Jesus better.

Reach Out

1. Read Philippians 3:7–9 to find out how Saint Paul describes what Jesus means to him. Then answer these questions to yourself:
   - How much does Jesus mean to me?
   - Do I treasure Jesus' friendship enough to spend time with him every day?
   - How would I rate my own openness to Jesus?
   - What will I do to know Jesus better?

2. Interview three teenagers or adults who seem to have a strong friendship with Jesus. Ask them to share how Jesus reveals himself to them in their daily lives.

3. Inquire about the process of becoming a lector in your parish. Reflect on whether you might be called to be a lector and proclaim the Word of God in your Christian community.

4. Think of something Jesus said or did. Write it in your reflection notebook. That statement is Jesus' message to you. He is telling you something about himself. He wants its meaning to grow in your heart and move you to love him more.

Write about Jesus' message, including some of these ideas:
   - What it means to you
   - How it makes you feel about yourself
   - How you think Jesus would like you to respond
   - Something you will do to respond
   - Your thanks that Jesus has spoken to you.

Words to Know

Evangelist   synoptic

Meet the Gospels   Write the letter of the Gospel being described.

a–Matthew   b–Mark   c–Luke   d–John

___d___   1.   The last Gospel

___b___   2.   Probably the first Gospel written

___a___   3.   For Jewish converts

___d___   4.   Is poetic and has discourses

___c___   5.   Shows Jesus as friend to all, including sinners and women

___b___   6.   Is short and fast-moving

___b___   7.   The Synoptic Gospels

___d___   8.   Proclaims Jesus as the Messiah, the Son of God who saved us

___c___   9.   Especially for Gentiles

___d___   10. The symbol of its Evangelist is an eagle.

❮ Matthew.

Scripture Mount   Write the missing word or number in each sentence on the corresponding blanks of the pyramid below.

1.   Most of the New Testament books were probably written by the end of the _____st century A.D.

2.   The Old Testament has 46 books; the New Testament has _____ books.

3.   _____ is the author of the Bible.

4.   The _____ of the Apostles is the book that tells the story of the early Church.

5.   The Gospels are not biographies, but documents of _____.

6.   _____ means "good news."

7.   Most _____ were written before the Gospels and apply Jesus' message to life.

8.   The first three Gospels are so similar they are called _____.

9.   A long speech in a Gospel is a _____.

10. The last book in the Bible, a symbolic book about the end of the world, is the Apocalypse or the Book of _____.

11. The Gospels' writers are the _____.

12. _____ is the action of God that moves people to communicate what God wants made known.

1. __
2. __ __ __
3. __ __ __ __ __
4. __ __ __ __ __ __
5. __ __ __ __ __ __ __
6. __ __ __ __ __ __ __ __
7. __ __ __ __ __ __ __ __ __
8. __ __ __ __ __ __ __ __ __ __
9. __ __ __ __ __ __ __ __ __ __ __
10. __ __ __ __ __ __ __ __ __ __ __ __
11. __ __ __ __ __ __ __ __ __ __ __ __ __
12. __ __ __ __ __ __ __ __ __ __ __ __ __ __

Gather and Go Forth

CHAPTER 3

Know and Proclaim

As Catholics, we learn the Good News of the Gospels and share it with the world.

We Know Our Faith	We Proclaim Our Faith
The Gospels tell us about the life, Death, Resurrection, and teachings of Jesus.	Catholics honor the Gospels by standing at Mass while the Gospel is proclaimed by a priest or deacon and by saying "Praise to you, Lord Jesus Christ" after it is read.
The Gospels were written by four Evangelists—Matthew, Mark, Luke, and John—under the inspiration of the Holy Spirit.	Catholics read, study, and pray with the Gospels to come to know and love Jesus more. Many parishes offer Bible studies to help Catholics know Jesus and understand his message.
The New Testament consists of the Gospels, the Acts of the Apostles, Letters, and the Book of Revelation.	Catholics read the Word of God. Some serve as lectors at Mass, proclaiming the Word of God to the assembly. Many Catholics pray and meditate on the Scriptures.

Jesus came to reveal the mystery of God's saving love. The Gospels reveal the Good News of Jesus. As Catholics, we are inspired by his love to share the Good News with others.

"No one knows the Son except the Father, and no one knows the Father except the Son and anyone to whom the Son wishes to reveal him."

Matthew 11:27

Test Your Catholic Knowledge

Fill in the circle that best completes the sentence.

The Gospels of Matthew, Mark, and Luke are called Synoptic Gospels because:

○ they were written by Jesus' friends.

○ they present similar stories of Jesus' life.

○ they present different stories of Jesus' life.

○ they were all written while Jesus was still alive.

A Catholic to Know

Saint Mark's Gospel is the shortest and oldest of the Gospels. Mark tells the story of Jesus to proclaim Jesus' message of love to the world. Mark wrote to early Christians to give them hope in the face of persecution for their faith. In Mark's view, Jesus was a man of action, and Mark's Gospel calls us to action. According to Mark, it is not enough to profess to believe in Christ without a willingness to live as he did. Mark's Gospel challenged the early Christians to follow Jesus' path to the Cross and to share in his Resurrection. Saint Mark, the earliest Gospel writer, offers the same challenge to Christians today.

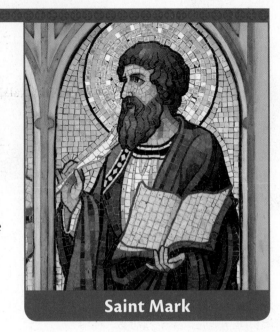

Saint Mark

Witness and Share

These sentences describe what Catholics believe. Listen carefully as they are read. Ask yourself, "How strong are my Catholic beliefs?"

My Way to Faith

- I share the Good News through my words and actions.

- I often hear God speak to me whenever I read or hear Scripture.

- I think about how Jesus lived and what he taught when I'm facing difficult decisions in my own life.

- I would like to learn more about Jesus by participating in a Bible study in my school or parish.

- I believe that Jesus is truly present in the Eucharist.

Share Your Faith

Think about a favorite Gospel story that inspires you to follow Jesus. What does Jesus say or do? What effect do his actions have on those present? Use the story to write your own prayer on the lines below or on a separate piece of paper. Then invite a family member or a friend to share his or her favorite Gospel story.

_____

_____

_____

_____

The World Jesus Lived In

Jesus the Nazarene

The Land Jesus Walked

You probably eat with knives, forks, and spoons, and not your fingers. Your parents will not be choosing a husband or wife for you. Some customs that you would find strange are perfectly normal for people in other times and countries. The way you live, your attitudes, and values are largely determined by the country and time in which you live. What else determines what you are like?

When the Son of God became man, he chose to live 2,000 years ago in a country in the Middle East called Palestine. The United States is more than 230 years old, but consider how life has changed since the time of George Washington. Imagine then the difference between the world that shaped Jesus and your world. Knowing about life during his time will help you understand Jesus and the Gospels.

During Jesus' time, Palestine was as large as Vermont and had three main areas: Galilee in the north, Samaria, and Judea in the south. (To remember the order of **G**alilee, **S**amaria, and Judea, think "**G**od **S**ent **J**esus.") Nazareth, a town in the hills of Galilee, was the place where Jesus grew up. During his public ministry, his home base was Capernaum, a town near the Sea of Galilee. Jesus' life began in Bethlehem and ended in Jerusalem, both in Judea.

Galilee is mountainous and beautiful. The Sea of Galilee (also called Lake Gennesareth) is to

the east, and Mount Hermon is to the north. Although most of Galilee was rural during Jesus' time, major trade routes passed through its large trading cities. Greek and Roman culture were popular in Galilee. Many Galilean Jews were originally of non-Jewish origin. For this reason, Judeans looked down on Galileans.

Samaria was avoided by Jewish people when they traveled. The Samaritans were considered heretics because they had intermarried with foreigners and worshiped in their own temple on Mount Gerizim instead of at the Temple in Jerusalem.

Judea is a dry, hot land. The Dead Sea is to the east, and wilderness is to the south. Jerusalem was the capital city where Israel's kings had lived. It was also the holy city because the Temple was there. Jerusalem is sacred to Jews, Christians, and Muslims.

To the west of Palestine is the Mediterranean Sea. Within Palestine the Jordan River flows south through the Sea of Galilee and into the Dead Sea.

When Jesus lived, towns in Palestine were surrounded by walls. Food and crafts were sold in markets just outside the walls. Every night the city gates were locked, and guards kept watch.

❮ The Western Wall in Jerusalem.

to keep any money they collected beyond their quota.

Some Religious Groups

The **Pharisees** were largely middle-class Jews. They were known for their love of the Torah, or the Law, the first five books of the Bible. Some schools of Pharisees interpreted the Law strictly and added 613 regulations. The Pharisees believed in angels and in our resurrection. The Gospels show Jesus scolding some of them for stressing external observances instead of a spirit of love and worship. The Pharisees, however, were sincerely seeking holiness. They preserved the Jewish religion after Jerusalem was destroyed by Rome in A.D. 70. The scholarly teachers among the Pharisees were called scribes.

The Sadducees were wealthy and powerful political leaders. Most were priests. They worked closely with Rome and, unlike the Pharisees, did not believe in resurrection or in adding to the Law. The Sanhedrin was a group of 71 Jewish men in Judea who served as a supreme council. The chief high priest presided over it. He was not only a spiritual leader but almost a king. Caiaphas was the high priest at the end of Jesus' life, assisted by his father-in-law, Annas.

Zealots were freedom fighters who sometimes used violence to overthrow Rome's control of Palestine. The Essenes were men unhappy with the way Jewish faith was lived. Seeking a pure life, many withdrew to the desert. There they lived in communities, doing penance and waiting for the coming of God.

The Political Scene

When Jesus lived, Palestine was occupied by Rome, which had conquered it in 63 B.C. During Jesus' lifetime, Augustus Caesar and then his stepson, Tiberius Caesar, were the Roman emperors. Herod the Great was king of Palestine until shortly after Jesus' birth. Although he was a great builder and rebuilt the Temple, he is remembered most for his cruelty. He killed many of his family for fear that they would overthrow his rule. After his death, Palestine was divided among his three sons: Archelaus, Herod Antipas, and Philip. Archelaus ruled Judea and Samaria until Augustus replaced him with Roman procurators such as Pontius Pilate, who sentenced Jesus to death. Herod Antipas, whom Jesus called "the fox," ruled Galilee. Philip ruled the region east of Galilee.

In general, Rome respected Jewish religious practices. Jewish men, for instance, did not have to serve in the army because their religion did not permit them to mix with **Gentiles,** or non-Jews. However, the Jewish people resented the presence of Roman troops, Roman laws, and Roman taxes. Jewish men who collected taxes for Rome were the least popular men in town. These tax collectors, also called publicans, were allowed

Augustus Caesar.

Jesus' Religion

Jesus was Jewish. Jewish families prayed many prayers together at home. They prayed before and after eating. Morning and evening they prayed the Shema, the main commandment:

> Hear, O Israel! The LORD is our God, the LORD alone! Therefore, you shall love the LORD, your God, with all your heart, and with all your soul, and with all your strength.

Deuteronomy 6:4–5

A Moment with Jesus

Pause for a moment and silently read the Scripture passage above. Imagine Jesus learning this prayer and praying it each day. Take a moment to reflect on how you express your belief in God each day. Ask Jesus to help you love God with all your heart, soul, and strength.

On entering and leaving a house, Jewish people touched the mezuzah. It was a small case on the right post of a doorway that held a copy of the Shema. At prayer, devout men put a prayer shawl on their heads and strapped small boxes (phylacteries) to their foreheads and arms. These boxes contained the Word of God. People greeted one another by saying *shalom,* which means "peace."

Everyone who was able traveled to the Temple in Jerusalem to observe the three major feasts: Passover, Pentecost, and Tabernacles. The Temple, the symbol of the Jewish faith, was the only place where sacrifices were offered. It was a huge and majestic building. Twenty men were needed to open one of its thirteen gates. Twenty thousand people worked there. During Jesus' time, the Temple was undergoing an expansion ordered by Herod the Great. In

‹ Mezuzah.

A.D. 70, Rome attacked Jerusalem and destroyed the Temple. All that was left standing was an outer western wall that still exists today. At this wall, called the Western Wall, Jewish people pray and grieve over the destruction of the Temple. They insert prayer petitions between the giant stones.

Sabbath, the Lord's Day, was a day of strict rest. Among forbidden activities were tying a rope, putting out a lamp, and walking more than a half mile. Sabbath services were held at local synagogues. These were the centers of prayer, education, and social life in the towns. The scrolls of the Torah were read and preached there.

The Law declared what made a person unclean or unfit for worship. Actions such as touching a sick or dead person and dealing with Gentiles required special prayers, washings, or passage of time before the person became clean.

Maurice Denis, *Jesus Christ, Mary and Joseph,* early 20th century. ›

Daily Life in Palestine

Imagine that you lived in Palestine when Jesus did. Your house is made of clay bricks or stones held together with mud and straw. Its one room has a dirt floor. At night, you sleep on a mat on the dirt floor. Your pillow is a piece of wood or a stone. In hot weather, you climb the outside steps up to the roof to sleep. The roof is made of sticks bound by long grass and covered with earth. In your house are a table, a spinning wheel, and a wooden bowl for measuring grain. Since there are no windows, an olive-oil lamp burns all day on a stand. At the far end of your house, a cave shelters your goat and donkey.

You probably belong to a large family. Your father is a farmer, a craftsman, or a fisherman. He has a beard and large brown eyes. He wears a sleeveless gown covered by a long tunic that is fringed at the bottom and tied with a belt. A white cloth on his head is held in place by a cord. A heavy cloak made of camel hair or goat hair serves him as a coat or a blanket. He leads the family prayers. You and your mother are considered his property.

Your mother cooks outside, grinding grain and baking bread. She wears a decorated tunic and sandals, and she never goes out without a veil over her face. She looks forward to her daily walk to the town well. There she meets and chats with other women before carrying home  her water jug on her head. Your mother is not allowed to know how to read or write, but she memorizes Scripture from the synagogue service.

If you are a boy, you go to synagogue school. There a rabbi teaches you to read and write by studying Scripture. Your father teaches you his trade. If you are a girl, your mother prepares you to be a good wife. You hope to have many sons. Your parents will arrange a marriage for you. You might not see your husband until your wedding day.

You do not attend public entertainment because the Gentiles are there. Your life revolves around prayer and religious celebrations, especially those that mark stages of life. Weddings can last seven days. For funerals, even poor people hire flute players and mourners for a procession to the stone tombs.

You eat twice a day while sitting cross-legged outside on the ground. Instead of a fork or spoon, you use your hands. Besides bread, your meals include honey, spiced foods, cheese, vegetables, fruit, and fish. You seldom have meat or eggs. Water and wine are the usual drinks.

You probably speak Aramaic, but you also know some Hebrew for prayer and perhaps some Greek, which is the language of the land.

❮ James Tissot, *The Presentation of Christ in the Temple,* 1886–1894, watercolor.

Summary

Remember

Who do we believe Jesus of Nazareth is?

> And the Word became flesh
> and made his dwelling among us,
> and we saw his glory,
> the glory as of the Father's only Son,
> full of grace and truth.

John 1:14

Respond

Create this scene in your mind. You are sitting with Jesus on a grassy hillside overlooking the Sea of Galilee. Hundreds of brilliant wildflowers surround you. Before you the blue lake sparkles in the sun. You hear the water lapping against the shore. The hills across the lake are also blue. You feel very comfortable and relaxed next to Jesus.

What would Jesus say to you? What would you say to him? Think about it. Then write your conversation in your reflection notebook.

Reach Out

1. Find out what the Holy Land is like today. Write a report that includes geographical, political, religious, and cultural aspects of the Holy Land.

2. Ask a Jewish person to tell you about his or her religious customs and feasts. You might be able to visit a Jewish temple, or synagogue.

3. Make a relief map of Palestine out of dough and paint it.

4. The Gospel of Mark has Aramaic phrases scattered throughout. Find the meaning of these by looking up the references:

   Talitha koum (Mark 5:41)

   Ephphatha! (Mark 7:34)

   Golgotha (Mark 15:22)

   Eloi, Eloi, lema sabachthani? (Mark 15:34)

5. Research how the Christian religion has been adapted to other cultures.

   Visit a Byzantine Catholic church or other Eastern rite church.

   Attend a liturgy in a parish where the dominant culture is different from yours.

   Ask people about Catholic customs in other countries.

6. Write the story of Jesus' life as if it were set in our country. What if Jesus had been born in our country and was living now? Where would he live? What would his life be like? How would he teach people? How would he die?

Words to Know

Gentiles   Pharisees

Who Am I? Write the letter of the person who fits each description.

1. I work to overthrow Rome, sometimes by violence. _____
2. I am a Roman emperor. _____
3. I seek a pure life in a desert community. _____
4. I believe in interpreting the Law strictly. _____
5. I am a priest who does not believe in resurrection. _____
6. I am a tax collector. _____
7. I am a scholarly teacher among the Pharisees. _____
8. I am despised by Jewish people for not worshiping at the temple in Jerusalem. _____

a. **publican**
b. **Sadducee**
c. **Augustus Caesar**
d. **zealot**
e. **Essene**
f. **Samaritan**
g. **Pharisee**
h. **scribe**
i. **Pontius Pilate**

What Do I Mean? Circle the related word or phrase.

1.	**Sabbath**	day of rest	work day
2.	**shalom**	"Rejoice!"	"Peace!"
3.	**Jerusalem**	holy city	Jesus' birthplace
4.	**Torah**	king	Law
5.	**Shema**	clothing	prayer
6.	**Galilee**	northern region	southern region
7.	**synagogue**	home	church
8.	**Gentile**	non-Jew	priest
9.	**Sanhedrin**	council	army
10.	**mezuzah**	prayer container	prayer shawl

❮ Counterclockwise from top:
Torah scroll bound by wooden rollers,
ancient Roman coin, and Galilee.

Gather and Go Forth

CHAPTER 4

Know and Proclaim

Catholics share a common heritage with the Jewish people.

We Know Our Faith	We Proclaim Our Faith
Jesus was born into a Jewish family in the town of Bethlehem, part of the kingdom of Judea, which was controlled by the Roman Empire.	Catholics have profound respect for Judaism and seek to learn more about its traditions, many of which influence Catholic practice today.
Jesus practiced Jewish religious customs. He went to the Temple in Jerusalem for major feasts.	Catholics go on pilgrimages to holy sites such as cathedrals. This practice echoes Jewish pilgrimages to the Jerusalem Temple in Jesus' day.
The Sabbath is a day of strict rest observed by Jews.	The Sabbath is a day of strict rest observed by Jews. Since Christ rose from the dead on Sunday, the Catholic celebration of the Lord's Day replaces the Sabbath. Catholics keep the Lord's Day holy by going to Mass on Sunday and holy days of obligation and by being mindful of God throughout the day.

Jesus lived in a particular time and place in the history of God's Chosen People. He was a Jewish man and lived according to Jewish laws and customs. His message is, however, for all times, all places, and all people.

While the law was given through Moses, grace and truth came through Jesus Christ.

John 1:17

Test Your Catholic Knowledge

Fill in the circle that best answers the question.

Who was most upset that Jesus taught that a spirit of love and worship was more important than external observations of the Law?

○ the Samaritans

○ the Pharisees

○ the Romans

○ the Essenes

A Catholic to Know

Mary Magdalene has been called the "Apostle to the Apostles." Mary of Magdala, as she was also known, was one of Jesus' first disciples in Galilee. She was present at Jesus' Crucifixion, and when the male disciples fled in fear following Jesus' Death, Mary Magdalene was among the women standing before the empty tomb. She was the first person to witness the risen Christ and the one who proclaimed the Good News of the Resurrection to the twelve apostles. Each year we honor Saint Mary Magdalene's faithful witness to the Paschal Mystery on her feast day, July 22.

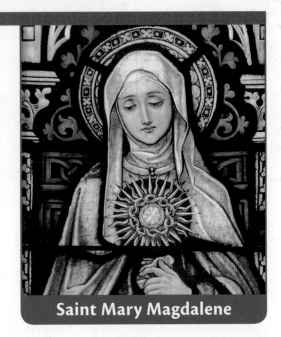

Saint Mary Magdalene

Witness and Share

These sentences describe what Catholics believe. Listen carefully as they are read. Ask yourself, "How strong are my Catholic beliefs?"

My Way to Faith

- I respect people of other faiths in my thoughts or actions.

- I find that offering my day to God each morning helps me to live my faith.

- I keep the Lord's Day holy by attending Mass every Sunday and by being mindful of God.

- I believe it is important to have an awareness of Jewish history and customs so that I can understand Scripture better.

- I value sacred spaces in my home, parish, and larger Catholic community.

Share Your Faith

Think about the world in which you live. What events have affected your life? How do those events affect your faith? Write your ideas in your own words on the lines. Invite a family member or a friend to share how the values and attitudes of today's culture impact his or her life.

_____

_____

_____

_____

The Early Life of Jesus

Jesus the Son of Mary and Joseph

Stories of an Infant God

What does Christmas mean to you?

If Jesus had not died and risen, we would have nothing to celebrate at Christmas. But Jesus did rise, showing himself to be the Son of God, our Savior. That is why we celebrate his birthday. The first Christians, however, did not. The recent astounding events of his Death and Resurrection were uppermost in their minds. As time went on, Christians wondered about Jesus' origins and early life. Soon stories were circulating.

Stories about Jesus' birth and early life are in the Gospels of Matthew and Luke. They are called **Infancy Narratives.** The evangelists wrote them in a way that shows who Jesus was. They present the mystery of his coming through beautiful and miraculous events:

- The Annunciation—Jesus' conception in Mary by the power of the Holy Spirit

- The Visitation—the recognition of his presence by Elizabeth and John

- The Nativity—Jesus' birth

- The Presentation—the offering of Jesus to God in the Temple

Biblical scholars have theories about the Infancy Narratives. For instance, they discuss who the magi were and whether the story is historical or symbolic. It does not matter if there were three kings or not. The Church teaches that the Scriptures contain the truth that is necessary for us to know for our salvation. This is called **inerrancy.** The all-important truth in the Infancy Narratives is that Jesus came to save us.

At Jesus' birth around 4 B.C., there was no video equipment to capture the events. Maybe Mary told Luke the stories of Jesus' birth. Maybe the evangelists added events and symbols to make a point or to fulfill prophecies. What we do know is that the Infancy Narratives are God's Word. They proclaim the meaning of who Jesus is for us.

Mini-Gospels

The Infancy Narratives are known as the "Gospels in miniature" because they tell the same Good News as the whole Gospels. They show all the aspects of Jesus' love. They reveal Jesus' identity, his mission, the role of the Holy Spirit in his life, Jesus' concern for all, his suffering, and his rejection. The main message of the narratives is the same as the Easter message: *Jesus is Lord, the Son of God who saved us.* That message is proclaimed in many ways. As you review the stories, listen for it and for other messages God may be sending you.

An Album of Jesus

Each picture in this album matches a story from the Infancy Narratives. Look up the Scripture citations and read the verses. Then write a title for the picture.

_____
1. Luke 1:26–28

_____
2. Matthew 1:18–25

_____
3. Luke 1:36, 39–56

_____
4. Luke 2:1–20

_____
5. Matthew 2:1–12

_____
6. Matthew 2:13–15

_____
7. Luke 2:22–38

_____
8. Luke 2:41–52

Gospel Truths

The Infancy Narratives contain the following Gospel truths. Think of each story identified above and write its number in front of any truth it conveys. Be ready to explain your answers.

_____ a. Jesus is God, so extraordinary signs accompany his birth.

_____ b. Mary, the Mother of God, is someone special.

_____ c. Jesus is the Messiah.

_____ d. Jesus is sent by the Father.

_____ e. The Holy Spirit acts for our salvation.

_____ f. Jesus is Savior of all people, not only Jewish people.

_____ g. Some people reject Jesus.

_____ h. Jesus suffers.

_____ i. Jesus comes for the poor and the outcast.

Mary, a Listener

The heroine of the Infancy Narratives is Mary, a woman who was always open to God. By her faith, expressed when she answered yes, Mary became the mother of Jesus. Because Jesus is God, Mary is *Theotokos,* or the **Mother of God.** When the Son of God became the Son of Mary, he took the substance of his flesh from her. Jesus bore her features. He lived with her for about 30 years. She made his clothes, cooked his food, and taught him to walk and talk. He took care of her, obeyed her, and loved her. She witnessed his growth, his joys and sorrows, and his prayer. She knew his smile, the touch of his hand, and his thoughts and feelings. Forever he will call her Mother.

Mary listened to God, which led to action. She was prepared to risk all she had for love of God. She responded to Gabriel, "Let it be," *(fiat)* calling herself God's handmaid. She willingly became the Mother of the Redeemer, a dangerous and painful mission. After the Annunciation, Mary did not just sit and think about herself. She went to help Elizabeth. At all times, she cooperated with the work of her Son, even when it meant standing at the foot of the Cross.

Mary's "Let it be" echoed God's "Let it be" that began creation. She made possible the new creation that Christ brought about. As Saint Irenaeus put it, "Mary's obedience helped untie what Eve's disobedience had tied."

Do you *listen* to God speak to you in quiet prayer time? through your parents, teachers, brothers, and sisters? Do you listen to your friends' needs? to calls to share your money or time with the poor? Do you *act?*

It is said that Mary bore Jesus in her heart before she bore him in her womb. How can you be a Christ-bearer today?

_____

_____

We believe that because Mary is the Mother of God, she was given special gifts. These privileges of Mary are Catholic **doctrines.**

- The Immaculate Conception—Mary was never in the state of sin, neither Original Sin, nor personal sin.
- The Virgin Birth—Mary conceived Jesus solely through the power of the Holy Spirit. (We believe she was always a virgin.)
- The Assumption—Mary went to heaven body and soul at the end of her life.

A Modern Mary

After raising four children, Rosemary Koenig felt God calling her to serve others. With little money and at the age of 65 she opened the Shelter of God's Love in Chicago. It was a home for eight people with disabilities like Pam, who is blind; Margie, a young girl with cerebral palsy; and Evelyn, a grandmother who has multiple sclerosis. Each evening after dinner, the community prayed for the world. A few years later, Rosemary started another Shelter where senior citizens could live together. Rosemary trusted God for everything. In surprising ways, the Shelters' needs were met: a van, a computer, an assistant director. Like Mary, Rosemary listened to God and then acted. She let God do great things through her. Rosemary died in 2005 at the age of 92.

Honoring Mary

Throughout the centuries, the Church has honored Mary. The early Church saw her as the new Eve. Eve was disobedient to God; Mary obeyed God with her whole heart and soul.

During the centuries of the Middle Ages, from about 900 to 1500, Mary became even more important to Christians. Europe was going through difficult times with wars and sickness. To the people, Mary was seen as a tender and caring Mother of Mercy and refuge of sinners.

The people felt that they had a special friend in Mary. God chose his mother not from the palaces of kings and queens, but from a quiet, small village. Mary was a young girl from a humble family. She was honored with the title of Queen of Heaven and Refuge of Sinners.

Many cathedrals were built in Europe and named after Mary. She was celebrated in poetry, hymns, prayers, and sermons. Mary's Assumption into heaven was especially celebrated. Since Mary is the Mother of Christ, it was only fitting that after her time on earth she would be assumed body and soul into heaven. There are many examples of appearances Mary has made to help people and to encourage them to pray.

Our Lady of Guadalupe

In 1521 Mary appeared to Juan Diego in Mexico. She told him that she wanted a church built in her honor. When Juan Diego brought her request to his bishop, the bishop asked for a sign. In response to the bishop's request, Mary filled Juan Diego's cloak with roses. When Juan Diego opened the cloak for the bishop, they discovered the beautiful image of Our Lady of Guadalupe on the cloak. This image is still on display in Mexico and is visited by thousands of pilgrims every year. Our Lady of Guadalupe is the Patroness of the Americas.

Our Lady of Lourdes

In 1858 Mary appeared to Bernadette Soubirous, a girl from a poor family in France. Bernadette

St. Bernadette of Lourdes.

received 18 messages from Our Lady in the grotto of Lourdes. Mary proclaimed to Bernadette that she was the Immaculate Conception. The teaching of the Church is that Mary was conceived without Original Sin. Obediently following the instructions of Mary, Bernadette discovered a spring that proved to be a source of miraculous healing. Since that time, millions of people have visited Lourdes. Many continue to visit today to honor Mary and to pray for healing.

Under the title of the Immaculate Conception, Mary is also the Patroness of the United States. She continues to intercede for us, her children, today.

Our Lady of Guadalupe.

A Moment with Jesus

God chose Mary, a young girl from a poor family, to be the Mother of God. Pause and think about this for a moment.

Her yes to God is an example for us. Take a moment and ask Jesus to show you how you are being called to say yes to God at this time in your life. Thank Jesus for the gift of Mary to the Church.

Remember

What do the Infancy Narratives proclaim?

The Infancy Narratives proclaim the Good News that Jesus is the Son of God and Savior of the world.

What privileges did God give Mary because she was the Mother of God?

Mary's privileges are the Immaculate Conception, the Virgin Birth, and the Assumption.

Why did Jesus come?

Jesus said, "I came so that they might have life and have it more abundantly." (John 10:10)

Respond

What might God be saying to you through a person or symbol in the Infancy Narratives? Spend some time in quiet reflection, then write your thoughts in your reflection notebook. (Ideas: Mary, star, Joseph, angel's song, Elizabeth, Magi, innkeeper, manger, shepherd, Simeon, holy innocents, Anna.)

Reach Out

1. Find out how the celebration of Christmas by your family came to be the way you know it.

2. Research the Christmas customs of another country and culture. Look for information about food, decorations, activities, and music.

3. Share the Good News of the story of Christmas:
    - Tell a child the story.
    - Design a Christmas card based on the Gospel story of Christmas. Give it to someone special.
    - Make a mural of the events surrounding Jesus' birth or a mobile of Christmas symbols. Put your mural or mobile where it can be seen.
    - Prepare a creative presentation to tell the Christmas story.

4. Ask at least 12 people of different ages what Christmas means to them, and write down their responses.

5. Pray Mary's Magnificat in Luke 1:46–55. Notice that Mary praises how God treats the poor and lowly.

6. Use a liturgical calendar or a reference book to find the dates we celebrate the Annunciation; the Visitation; the Nativity; the Presentation; the Epiphany; the Solemnity of Mary, Mother of God; and the feasts of the Holy Innocents and the Holy Family.

Words to Know

doctrine

inerrancy

Infancy Narratives

Mother of God

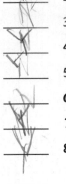

The Honest Truth Write Y for yes or N for no in answer to each question.

Y **1.** Was Easter more important than Christmas to the early Christians?

N **2.** Does the Gospel of John include Infancy Narratives?

3. Are all of the details in the Infancy Narratives historically true?

4. Do the Infancy Narratives proclaim that Jesus is Lord, the Son of God, who saved us?

5. Were the writers of the Infancy Narratives inspired by God?

6. Was Elizabeth present at the Annunciation?

7. Was Mary always free from sin, even Original Sin?

Y **8.** Is the Assumption, Mary's being taken into heaven body and soul, a Catholic doctrine?

A Christmas Crossword Fill in the puzzle.

Across

2. A Galilean woman who was sinless and full of grace

5. The holy man who was allowed to see the Messiah before he died and who prophesied sorrow for Mary

7. The king who wanted to put the newborn king to death

8. The holy family fled to this place.

11. The messenger at the Annunciation

12. Mary was betrothed to this man.

14. When Mary became pregnant, Joseph intended to take this action allowed by Jewish law.

Down

1. Men who followed a star to Bethlehem

3. A relative of Jesus who was six months older than Jesus

4. Jesus was conceived by this power.

5. The first to hear the good news of Jesus' birth

6. Mary helped this older relative during the woman's pregnancy.

9. When Jesus was lost in Jerusalem, his parents found him here doing his Father's work.

10. When Jesus was born, he was laid in this.

13. Mary's child was his Son.

Gather and Go Forth

Know and Proclaim

Catholics bring the Good News of the Gospel to life in the way they live out the teachings of the faith.

We Know Our Faith	We Proclaim Our Faith
The Infancy Narratives tell us the stories of Jesus' birth and early life. They can be found in the Gospels of Matthew and Luke.	Catholics display scenes of the Nativity at Christmas. These displays remind people that Jesus came to save the whole world.
Mary listened to God, which led her to bring Jesus into the world.	As Catholics, we seek to bring the Good News to the world through our words and interactions with others.
Mary is the Mother of God because she is the mother of Jesus. Mary has a privileged place in the Church.	Catholics honor Mary with special celebrations, such as the May Crowning, when a statue of the Blessed Virgin Mary is crowned with a wreath of flowers.

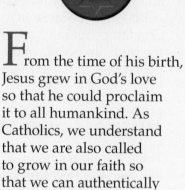

From the time of his birth, Jesus grew in God's love so that he could proclaim it to all humankind. As Catholics, we understand that we are also called to grow in our faith so that we can authentically proclaim Christ.

The child grew and became strong, filled with wisdom; and the favor of God was upon him.
Luke 2:40

Test Your Catholic Knowledge

Fill in the circle that best completes the sentence.

When Mary said yes to the angel Gabriel, she agreed to:

○ marry Joseph.

○ become the Mother of God.

○ be written about in the Gospels.

○ be the mother of John the Baptist.

A Catholic to Know

Juan Diego (1474–1548) was a reluctant saint. When the Blessed Virgin Mary appeared to him at Tepeyac in Mexico, he asked her to find someone more worthy to take her message to the bishop. She appeared three times, always with the dark skin of the native people, adorned with native and Christian symbols, and speaking Juan's own Nahuatl language. Juan convinced the bishop when an image of Mary miraculously appeared on the inside of his cloak. Because Juan Diego said yes, Our Lady of Guadalupe remains a sign of hope and compassion for the Mexican people and for millions of believers around the world.

Saint Juan Diego

Witness and Share

These sentences describe what Catholics believe. Listen carefully as they are read. Ask yourself, "How strong are my Catholic beliefs?"

My Way to Faith

- I am familiar with the Scripture stories of Jesus' birth.

- I believe that Mary is the Mother of God.

- I pray prayers like the Hail Mary and other prayers that honor Mary.

- I share the message of Christmas throughout the year through my words and interactions with others.

- I welcome Jesus into my own life.

Share Your Faith

Think about how you can make Jesus' presence more evident for yourself and those around you. Where do you see Jesus acting in your life? Write your ideas in your own words on the lines. Invite a family member or a friend to share how Jesus is present in his or her life.

_____

_____

_____

_____

The Mission of Jesus

Jesus the Christ

The Role of Messiah

All of us have a number of roles in life. Your favorite aunt, for instance, might also be a wife, a mother, a lawyer, and the captain of her bowling team. List some of your roles.

_____

_____

_____

In addition to being God's Son, Jesus is the Christ. *Christ* means "anointed one." The Israelites anointed their prophets, priests, and kings with oil. As God's anointed one, Jesus was a prophet, priest, and king.

Christ is another name for *Messiah.* Jesus was not the Messiah many Jewish people expected. In their minds, the Messiah would help them overthrow Rome. Jesus' mission as Messiah, however, was to proclaim and make present the reign of God. He was to bring about the Kingdom of God, in which all people live in peace and love.

God's kingdom is not a place. It is the rule of God over our hearts.

Jesus was the Messiah who preached humility and love of neighbors and enemies. He was the Messiah who suffered and died for us.

Jesus began this mission when he was about 30 years old. The Gospels tell how the Holy Spirit strengthened Jesus for his mission and how he accepted it.

A prophet hears God's Word and proclaims it. Jesus delivered the Good News that the Father wanted made known. He proclaimed, "Repent, the kingdom is at hand." Like many prophets before him, Jesus was killed for proclaiming God's words.

A priest represents people in offering sacrifice to God. Jesus stood for all of us when he offered himself to the Father on the Cross.

A king is a man who rules in God's name. Jesus is Lord of the universe as a result of his incarnation, Death, Resurrection, and Ascension.

Launching the Mission

In the Gospel of Luke when Mary, pregnant with Jesus, came to help her relative Elizabeth, Elizabeth's baby leaped for joy. The baby grew up to be John the Baptist, the prophet who prepared the way for Jesus. The following is a news report about Jesus' baptism by John.

Newscaster: We are on location at the Jordan River to find out what attracts the people of Judea to John the Baptist. Let's ask them about this strange man from the desert, who lives on nothing but grasshoppers and honey. Pardon me, may I ask you a few questions?

Woman: Certainly.

Newscaster: When did you first hear about John the Baptist?

Woman: The day he started to preach here. When I heard he was here, I just had to come to hear him.

Newscaster: What kinds of things does John say?

Woman: He says to repent for our sins because the Kingdom of God is near.

Newscaster: Do you think John is the Messiah?

Woman: No. He says that the Messiah is greater than he is and that he's not even worthy to untie the Messiah's sandal.

‹ John the Baptist.

Newscaster: Thank you. *(turns to a man passing by)* Sir, may I have a word with you?

Man: Only a minute. I want to get down there before John stops baptizing.

Newscaster: Why do you want to be baptized?

Man: To show that I am sorry for my sins and be ready for the Messiah when he comes.

Newscaster: Do you think that will be soon?

Man: I sure do. John says so.

Newscaster: Thank you, sir. *(turns toward the riverbank)* Just one more man is waiting for baptism. He's going to the river. Something seems to be wrong. John is hesitating. *(pause)* I guess it's all right now. They're wading out into the river . . . the man is under the water . . . there, he's up . . . they're back on the riverbank, but look at their faces! *(stops a boy)* Pardon me. Do you know the young man whom John just baptized?

Boy: That's Jesus. He comes from Nazareth.

Newscaster: Thank you. We'll try to find out what happened. Here comes John. Pardon me, sir. What happened? You look as if you've seen something extraordinary.

John: You're right. I just baptized the Messiah.

Newscaster: How do you know?

John: After Jesus was baptized, the heavens opened up. I saw a dove come down and hover over his head. Then I heard a voice saying, "This is my beloved Son, with whom I am well pleased." Don't you see what that means? Jesus is the Messiah. Praised be the God of Israel!

Newscaster: Praised be the God of Israel! What more can be said? No doubt, we'll be hearing more about this Jesus from Nazareth. This is Isaac Jacobs reporting from Judea.

The Jordan River.

Anointed for the Mission

Jesus was sinless. Why then did he go to John for baptism? The baptism of Jesus was a sign that he accepted his mission as Messiah. He was ready to proclaim and make present the Kingdom of God. Also, Jesus took on the sins of the world. Jesus' going into the water symbolized that he was ready to die for us.

The Gospels proclaim the identity of Jesus by describing an epiphany that occurred after his baptism. An epiphany is a revelation or manifestation of God. The Father's voice, the Holy Spirit like a dove descending upon Jesus, and Jesus the Son are a revelation of the Trinity—the three Persons in one God. The Father strengthened Jesus for his mission, and the Spirit anointed him for his work.

A Moment with Jesus

Jesus' baptism marked the beginning of his mission. Take a moment now to reflect silently on the story of Jesus' baptism. What do you imagine it was like for Jesus to begin his mission of proclaiming God's kingdom? Pause for a moment to reflect on how your Baptism calls you to live. Ask the Holy Spirit to help you be a faithful witness of God's love in the world.

The Messiah's Test

After his baptism, Jesus was led by the Spirit into the desert. There, alone, he prayed and fasted for 40 days to prepare for his mission. His ancestors, the Hebrews, had been formed into God's people by 40 years in the desert. Now Jesus would grow into his role in the same way. While the Hebrews, however, often failed their tests, Jesus overcame Satan and refused to compromise with evil. Faithful to his Father, he proved to be the true Messiah whose kingdom was spiritual and based on faith and love. He walked out of the desert stronger and ready to live his role fully.

The temptations according to Matthew are shown below.

The Temptations

Temptation to physical pleasures

Jesus is hungry after fasting.

Satan: *"If you are the Son of God, command that these stones become loaves of bread."*

Jesus: *"One does not live on bread alone, but by every word that comes from the mouth of God."*

The Kingdom of God is not based on material goods.

Temptation to pride

Satan takes Jesus to the tower of the Temple.

Satan: *"If you are the Son of God, throw yourself down. Scripture says that the angels will support you with their hands."*

Jesus: *"Scripture says, 'You shall not put the Lord, your God, to the test.'"*

The Kingdom of God is not based on magic tricks.

Temptation to power

Satan takes Jesus to a high mountain and shows him all the kingdoms of the world.

Satan: *"All these I shall give you if you will prostrate yourself and worship me."*

Jesus: *"Get away, Satan! Scripture says, 'The Lord, your God, shall you worship and him alone shall you serve.'"*

The Kingdom of God is not based on a show of political power.

Our Test

You will never meet the devil dressed in a red suit and carrying a pitchfork. However, the power of evil is real. Satan, the world around us, and our own weak nature tempt us to sin. Temptations are people, circumstances, and things that entice us to do what is wrong or to omit doing what is good. We can recognize temptations because they are contrary to Jesus' teaching. Of themselves, temptations are not sins. Sin is actually choosing to do what is wrong or to omit what is good.

Sin offends God and hurts our relationships with him and other people. Sins are called venial when they weaken our relationship with God. Sins that are more serious and completely break our relationship with God are called mortal (deadly) sins. The degree of our guilt for sin depends on

- the seriousness of the matter
- our knowledge
- pressure from outside forces
- circumstances that weaken our willpower
- our intentions

Who seems to be guiltier: someone who steals money to provide food for his family or someone who steals money so she can buy an expensive car?

Because of Original Sin, the consequences of the sin of our first parents, we are left weak, and doing what is right often involves a struggle. Our means for resisting temptation are fasting, self-control, the sacraments, prayer, and friendship with Jesus, who knows what it is like to be tempted. Also, the Trinity dwells in us since our Baptism. We can rely on God's grace to help us meet the challenge of evil. When we overcome temptation, we fulfill our roles in life—especially our role as baptized Christians.

Resisting Temptation

Below is a temptation to keep you from fulfilling your role as a son or daughter. Write a response to the temptation. Then choose a role from the list you made on page 43 and write your own test.

Role: Son or daughter

Tempter: What your mom wants this time is unreasonable. No one else your age would do that. Don't do what your mom wants.

You: _____

_____

Role: _____

Tempter: _____

_____

You: _____

_____

Summary

Remember

What are Jesus' three roles as the Christ?
Jesus' three roles as the Christ are prophet, priest, and king.

What was Jesus' mission?
Jesus' mission was to proclaim and make present the reign of God.

What do we learn from Jesus' baptism?
From Jesus' baptism, we learn that there are three Persons in one God—the Father, the Son, and the Holy Spirit.

What is temptation?
Temptation is any person or thing that entices us to do what is evil or to omit doing what is good.

Respond

Author Pearl Buck said, "Youth is the age of temptation." Here are some questions for you to reflect on and respond to in your reflection notebook.

- What is my biggest temptation right now?

- What am I doing to resist it?

- What does Christ expect of me?

- With Christ's help, what more can I do to overcome this temptation?

Reach Out

1. At times, we need to get away from it all, to find a quiet place to pull ourselves together, to think, and to pray. Your "desert place" might be a special place where you can be alone. It might be the early morning, at night before going to bed, or a quiet Sunday afternoon. Plan a visit to your desert place. Decide when you will go there and what you will think about or pray about. Write about your desert experience in your reflection notebook.

2. Read Philippians 1:27–28. What do you think Saint Paul meant by this advice? How does it apply to your life right now? Think about that during a desert experience, then discuss it with members of your family. Ask them how they interpret Saint Paul's advice.

3. Conduct a round-robin discussion with a small group of friends or family members. Write a thought-provoking question on the bottom of a sheet of paper. Then pass the paper around. Each person writes a response at the top of the paper and folds it over before handing it to the next person. After the paper has circulated, unfold it and read aloud the answers, allowing time for comment.
    Sample questions:
    - How would you reply if someone said, "The devil made me do it!"?
    - At times, we all face the temptation to do something to be popular or admired. How do you handle this temptation?

4. Show you belong to God's kingdom by doing something to oppose an injustice. Talk with your family about an issue that affects your community or members of your family. Together, write a letter to the editor, write or e-mail your state senator or representative, or make a phone call to a local official to express your opinion as a disciple of Jesus.

Identification   To what do the following phrases refer?

1. Jesus' mission: _____

2. Jesus' anointing for his mission: _____

3. Jesus' test: _____

4. Jesus' type of kingdom: _____

5. A person who speaks for God: _____

6. A manifestation of God: _____

Temptations   In each situation, decide if the person is guilty (G) or only tempted (T). Write the correct letter for each situation.

___G___ **1.** Sue Ellen shoplifts a necklace and does not get caught.

___G___ **2.** Robert has a bad cold. When his brother picks on him, Robert punches him.

___T___ **3.** Jill does not like Patty. She always has the urge to avoid her and to say things to hurt her.

___T___ **4.** Jane considers going to a party where she knows there will be beer.

___G___ **5.** Mark joins in when boys on the bus make fun of a student in special education classes.

___G___ **6.** The Sunday after Ann's family returns from camping, Ann says she is too tired to go to Mass. Her mother tells her to stay home, so she does.

___G___ **7.** Frequently during the day, the sexy scenes in a video Carl saw come into his mind without his willing it.

Three of a Kind   Write a short description that identifies each set of words.

1. _____
prophet • priest • king

2. _____
material goods • magic tricks • political power

3. _____
pleasure • pride • power

4. _____
mortal • venial • original

5. _____
Satan • the world • human nature

6. _____
knowledge • circumstances • intention

7. _____
self-control • sacraments • grace

Gather and Go Forth

Know and Proclaim

We grow strong in the knowledge of our faith to proclaim Jesus as Messiah with courage and conviction.

We Know Our Faith	We Proclaim Our Faith
Jesus' mission was to proclaim and make present the Kingdom of God, in which all people live in peace and love.	Responding to the beatitude "Blessed are the peacemakers," Catholics pray for peace in the world during the Prayer of the Faithful.
Jesus' baptism revealed the Trinity. The Father, the Son, and the Holy Spirit are three Persons in one God.	Catholics pray the Glory Be to the Father (Doxology) to give praise to the Trinity. Catholics also praise the Trinity whenever they pray the Sign of the Cross.
Sin offends God and hurts our relationship with him. Sin also hurts our relationships among people.	Fasting is a practice many Catholics use to try to resist the temptation to sin. One common form of fasting is to abstain from eating meat on Fridays, especially during Lent. Catholics also fast by giving up things they enjoy as a sacrifice to God.

Jesus understands the tests we face. Catholics rely on God's grace, which is present in the sacraments, to meet the challenge of evil.

For we do not have a high priest who is unable to sympathize with our weaknesses, but one who has similarly been tested in every way, yet without sin.

Hebrews 4:15

Test Your Catholic Knowledge

Fill in the circle that best completes the sentence.

As Catholics, we believe sin:

○ is a conscious choice to do what is wrong.

○ makes God stop loving us.

○ can never be forgiven.

○ is always mortal.

A Catholic to Know

Peter Claver (1581–1654) ministered to the African slaves in South America for more than 40 years. These slaves suffered incredible cruelty. They were crowded together in the lower holds of ships for the long voyage to what is now Colombia, during which approximately one-third would die from mistreatment. Peter Claver treated their wounds and supplied fresh food and drink upon their arrival. Despite their miserable travel, living, and work conditions, Peter Claver wanted to help restore their dignity and let them know they were children of God and precious in God's sight. We honor Saint Peter Claver's tireless ministry to African slaves on September 9.

Saint Peter Claver

Witness and Share

These sentences describe what Catholics believe. Listen carefully as they are read. Ask yourself, "How strong are my Catholic beliefs?"

My Way to Faith

- I believe that God loves me even when I sin.

- I act as a peacemaker between my friends when they argue.

- I believe that I am called to share in Jesus' mission to build the Kingdom of God among people today.

- I pray to God for the grace to avoid temptation and sin.

- I seek to correct injustice when I see it.

- I work to restore human dignity when I see it being denied.

Share Your Faith

Think about ways in which you can take a more active role in your parish community—through prayer, service, or study with others. Write your ideas on the lines and plan to implement at least one of them in the next month. Invite a friend or family member to participate with you.

_____

_____

_____

_____

The Apostles, Mary, and Others

Jesus the Master

You have probably heard of the great teachers Socrates of Greece (left) and the Buddha of India. Every once in a while, someone very wise such as those men appears on earth. The person attracts people who want to explore the mysteries of life. The teacher is called a master, and the followers are called **disciples,** which means learners. Jesus, the world's greatest teacher, had many disciples who were dedicated to him. Excited by what they heard and saw, they followed Jesus and brought other people to him.

The First Disciples

John's Gospel tells how Jesus met his first disciples after his baptism:

> The next day John [the Baptist] was there again with two of his disciples, and as he watched Jesus walk by, he said, "Behold, the Lamb of God." The two disciples heard what he said and followed Jesus. Jesus turned and saw them following him and said to them, "What are you looking for?" They said to him, "Rabbi" (which translated means Teacher), "where are you staying?" He said to them, "Come, and you will see." So they went and saw where he was staying, and they stayed with him that day. It was about four in the afternoon.

> John 1:35–39

Something about Jesus attracted the disciples to him. They responded to his invitation, "Come, and you will see." For many months after their first meeting, the disciples walked with Jesus from town to town. They enjoyed his company. Their understanding of him grew day by day. First they called him teacher. At the Last Supper, Jesus called them friends. Eventually they called him Messiah.

The Twelve

Jesus chose 12 men to accompany him on his mission. They are called the apostles. The word *apostle* comes from words that mean "send" and "messenger." The apostles were to share the ministry of Jesus and preach the Good News of the risen Lord. They and their successors, the bishops, would be empowered by Christ to carry out his mission. Because 12 was the number of the tribes of Israel, the 12 apostles symbolized the new People of God.

There is a saying that you can tell a lot about a person by the friends he or she keeps. The apostles were political nobodies. They were ordinary people, such as fishermen and a tax collector. All of them were sinners. Sometimes they were jealous and ambitious. Sometimes they were afraid. Sometimes they did not understand Jesus, yet Jesus loved them. They were with him at the Last Supper, and he sent them to act in his name.

When Jesus looked at Simon, he saw a fisherman who often spoke without thinking. He also saw Simon as a future leader. Simon would be the first person to proclaim the Gospel on the morning of Pentecost. When Jesus looks at us, he sees us as we really are, with our good qualities and our flaws. He also sees in us what we can become.

The apostles and all the other disciples found compassion and strength in Jesus. Jesus challenged them to continue his mission. Jesus continues to touch the hearts of people today and to challenge them. Unlike Socrates and the Buddha, Jesus is still with us, inviting us to "come, and you will see." His influence is stronger and more real today than when he walked the roads of Palestine.

Portraits of the Apostles

The following sketches of the 12 apostles are drawn from Scripture and Tradition.

Peter
Feasts: February 22, June 29, November 18

Peter was the apostle Jesus chose to be the first leader of his Church. When Peter met Jesus, he was known as Simon. Jesus changed his name to *Cephas,* or Peter, the Greek word for "rock." Jesus said he would build his Church upon that rock.

Peter and his brother Andrew were fishermen from Bethsaida. Later they lived in Capernaum, a city on the northern shore of the Sea of Galilee. Peter often spoke and acted impulsively. He loved Jesus very much and said he would follow Jesus even to death. According to Tradition, Peter arrived in Rome during a great persecution of Christians. He was arrested and crucified upside down. Most pictures of Peter show him carrying a pair of keys. In Matthew 16:19, Jesus gives Peter the keys of the kingdom of heaven when he makes Peter head of his Church.

Andrew

Feast: November 30

Andrew was one of the first men Jesus called to follow him. After Andrew met Jesus, he brought his brother Peter to meet Jesus. Andrew's name means "manly" and "courageous." His symbol is an X-shaped cross, because it is believed that he died on one. Centuries after his death, missionaries taking his relics to Scotland were shipwrecked. They reached shore safely and introduced the Scots to Jesus. Because so many people came to follow Christ, Andrew was named the patron saint of Scotland. He is also the patron saint of Russia.

James the Greater

Feast: July 25

Two apostles were named James. James the Greater was the brother of John. James and John were sons of Zebedee and Salome. With their father, they worked as fishermen and were partners with Peter.

James and John once asked Jesus to give them places of honor in his kingdom. Peter, James, and John were the only apostles chosen to witness the Transfiguration of Jesus and the raising of Jairus's daughter from the dead. They were the only three to be near Jesus during his agony in the garden. James was the first apostle to be martyred for Christ. He was beheaded in Jerusalem at the command of King Herod. His symbols are a traveler's staff and a pilgrim's bell. James is the patron saint of Spain.

John

Feast: December 27

John is sometimes called the teenage apostle. Unlike the other apostles, he was not married. Although at one time Jesus called James and John "sons of thunder," John developed into a gentle, sensitive man, an apostle of love. We think John is the person referred to in John's Gospel as "the disciple Jesus loved." John was the only apostle to stand beneath the Cross, and Jesus asked him to take care of Mary. The story is told that whenever John was asked to speak in his old age, all he would ever say was "Little children, love one another. Love one another." He was the only apostle to die a natural death. According to Tradition, John was the fourth Evangelist. His symbol is an eagle.

Philip

Feast: May 3

Philip, like Peter and Andrew, came from Bethsaida. He received a direct invitation from Jesus to follow him. Convinced that Jesus was the one Moses and the prophets had written about, Philip told his friend Nathanael to come and see. We learn from writers of the early Church that Philip did great missionary work in Asia Minor, where he is buried. (Asia Minor roughly corresponds to the Asian portion of present-day Turkey.) Philip's symbol is a column or pillar because of the tradition that he died hanging from one of these.

Bartholomew

Feast: August 24

Bartholomew is believed to be Nathanael, the man whom Philip introduced to Jesus. *Bartholomew* may mean "son of Tolomai," in Hebrew, *bar Tolomai*. Jesus, who knows the thoughts of all hearts, spoke of him as an Israelite without guile. That means he was straightforward and honest and did not try to deceive people. Bartholomew traveled east to preach the Gospel. While in Armenia (a country east of present-day Turkey), he was arrested, tortured, and finally put to death. His symbol is a knife, the instrument of his torture.

Matthew

Feast: September 21

Matthew, also called Levi, was a tax collector. He lived in Capernaum, where Jesus did much of his public ministry. Matthew is remembered for his prompt response to Jesus' call. He immediately left his money booth and followed Jesus. The Gospel according to Matthew was often quoted by the early Christians and is presented as the first of the four Gospels in the New Testament. Tradition tells us that Matthew died a martyr's death, probably in Ethiopia in eastern Africa. His symbol as an Evangelist is the head of a man.

Thomas
Feast: July 3

The apostle Thomas is best remembered as "doubting" Thomas. He was not with the other apostles when Jesus came to them after the Resurrection.

Thomas claimed that he would not believe that Jesus had truly risen unless he could touch his wounds. Once he saw Jesus, however, Thomas immediately fell to his knees and exclaimed, "My Lord and my God!"

Thought to be a house builder by trade, Thomas is usually shown carrying carpenters' tools. He is the patron saint of carpenters, architects, and people who are blind. Thomas is thought to have brought the Good News to India, where he died a martyr and was buried.

James the Less
Feast: May 3

James the Less is the brother of the apostle Jude. He was given the title "the Less" to distinguish him from the other apostle James. Perhaps he was shorter or younger than the other James. His mother was Mary of Clopas, a follower of Jesus and possibly a cousin of the Blessed Virgin Mary.

According to Tradition, James the Less was the first bishop of Jerusalem. Some scholars believe that the letter bearing his name may not have been written by him. James is said to have been beaten to death by Jews who were angry that Paul had escaped death by appealing to Caesar. James's symbol is a cudgel, or club.

Jude
Feast: October 28

A brother of James the Less and perhaps a cousin of Jesus, this apostle is also known as Thaddeus. For reasons unknown, Saint Jude has become popular as the patron of hopeless cases. He preached the Gospel in the region between the Tigris and Euphrates Rivers and Persia (Iran), and one of the letters in the New Testament bears his name. Some pagan magicians are believed to have killed him for exposing how they were fooling the people. His symbol is an ax, the instrument used in his martyrdom.

Simon
Feast: October 28

Simon from Cana was the only apostle who was a Zealot. When Simon chose to follow Jesus, he had to channel his zeal into the peaceful pursuit of the Kingdom of God. He first preached the Gospel in Egypt and then went to Persia with Jude. It was there that he suffered martyrdom when he was beaten with clubs and then sawed into pieces. His symbol is a saw.

Judas
Feast:

From his name, Judas Iscariot is believed to have come from a town in Judea. He was entrusted with the care of the common funds. He helped himself to some of the money that belonged to all. He also betrayed Jesus for 30 pieces of silver. When he realized what he had done, he did not return to Jesus to receive his loving forgiveness as Peter did. Instead, Judas hanged himself. According to the Acts of the Apostles, Judas fell and died in a field he had bought with his blood money.

Matthias
Feast: May 14

We learn from the Acts of the Apostles that Matthias was selected to take the place of Judas. Matthias was a follower from the beginning of Jesus' ministry and had been a witness of the resurrected Lord. It is believed that he preached in Palestine and was martyred by crucifixion. His symbol is a lance.

A Moment with Jesus

Each of the sketches above gives a glimpse of the men whom Jesus chose to be his apostles. Pick one of them, reread the sketch of him, and reflect on how he carried out the mission of Jesus. What does his symbol tell you about his relationship with Jesus?

Pause for a few moments and ask Jesus to help you deepen your relationship with him and his Church. Thank Jesus for calling you to follow him.

Pilgrims at World Youth Day, Germany, 2005. ❯

Successors of the Apostles

The primary role of the apostles was to witness to the life, Death and Resurrection of Jesus Christ. Our Catholic faith is built on the foundation that the apostles have given to us.

Jesus intended that the faith of the apostles be proclaimed to the end of time. So the teaching of the apostles is carried on by their successors—the pope and the bishops of the Catholic Church.

The pope, the bishop of Rome, is the successor of Peter, who was appointed by Jesus to be the head of the Church. The pope is the pastor of the whole Church and has the universal power in the care of souls.

The bishops of the Catholic Church are successors of the apostles and are the principal pastors of their local churches (dioceses). The bishops are the visible source and foundation of unity in the local Church.

With the pope, the college of bishops exercises the authority of Jesus Christ over the whole Church. They keep alive the faith in Jesus witnessed by the first apostles in their lives and in their deaths.

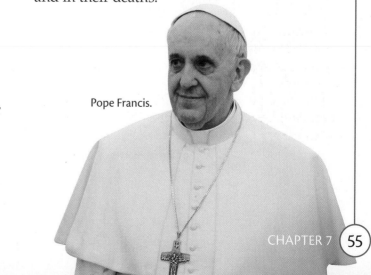

Pope Francis.

The First and Best Disciple

The Acts of the Apostles tells us that on Pentecost when the Spirit came, Mary, the mother of Jesus, was with the disciples. Her presence was fitting because she was the first one to believe and follow Christ. Her faith and obedience made her open to God's will in her life. Mary brought Jesus into the world through the power of the Holy Spirit. She devoted her life to him for 30 years before he began his public ministry. One of her titles is Queen of Apostles.

The highest praise of Mary is that she fits her Son's description in Luke 8:21. Write Jesus' words here:

_____

_____

_____

True disciples, the real members of Christ's family, believe and act on their beliefs. Someone whose life gives testimony to his or her beliefs is called a witness. Mary was a witness. At a wedding feast, she trusted that her Son would help when the wine ran out. She told the servants, "Do whatever he tells you." During the suffering and Death of Jesus, many followers fled in fear. Mary, however, stood faithful at the foot of the Cross. There Jesus called her the mother of John, the beloved disciple. From the moment of the Incarnation, when she became the mother of Jesus, Mary became the mother of all believers. Mary is the mother of Jesus and the Mother of the Church, his mystical body.

Mary is the model for everyone who seeks Jesus Christ. In our struggles to be faithful

❮ Statue of Mary, Cartagena, Colombia.

disciples, she not only inspires us, but she also prays for us and loves us.

The Way of the Witness

1. Read the concerns junior high students have about seriously following Jesus. Write a concern of your own. Then rank the concerns from the greatest (8) to the least (1).

   _____ They will not have as much fun.

   _____ They may lose their friends.

   _____ They will have to treat everyone kindly.

   _____ They will be made fun of.

   _____ Their families will not understand them.

   _____ They will have to work too hard.

   _____ They will have to give up too many things.

   _____ Other: _____

Think about how you would answer each question. For each question, write your answer below.

2. If people your age decided to be real friends of Jesus, what things would they most likely have to change in their lives?

   _____

3. If people your age decided not to grow in their love for Jesus, what things would they be giving up?

   _____

4. What do you think is the best way for junior high students to witness to one another? to the world?

   _____

Summary

Remember

Who were the apostles?

The apostles were the 12 men chosen by Jesus to share his ministry and preach the Good News of the risen Lord.

What is a disciple of Jesus?

A disciple of Jesus is a follower of Jesus who is dedicated to him.

What is a witness?

A witness is someone whose life gives testimony to his or her beliefs.

Why is Mary a disciple?

Mary is a disciple because she was open to God's will and lived it faithfully.

What did Jesus demand of his disciples?

Jesus said, "Whoever wishes to come after me must deny himself, take up his cross, and follow me." (Matthew 16:24)

Respond

Jesus' invitation to you to become his disciple includes an RSVP. It requires a response. Write a letter in your reflection notebook, responding to Jesus' invitation.

Reach Out

1. Make a flash card for each of the apostles. Write the name on one side and three interesting facts on the other side. Ask someone at home to work with you, then test each other on your knowledge of the apostles. On each apostle's feast day, display the card where your family will see it.

2. Gather with one or more family members and read aloud Luke 8:21. Then together name members of your extended family who exemplify Jesus' message in the Scripture passage.

3. Think of someone in your family or a close family friend whom you think has been a faithful witness to Jesus in his or her life. Spend some time with that person and ask him or her to share with you the joys and difficulties he or she has experienced in following Jesus.

4. Jesus prepared for important events, such as choosing his apostles, by praying. Read Luke 6:12–13, 22:31–32, and 22:39–46. When do you pray? If a friend asked you why you pray, what would you say? Use your own words to ask Mary in prayer to help you be a better disciple.

5. At the end of the day, think of all the good things you have seen and heard during the day. Decide on one specific thing you will do the next day to bring the light of Jesus to others.

Word to Know

disciple

Disciple Rhymes Fill in the name of the disciple described in each verse.

1. Nathanael might be called _____ too.
   Jesus described him as honest and true.

2. Jesus made _____ the head of his flock.
   He renamed Simon the fisherman "rock."

3. Peter's brother named _____ was called from his nets.
   He died on a cross in the shape of an X.

4. The publican _____ said yes to the Lord.
   He left all that he had, followed Christ, and wrote God's Word.

5. _____ was one of the favored three,
   First martyred apostle, and son of Zebedee.

6. The evangelist _____ was James's brother.
   He stood by the Cross and received Mary as mother.

7. Apostle to India, Saint _____ once doubted.
   To Jesus, "My Lord and my God," he later shouted.

8. The brother of Jude, _____, an early Church leader,
   Was Jerusalem's bishop and known for his letter.

9. Saint _____ preached in Persia. A letter bears his name.
   To do the impossible is his great fame.

10. From Cana came _____, a Zealot all-fired.
    In Egypt, then Persia he preached and was martyred.

11. _____ invited a friend, "Come and see,"
    Right after he answered Christ's "Come, follow me."

12. By _____ Iscariot Christ was betrayed.
    To him 30 pieces of silver were paid.

13. _____, our model in answering God's call,
    Was the best of disciples and first of them all.

14. _____ was chosen by lot to replace
    Judas, the traitor who died in disgrace.

15. "Be my disciple," the Lord calls to _____.
    "So take up your Cross, and love and serve too."

The disciple who betrayed Jesus was paid with thirty Roman coins such as these.

Gather and Go Forth

Know and Proclaim

Knowing the teachings of the Church enables us to proclaim the truth of Christ.

We Know Our Faith	We Proclaim Our Faith
The apostles shared in the ministry of Jesus and preached the Good News of the Resurrection.	Many Catholics share in the ministry of Jesus by teaching religious education classes in their parish. They help pass on the truth of the Church to another generation of Catholics.
The pope is the Bishop of Rome. He is the successor of Peter, who was chosen by Jesus to be the head of the early Church.	Catholics pray for the pope and bishops during the Eucharistic Prayer at Mass. Many Catholics have a picture of the current pope in their home.
Mary is the model for discipleship. She is the mother of Jesus, the Mother of the Church, and the mother of all believers.	Catholics may show their devotion to Mary by placing a statue of her in a flower garden or by planting a Mary garden. They may wear a medal as a sign of devotion to Mary.

As disciples, Catholics desire only to follow Christ, share in his mission, and live with him forever. This desire leads us to know and proclaim him with our lives.

For his sake I have accepted the loss of all things and I consider them so much rubbish, that I may gain Christ.

Philippians 3:8

Test Your Catholic Knowledge

Fill in the circle that best completes the sentence.

The bishops of the Roman Catholic Church:

○ are elected by representatives of parish churches.

○ can choose any diocese they wish to serve.

○ are the principal pastors of their dioceses.

○ have universal power in the care of souls.

A Catholic to Know

Andrew and his brother, Simon Peter, were fishermen when Jesus promised to make them "fishers of men." Andrew was originally a follower of John the Baptist but, at Jesus' baptism, he recognized the truth of John's proclamation—that Jesus was truly the Lamb of God. Following the Ascension of our Lord, Andrew traveled to Greece, where he preached the Good News of Jesus' Resurrection. Around the year A.D. 70, Andrew was crucified and tied to an X-shaped cross for two days, proclaiming Christ to the crowds as he died. The X-shaped cross remains Saint Andrew's symbol, along with fish and a fisherman's net.

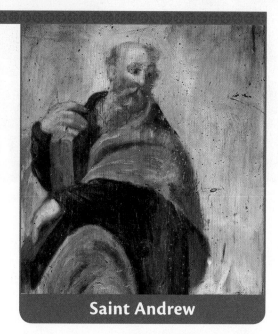

Saint Andrew

Witness and Share

These sentences describe what Catholics believe. Listen carefully as they are read. Ask yourself, "How strong are my Catholic beliefs?"

My Way to Faith

- I answer the call to live as a disciple of Jesus Christ.

- I honor Mary by praying Marian prayers such as the Hail Mary and the Rosary.

- I look to the pope, the Church, and its leaders to help me deepen my relationship with Jesus.

- I follow Jesus, even though some friends do not believe.

- I share my experiences of faith in Jesus with my friends and family.

Share Your Faith

Do you know a friend or family member who does not go to church very often? Think of one way you might invite that person back to Jesus. Write your ideas on the lines and then invite that person to attend Mass with you.

_____

_____

_____

_____

_____

Baptism and Confirmation

Jesus the Savior

The Seven Sacraments

Friendships are built by signs and words. Signs and words celebrate and seal our relationships. Our friendship with Jesus grows through the signs and words of the seven sacraments that he entrusted to his Church. Sacraments are special encounters with Jesus Christ at key times during our journey of life. We celebrate our relationship as the **Mystical Body of Christ.** Through the sacraments, Christ acts in us to save us; we celebrate his grace, his divine life in us. The sacramental grace we receive through the work of the Holy Spirit enables us to carry out our mission as his disciples.

The sacraments give us the grace that they signify. The grace is always present and does not depend on the worthiness of the minister. However, a sacrament will only accomplish what it intends if the person receiving the sacrament is open to cooperating with God's grace. Baptism, Confirmation, and Holy Orders confer a permanent character or seal, so they are celebrated only once.

Christian Initiation

Adolescents and adults become disciples of Jesus and join the community of believers through a process called the Rite of Christian Initiation of Adults (RCIA). The RCIA takes place in the midst of the parish community. It has three steps: catechumenate, election, and initiation. The last step is the celebration of the Sacraments of Baptism, Confirmation, and the Eucharist. The people preparing for initiation are already part of God's household. They are assured of salvation even if they should die before being baptized. They have the baptism of desire. The following story tells how Joe began participating in the RCIA process.

Chris and Joe, high school juniors, rang the doorbell at St. Jude's rectory.

"Relax, Joe. Father Shea's great," Chris encouraged. Before Joe could reply, the door opened and there was Father Shea.

"Hello, Chris, how are you?"

"Fine," Chris replied. "Father, this is my friend Joe. We'd like to talk with you."

"Sure, come in." Father led them to his office.

Chris spoke first. "Joe wants to become a Catholic, Father, and I would like to sponsor him."

Father Shea smiled at Joe, "What made you decide this, Joe?"

Joe began his story. He and Chris had met at basketball. Joe often stayed at Chris's house for supper. He sensed that the spirit he enjoyed so much there was connected with the family's religious beliefs. One day Joe asked Chris about his religion. Chris explained that faith in Christ helped him understand life and gave him a desire to serve others. He told Joe about the Church. Their conversations led to this meeting with Father Shea.

When Joe finished speaking, Father said that Joe could begin the Rite of Christian Initiation. Chris would be his sponsor and assist him.

Responding to the Call

Here is part of the journal Joe kept during the RCIA process.

Thursday, September 8

All of us who want to be Catholics met in the church hall tonight with our sponsors. We prayed and were introduced. The leader told us how he came to the faith, and then he had us tell our own stories. We're called inquirers, ones who are studying the faith. We'll meet once a week.

Saturday, October 10

Tonight we became catechumens. Before Mass we and our sponsors met at the church entrance. Father Shea called our names and asked, "What do you ask of God's Church?" We said, "Faith." He asked, "What does faith offer you?" We answered, "Eternal life." Then he prayed that we would follow the Gospel under Christ's leadership. He asked everyone if they were ready to help us. They answered, "We are." Father Shea made a cross on our foreheads, saying, "By this sign of love, Christ will be your strength. Learn now to know and follow him." We entered the church but stayed only until the end of the homily. After we're baptized, we'll stay for the whole Mass.

Friday, February 12

With school, basketball, and catechumen meetings, the months have really been busy. We catechumens know one another well because we have studied the life of Christ and the Church's teachings together and because we have prayed together. Father Shea told us that as followers of Christ, we should set a good example. I've been trying to play fair and watch my language.

Sunday, March 3

Today is the first Sunday of Lent. We had the Rite of Sending of the Catechumens for Election at Mass. After the Homily, Father Shea called the sponsors and us catechumens to the altar. He asked the sponsors if we were taking our formation seriously and if we were ready to be presented to the bishop for the rite of election. They said we were. That afternoon we stood before the bishop as he asked us similar questions. Then the bishop declared that the Church called us to the Sacraments of Baptism, Confirmation, and Eucharist. We wrote our names in the book of the elect. We are now the elect.

Sunday, March 10

On three Sundays in Lent, we have scrutinies at the 10:00 A.M. Mass. They are petitions and exorcisms. Exorcisms are prayers against the evil spirit. They teach repentance, the mystery of sin, and how Christ the Redeemer saved us. The scrutinies strengthen our decision to live for Christ. After the scrutinies are presentations. Today Father Shea presented us with the Creed. On the last Sunday, he will give us the Lord's Prayer.

Sacraments of Initiation

The night of the Easter Vigil is momentous for Joe, Chris, and the community of St. Jude's. Joe and Chris together with others have walked a journey of faith in response to God's call.

This is a very decisive moment in Joe's life. Following Christ and living his values will be difficult. That is why the faith community is there for support. Joe and the community listen to Saint Paul's words about "dying to sin."

After the Homily, Joe and the other elect go to the baptismal font for a profession of faith. They make their baptismal vows, publicly rejecting Satan and evil and declaring their faith. As the water of Baptism flows over Joe, he remembers that water is a sign of death and life. He is entering into the Death of Jesus and experiencing a new life of grace. He becomes alive in the life of Jesus and shares in the glory of his Resurrection. When Joe's godparents put a white robe over his head, he is being "clothed with Christ." His sins are forgiven, and he has new life in Jesus Christ. His godparents hand him a lighted candle, a symbol of his life in Christ. Joe is now a full-fledged member of the Church. He may stay for the whole liturgy.

Next Joe celebrates Confirmation. He is anointed with a mixture of olive oil and balsam called chrism. He knows that now he is expected to proclaim his faith and that the Holy Spirit will strengthen and guide him.

The Mass continues. During the Liturgy of the Eucharist, Joe recalls that Christ died and rose so that he could live. When he receives the Body and Blood of Jesus, Joe makes an act of faith. He is not afraid. The community of believers will help him grow spiritually. They will help him live his faith during the coming months of **mystagogy,** a time to learn more about his faith and how to live it.

The signs and words of the Sacraments of Initiation express our relationship with Jesus as Savior. In Baptism, Confirmation, and the Eucharist, we receive the new life Jesus won for us. Through each of these sacraments, he becomes our personal Savior, and we commit ourselves to him.

Baptism: Water and Spirit

Jesus said you must be born of water and the Spirit to enter the Kingdom of Heaven. When the priest or deacon pours water over you at Baptism and says "I baptize you," you enter into the dying and rising of Jesus through the Holy Spirit. You are removed from the reign of evil and strengthened against it. You receive divine life, and you are invited to share eternal life with Jesus. You become a new creation. You become a Christian, willing to give witness to Christ, eager to share his teachings with others, prepared to sacrifice all for him. Because Baptism marks you forever as a follower of Jesus, you can be baptized only once.

A Moment with Jesus

No matter how old we are when we are baptized, our responsibilities as members of the Church are the same. Pause for a few moments and reflect silently on these questions: How do I live my baptismal call in my daily life? How can I give witness to Christ in my life at home and school?

Ask the Holy Spirit to help you be aware of how you can follow Jesus more closely today. Then thank Jesus for calling you to be a member of the Church.

A Flood of Gifts

Are you aware of all the tremendous gifts you receive through Baptism?

You become

- a temple of the Trinity and share in God's life (grace)
- a child of God and heir to heaven
- a member of the faith community, the Church.

You

- are forgiven Original Sin and any personal sins
- receive the Holy Spirit and his gifts
- share in the priesthood of Christ
- receive the virtues of faith, hope, and love.

Signs of Baptism

See how many signs and symbols used at Baptism you understand by matching them with their definitions.

a–oil   *b–candle*   *c–water*   *d–profession of faith*   *e–chrism*   *f–cross*   *g–white robe*   *h–godparents*

_____ **1.** Symbol of being clothed with Christ and sign of new dignity

_____ **2.** Two people who represent the Christian community and promise to assist the newly baptized to grow in faith

_____ **3.** Symbol that shows that the newly baptized is cleansed of sin, dies with Christ, and is raised up with him to eternal life

_____ **4.** Sign of being strengthened and healed

_____ **5.** Promises the newly baptized makes to reject evil and to believe in the Trinity and the truths of the faith

_____ **6.** Symbol of the light of faith and the call to walk as children of light

_____ **7.** Sign made on the forehead of the newly baptized as a reminder of the saving power of Christ's Death and Resurrection

_____ **8.** Sign used in anointing that shows that the newly baptized has received the Holy Spirit and shares in the priesthood of Christ

Confirmation: Sealed with the Spirit

Confirmation always used to be celebrated with Baptism. Catholics of the Eastern rites still celebrate it that way. In Confirmation your baptismal gifts are deepened and perfected. The Spirit who came to the Church on Pentecost comes to you more fully. The bishop lays his hand on you, anoints you with chrism, and says, "(Name), be sealed with the gift of the Holy Spirit." You respond, "Amen." The anointing renews your call to witness to Christ through service. You are anointed to be priest, prophet, and king with Jesus and to share in his mission. You can be confirmed only once because Confirmation marks you permanently as God's special possession.

Through Baptism and Confirmation, the Holy Spirit empowers you to share your faith with others. You are Christ's follower, constantly growing in your understanding of his message and in your ability to love him and others. You are Christ's witness, showing by your actions his kingdom of justice and mercy.

Eucharist: Made One in the Spirit

The Eucharist completes and fulfills Christian Initiation. Christians gather together to celebrate the Lord's passion, Death, Resurrection, and Ascension and to join him in offering perfect worship to the Father. They become one with Jesus and with one another just as the grains of wheat become one in the bread and the grapes become one in the wine. At the Eucharist, the Christian community is strengthened by Jesus Christ's Body and Blood which it receives in Holy Communion. The members are prepared to carry on his work.

Remember

What is the Rite of Christian Initiation of Adults (RCIA)?

The Rite of Christian Initiation of Adults is the process through which people become disciples of Jesus and join the Catholic Church.

What are the Sacraments of Initiation?

The Sacraments of Initiation are Baptism, Confirmation, and the Eucharist. In Christian Initiation, a person is reborn in Baptism, strengthened in Confirmation, and nourished by the Eucharist.

Why are the Sacraments of Initiation important?

The Sacraments of Initiation make a person a member of the Church and empower him or her to carry out the mission of Christ in the world.

Respond

The Gifts of the Holy Spirit are wisdom, understanding, counsel (right judgment), knowledge, fortitude (courage), piety (reverence), and fear of the Lord (wonder and awe).

Choose one of the gifts and write a prayer asking the Holy Spirit to strengthen you in practicing that gift. Write your prayer in your reflection notebook.

Reach Out

1. Brainstorm with members of your family ways you can serve
   - one another
   - your parish community
   - other people

   Then write a family pledge that includes how you will do the above and have each member sign it. Place the pledge where everyone can see it.

2. Take a survey of five parish members you know, asking them the following questions:
   - What do you like best about your parish?
   - How does your parish help you?
   - How do you help your parish?

   Use the answers to prepare a report and share your findings in class.

3. Interview someone from another Christian faith tradition about how Baptism is celebrated in his or her church. Discuss with your classmates and teacher the similarities and differences between the two baptismal ceremonies.

Words to Know

mystagogy
Mystical Body of Christ

Write the Rite Words Identify the major terms of the RCIA defined below.

1. The person who assists a candidate in learning about the Catholic faith:

   — — — — — — — —

2. The rite involving petitions and exorcisms about repentance, the mystery of sin, and redemption for the "elect" during the third, fourth, and fifth Sundays of Lent:

   — — — — — — — — — —

3. The process of becoming a Christian (abbreviation):

   — — — —

4. The rite of celebrating the listing of names of catechumens preparing for the Sacraments of Initiation:

   — — — — — — — — —

5. People interested in studying about the Catholic faith:

   — — — — — — — — —

6. A person who has completed the catechumenate and is ready to enter the Lenten period of intense preparation for the Sacraments of Initiation:

   — — — — —

7. The Easter season experience when the newly baptized learn more about their faith and how to live it:

   — — — — — — — —

8. Prayers that the catechumen be delivered from the power of evil and receive the gifts of the Spirit:

   — — — — — — — —

9. The handing on of the ancient documents of the faith, the Creed, and the Lord's Prayer:

   — — — — — — — — — — —

10. People selected by the catechumen to help him or her prepare for Baptism and lead a genuine Christian life:

    — — — — — — — — — —

11. A person who studies the teachings of the Gospel and the Church and prepares to receive the Sacraments of Initiation:

    — — — — — — — — — —

12. Liturgical celebration at which a person celebrates the Sacraments of Initiation:

    — — — — —   — — — —

Sacrament Match Write the letter of the sacrament that corresponds to each statement: Baptism (B), Confirmation (C), or the Eucharist (E).

_____ 1. Laying on of hands by the bishop is a sign.

_____ 2. We receive the Holy Spirit and his gifts for the first time.

_____ 3. We are anointed with chrism and called to be a witness of Christ.

_____ 4. The community offers perfect worship to the Father.

_____ 5. The community is nourished by the Body and Blood of Jesus.

_____ 6. We become children of God and heirs to heaven.

_____ 7. The community celebrates the Paschal Mystery of Jesus and makes it present.

_____ 8. Original Sin is forgiven.

Gather and Go Forth

Know and Proclaim

Knowledge of our Catholic faith supports us as we proclaim our beliefs in what we say and do.

We Know Our Faith	We Proclaim Our Faith
The Sacraments of Initiation make a person a member of the Church, sharing in the mission of Christ.	Catholics rely on the Gifts of the Holy Spirit to carry out the mission of Christ. These gifts help Catholics live a moral life.
The Sacraments of Initiation are the foundation for life in the Catholic Church.	Newly baptized Catholics put on a white garment to show that they are a new creation in Christ, are anointed with chrism and sealed with the Holy Spirit at Confirmation, and nourished by the Body of Christ in the Eucharist.
The Rite of Christian Initiation of Adults (RCIA) is the process through which some people become full members of the Catholic Church.	Catholics participate as catechists and sponsors for the RCIA and pray for those entering the Church through the Sacraments of Initiation. The entire community participates in the formation of new Catholics.

Test Your Catholic Knowledge

Fill in the circle that best completes the sentence.

Baptism, Eucharist, and Confirmation are called the Sacraments of:

◯ Penance and Reconciliation.

◯ the Holy Spirit.

◯ Holy Orders.

◯ Initiation.

Catholics encounter Christ in the sacraments. Through them, we praise God as his chosen people.

But you are "a chosen race, a royal priesthood, a holy nation, a people of his own, so that you may announce the praises" of him who called you out of darkness into his wonderful light.

1 Peter 2:9

A Catholic to Know

Paul was a Jew who at first thought it was necessary to persecute Christians. On his way to Damascus, a blinding flash of light knocked him to the ground. Jesus spoke to him in an experience so powerful that Paul became one of Christ's most devoted disciples in an instant. As a convert, Paul became the "Apostle to the Gentiles," and he proved to be the right man to build a bridge between the Jews and Gentiles. Paul proclaimed Christ with a zealousness that profoundly influenced the first-century Church's understanding of discipleship in ways that continue to the present day. About half the epistles in the New Testament were written by Paul or attributed to him.

Saint Paul

Witness and Share

These sentences describe what Catholics believe. Listen carefully as they are read. Ask yourself, "How strong are my Catholic beliefs?"

My Way to Faith

- I believe that Christ is present today in the sacraments.

- I receive support from the faith community as I follow Christ.

- I give thanks for being a member of the Church.

- I live as a child of God and an heir to heaven living the Ten Commandments.

- I give witness to Christ by being merciful and forgiving toward others.

- I read Saint Paul's letters to help me understand how to live a Christian life.

Share Your Faith

The sacraments of the Church are signs of God's presence, but there are many other ways to recognize God's presence. Think of everyday people, things, or events that reveal God's presence and write them on the lines. Invite a family member or friend to share the times when he or she has encountered God.

_____

_____

_____

_____

Jesus Christ the Way

Looking Back

In Unit 1, you have looked at who Jesus is and who he is in your life. You have reflected on how the Son of God became man to save us from sin and death. You were reminded that Jesus calls you to friendship with him. You respond to that invitation to friendship through prayer, reading Scripture, and celebrating the sacraments. The purpose of this unit is to help you understand more fully how Jesus is the way to the Father, the way to everlasting happiness.

Before you continue with this chapter, ask yourself these questions. Write your answers on the lines below.

1. **How have your thoughts changed about Jesus? about yourself? about others?**

   _____

   _____

2. **How do you know Jesus can fill you with peace even when suffering enters your life?**

   _____

   _____

3. **What are two things you can do to know Jesus better and follow him?**

   _____

   _____

Workshop of Giovanni Bellini, *Christ Carrying the Cross*, 16th Century, oil on panel.

Personal Inventory

Use this inventory as a tool to reflect on how you are following Jesus. Write your answers in your reflection notebook. Choose one area that you would like to improve.

- ○ **Do you help your friends become the best people they can be?**
- ○ **Do you ask forgiveness when you have failed to be a good friend?**
- ○ **Do you open your heart to Jesus and spend time with him each day?**
- ○ **Do you listen to Christ's message proclaimed at Sunday Mass?**
- ○ **Do you follow in Christ's footsteps by sacrificing for others?**
- ○ **Do you give loving service to others?**
- ○ **Do you act for peace and justice?**

The Doughnut Priest

Following Jesus can lead to surprising roles. For one man, it meant becoming a priest who made doughnuts.

Father Joseph Valine, O.P. (1897–1992), ministered to people in Utah in an area larger than Rhode Island. At the age of 90 he was the pastor of three missions. He traveled only 300 miles a week, down from the 600 miles he used to drive.

Father Valine went to Utah in 1941 at the bishop's request. At that time, Catholics made up only 3 percent of the population of Utah, and they lived far apart. World War II barracks, a library, a trailer, and parishioners' homes all served as churches at different missions until a real church could be built. Father Valine built seven churches with donations and income from his hobbies. For years he catered dinners

and farmed more than 200 acres of alfalfa. Then he became a doughnut maker. Every Saturday Father Valine made doughnuts to sell. Farmers and tourists paid whatever they wished for a bag of 10 doughnuts.

In Milford, a town in which 90 percent of the people are Mormon, June 10, 1976, was proclaimed "Father Valine Day." It was a tribute to his love of God and people. In 1988 he received an award from the Catholic Church Extension Society. It was the Lumen Christi (Light of Christ) Award. What can you do to help spread the light of Christ to the world?

Testing Your Strength

How well do you understand what it means to follow Christ? Read each statement. If it is a Christian response, write C on the line. If it shows a selfish, unloving attitude, write S.

___S___ 1. I cannot volunteer for that task. I want to play basketball during noon recess.

___S___ 2. Here comes the principal! She always has a job for everyone she sees. Let's get away from here.

___C___ 3. I will sign up for the cleanup committee. I hate that kind of work, but I do not think anyone will volunteer for it.

___S___ 4. There is a boycott against grapes to support the grape pickers who are treated unjustly. It will not make a difference if I keep eating grapes, my favorite fruit.

___C___ 5. Mother, you look tired! Let me put the baby to bed.

___C___ 6. No, I am not going to take it. That is stealing!

___S___ 7. I do not have any money for the missions. I need this change to buy gum.

___C___ 8. I am good in art. I will volunteer to make the get-well card from our class.

___C___ 9. The yard is a mess after the storm. Maybe I can get it cleaned up before Mom comes home.

___S___ 10. I cannot do what Dad told me. Everyone will laugh at me.

Find the Truth Statements

Write an X before any true statements about Jesus.

_____ **1.** Jesus is too great to be a real friend.

__X__ **2.** Jesus is the Son of God, the second Person of the Trinity.

__X__ **3.** Jesus means "the anointed."

_____ **4.** Jesus only pretended to be a man.

__X__ **5.** Jesus saved us from sin and death by dying and rising.

__X__ **6.** Jesus showed us how to live.

_____ **7.** The Gospels agree on all the details about Jesus.

__X__ **8.** Jesus sent the Holy Spirit to help us understand him.

__X__ **9.** Jesus was Jewish.

_____ **10.** Jesus was accepted as the Messiah by everyone who knew him.

__X__ **11.** Jesus was tempted.

__X__ **12.** Jesus associated mostly with common people and those who were poor or outcast.

Sign Readers

What do these sacramental signs mean?

• water

_____

_____

_____

• chrism

_____

_____

Sacraments of Initiation

Baptism • Confirmation • Eucharist

Answer these questions in your reflection notebook.

1. How is Jesus present today in these sacraments?

2. How are the three Sacraments of Initiation related?

3. What gifts do we receive in Baptism?

Rite Order

Number the parts of the Rite of Christian Initiation of Adults in order.

__6__ Enlightenment

__1__ Time for Inquiry

__4__ Mystagogy

__5__ Rite of Election or Enrollment

__2__ Catechumenate

__3__ Initiation

• "I baptize you."

_____

_____

• laying on of hands

_____

• "Be sealed with the gift of the Spirit."

_____

Celebrating

Jesus the Way

Leader: Jesus Christ. Everyone who hears about him is faced with a decision. Either Jesus is God or he is not. Either he is our Savior or he is not. Whatever we decide about him involves a risk. Our whole life is at stake. Do you, like millions of others, choose to believe that Jesus is the Son of God? Or do you think he was a liar? a fool? a failure? In the Gospels, the first Christians share their faith in him.

Reader 1: A reading from the Gospel of John. (John 1:1,2,10–12)

In the beginning was the Word,
    and the Word was with God,
    and the Word was God.
He was in the beginning with God.
He was in the world,
    and the world came to be
        through him,
    but the world did not know him.
He came to what was his own,
    but his own people did not
        accept him.
But to those who did accept him
    he gave
    power to become children
        of God.

The gospel of the Lord.

All: Praise to you, Lord Jesus Christ.

Leader: People who knew Jesus reacted to him in different ways.

Side 1: John the Baptist said, "Behold, the Lamb of God, who takes away the sin of the world."

Side 2: The disciples said, "What sort of man is this, whom even the winds and the sea obey?"

Side 1: The Pharisees said, "He drives out demons by the prince of demons."

Side 2: His neighbors said, "Where did this man get such wisdom and mighty deeds?"

Side 1: Some said, "Look, he is a glutton and a drunkard, a friend of tax collectors and sinners."

Side 2: Peter said, "You are the Messiah, the Son of the living God."

Side 1: Nathanael said, "Rabbi, you are the Son of God; you are the King of Israel."

Side 2: The Samaritans said, "We know that this is truly the Savior of the world."

Side 1: The Pharisees said, "Look and see that no prophet arises from Galilee."

Side 2: Some Jewish people said, "We are not stoning you for a good work but for blasphemy. You, a man, are making yourself God."

Side 1: Martha said, "I have come to believe that you are the Messiah, the Son of God."

(Personal reflection: I say . . .)

Reader 2: A reading from the Gospel of Matthew. (Matthew 7:21,24–27)

"Not everyone who says to me, 'Lord, Lord,' will enter the kingdom of heaven, but only the one who does the will of my Father in heaven. Everyone who listens to these words of mine and acts on them will be like a wise man who built his house on rock. The rain fell, the floods came, and the winds blew and buffeted the house. But it did not collapse; it had been set solidly on rock. And everyone who listens to these words of mine but does not act on them will be like a fool who built his house on sand. The rain fell, the floods came, and the winds blew and buffeted the house. And it collapsed and was completely ruined."

The gospel of the Lord.

All: Praise to you, Lord Jesus Christ.

Leader: Jesus invites everyone to believe in him. If you believe in Jesus, you will believe in his words and act on them. As a friend and follower of Jesus, you will want to change anything in your life that is against the Father's law of love.

(Personal reflection: One thing that I can change is . . .)

Leader: Jesus is our way to the Father. He proclaimed the coming of the Kingdom of God. Let us pray with the words he taught us.

All: Our Father . . .

Leader: May the grace and peace of Jesus Christ, who is our Way, be with us now and always.

All: Amen.

Word Puzzle About Jesus

```
      W   A P O S T L E S            P
      I   H                    Z     A
      T   A      S                   S
    I N C A R N A T I O N            C
      E   I                R         H
      S   S            R   C     O   A
  P       S   E V A N G E L I S T    L
  A       E   M            A     S
  A     G O S P E L S      
  L             N      H              M
  S     J O H N     T H E   B A P T I S T
  T             S   M                 T
  I N F A N C Y   N A R R A T I V E S
  N       H                          R
  E     M A R Y          T R I N I T Y
          I
        D I S C I P L E
          T
```

How well do you know your friend? Write a clue for each word related to Jesus in the puzzle. Write your answers on a sheet of paper under the headings "Across" and "Down."

Gather and Go Forth

Know and Proclaim

We seek to know and proclaim Jesus by knowing and understanding our Catholic faith.

We Know Our Faith	We Proclaim Our Faith
Jesus is the Son of God who became man to save us from sin and death.	Catholics celebrate the lives of saints who set an example for how to participate in the mission of Christ and his Church. Saints' feast days are celebrated during the Mass and the Liturgy of the Hours.
Catholics respond to Jesus' friendship through prayer, celebrating the sacraments, and reading Scripture.	*Lectio divina* ("sacred reading") is a way Catholics pray using Scripture. In *lectio divina*, Catholics meditate on the Word of God and the mysteries of Christ.
God became man in the Person of Jesus to invite ordinary people to share in his divinity.	As sharers in Christ's divinity, Catholics are called to bring light to the world. Catholics hold lighted taper candles at the Easter Vigil on Holy Saturday to symbolize our call to carry the light of Christ to the world.

To know God, we must know and follow Jesus. As Catholics, we know Jesus through Sacred Scripture and Sacred Tradition. We meet Jesus in the sacraments and in one another.

Jesus said to him, "I am the way and the truth and the life. No one comes to the Father except through me."

John 14:6

Test Your Catholic Knowledge

Fill in the circle that best completes the sentence.

The Word became flesh in the event called the:

○ Passover.

○ Incarnation.

○ Assumption.

○ Resurrection.

A Catholic to Know

Vincent de Paul was born in 1580 in France. Vincent was appointed the court chaplain to Queen Margaret of Valois. For years, he lived a life of wealth and comfort. However, when he heard the confession of a dying servant, Vincent opened his eyes to the fact that the spiritual needs of the French peasantry were not being met. He devoted the remainder of his life to caring for those who were poor. He established societies and charities to perform the Spiritual and Corporal Works of Mercy by establishing hospitals, orphanages, and homes for those who were mentally ill. Saint Vincent de Paul is the patron of all charitable societies. Many parishes have a St. Vincent de Paul Society that serves those who are poor and in need.

Saint Vincent de Paul

Witness and Share

These sentences describe what Catholics believe. Listen carefully as they are read. Ask yourself, "How strong are my Catholic beliefs?"

My Way to Faith

- I believe that Jesus brings me peace even when I am hurting.

- I volunteer for tasks when I think I can be helpful.

- I share my gifts with people who are in need.

- I follow Jesus as my role model.

- I admire people who follow in Christ's footsteps by sacrificing for others.

Share Your Faith

We follow in Christ's footsteps by proclaiming his message with our deeds. Consider the things you do. How do they proclaim your faith? Write about one deed on the lines. Invite others to share their faith with you.

_____

_____

_____

_____

Jesus Christ the Truth

"The Little Way" Leads to Big Results

SAINT THÉRÈSE OF LISIEUX had none of the power that comes from controlling wealth or armies. Yet this humble young French saint has influenced Catholicism as few others have. After she died of tuberculosis at the age of 24 in the late 1890s, her meditations were published. She's most famous for outlining a spiritual path she called the "Little Way." It's the practice of doing small things with great love, finding spiritual sustenance and patience to make it through the day.

- As Thérèse once explained to novices at the convent, "You know well enough that Our Lord does not look so much at the greatness of our actions, nor even at their difficulty, but at the love with which we do them."

- Dorothy Day, a cofounder of the Catholic Worker Movement, was deeply devoted to Saint Thérèse. "No act, however apparently insignificant, is without meaning when done within the awareness of God's loving presence," she wrote. "Whatever our situation in life—a mother with children at home or a mother working, a store clerk, a scholar, a nursing home assistant, a suburbanite, an assembly line worker—all of us, in the ordinary and required activity of daily life, have available to us in the Little Way a means to holiness, to love as God loves us."

- Blessed Mother Teresa had more in common with Thérèse than her name. Like Dorothy Day, she dedicated herself to loving care of the world's poor. She wrote, "We can do no great things; only small things with great love." She also said, "Sometimes it is harder for us to smile at those who live with us, the immediate members of our families, than it is to smile at those who are not so close to us. Let us never forget: love begins at home."

Visit **www.christourlife.com** for more family resources.

Left to right: Saint Thérèse, Dorothy Day, Mother Teresa.

Love Anyway

People are often unreasonable, irrational, and self-centered. Forgive them anyway.

If you are kind, people may accuse you of selfish, ulterior motives. Be kind anyway.

If you are honest and sincere people may deceive you. Be honest and sincere anyway.

What you spend years creating, others could destroy overnight. Create anyway.

If you find serenity and happiness, some may be jealous. Be happy anyway.

The good you do today, will often be forgotten. Do good anyway.

Give the best you have, and it will never be enough. Give your best anyway.

—From a prayer on the wall in Mother Teresa's home for children in Calcutta, adapted from Dr. Kent Keith's "Paradoxical Commandments"

Parables: Stories Jesus Told

Jesus the Storyteller

Living in the Light

What is it like to walk in the dark without being able to see well? What might happen?

_____

_____

Jesus calls himself the Light of the World. He shows us the right path in life and helps us see where we are going. Jesus, the Son of God, is the source of all truth. All his life was a teaching. His teachings are the truth that light our way to the Father. They give us knowledge of how to be a better person in the light of God's commandments. Jesus revealed the love of God and God's plan for us. He proclaimed the message of salvation.

If we follow Jesus' teachings, we will know the happiness of his friendship. Walking with Jesus is the sure way of following God's will and eventually entering the kingdom. Walking with him, we live well on earth and arrive safely at the kingdom. What God has revealed, especially through Jesus, is the foundation of our faith.

Teachings of Twenty Centuries

Jesus commissioned his apostles to teach the Good News to all nations. Through their ministry of **evangelization,** the apostles handed on Jesus' message through the words they taught and the good example they gave to others. They shared Jesus' mission in stories, customs, prayers, and creeds, or professions of faith that we find based in the New Testament.

Bishops, the successors of the apostles, also have the right and duty to teach everything Jesus has revealed. The teaching authority of the Church is called the **Magisterium.** It is at work primarily in the pope and in the bishops teaching together and in union with the pope. The Magisterium is present in liturgy and in the practice of the faith—whenever doctrines contained in Scripture and Tradition are taught. A doctrine is a belief the Church holds and teaches. A doctrine that is officially defined by the Church as a truth revealed by God, an article of faith for Catholics, is a dogma. Some doctrines are more important than others. It is Church doctrine that Jesus is God and that Mary was sinless.

For 2,000 years the Church has preserved the doctrines Jesus taught and has gained new insights. Truth does not change, but the Holy Spirit continually leads the Church to a deeper understanding. On our journey of life, we can look to the Church for truths to guide us—the truths that Jesus taught.

Stories That Teach

Jesus was a master teacher. He used stories about the stuff of his everyday life: sowers and seeds, fishermen and nets, shepherds, thieves, and yeast. He spoke of ordinary happenings: looking for a lost object, getting paid for work, and asking a friend for help. The stories Jesus told about God and his kingdom are called parables. In a parable, a comparison is made between something familiar and the truth Jesus wants to bring to our attention.

A parable usually has an unexpected twist that shows the Kingdom of God in images we use in everyday life. It encourages us t o see things differently.

After hearing a parable, we make a judgment about the events in the story and then apply it to ourselves. Often we find that our way of thinking and acting is being challenged by God. The discovery challenges us to change our lives for the better.

How a Short Story Works

Read the Parable of the Rich Fool and then answer the questions on a sheet of paper.

> "There was a rich man whose land produced a bountiful harvest. He asked himself, 'What shall I do, for I do not have space to store my harvest?' And he said, "This is what I shall do: I shall tear down my barns and build larger ones. There I shall store all my grain and other goods and I shall say to myself, "Now as for you, you have so many good things stored up for many years, rest, eat, drink, be merry!'" But God said to him, 'You fool, this night your life will be demanded of you; and the things you have prepared, to whom will they belong?' Thus will it be for the one who stores up treasure for himself but is not rich in what matters to God."
>
> Luke 12:16–21

The Rich Fool, Jesus Mafa Collection, France.

1. **A story has a main character and other characters.** Who are the characters in this parable?
2. **A story has a setting.** Where does this story take place?
3. **A story has a plot, the action.** What happens in this story?
4. **The action centers around a struggle.** What problem does the main character face?
5. **A story's main character might have a flaw.** What is the rich man's flaw?
6. **Conversation in a story tells us what a character is like.** How do you know what the rich man is like?
7. **Some stories have surprise endings.** What happened to the rich man that he did not expect?
8. **Stories mirror real life.** Are there people like the rich man? Have you ever been like the rich man? Do you know of anyone who had an experience like the rich man's?
9. **Stories draw us into them and make us think.** How do you think the rich man felt when God spoke? Why was he a fool? What do you think happened after he died?
10. **Stories have a theme, a message.** What meaning do you find in this parable? What questions does the story make you ask yourself?

A parable has layers, like an onion. To reveal its meanings, ask questions like those above.

Probing the Parables

Read each parable and match it with a truth.

a. The Pharisee and the Tax Collector
(Luke 18:9–14), *image at right*
b. The Lost Sheep (Luke 15:4–7)
c. The Workers in the Vineyard
(Matthew 20:1–16)
d. The persistent friend (Luke 11:5–8)

_____ 1. God loves sinners and is glad
when they return to a good life.

_____ 2. Sinners who truly repent even at
the last minute will have the fullness of joy in heaven.

_____ 3. Beware of being proud of your
goodness and judging others.

_____ 4. Keep praying to God, and your
prayers will be answered.

Kingdom Parables

Jesus proclaimed the Kingdom of God, which is already here but not yet fully. In this kingdom, God and God's people live together in peace, justice, and love. The parables listed in the table below give insights into the kingdom. Read them and fill in the blanks in each statement. Notice which Gospel contains all of these kingdom parables.

THE PARABLE	A TRUTH IT TEACHES
The Mustard Seed Matthew 13:31–32 **The Yeast** Matthew 13:33	1. From a small beginning the kingdom _____.
The Net Matthew 13:47–50 **The Weeds** Matthew 13:24–30	2. On earth _____ and _____ live together until _____.
The Pearl of Great Price Matthew 13:45–46 **The Hidden Treasure** Matthew 13:44	3. The person who finds the kingdom feels _____. To possess it, he or she is willing to _____.
The Wedding Feast Matthew 22:2–14	4. The kingdom is open to _____. We are free to _____.

A Moment with Jesus

Pause for a moment and silently reflect on the kingdom parables and the truths that they teach about the Kingdom of God. Jesus used common images such as a wedding feast, weeds, or a small seed. Take some time to reflect on how you would describe the Kingdom of God. What common image would you use?

In your own words, ask Jesus to help you recognize the signs of the kingdom around you. Then thank him for the gift of his word in the Gospels.

Life or Death?

In Palestine, farmers probably scattered seed all over the land and then plowed it under. In the Parable of the Sower (Matthew 13:3–9, 18–23), Jesus told what happened to the seed sown by a farmer. Some seed fell on the edge of the path and was eaten by birds. Some fell on rocky ground. It grew, but then withered away for lack of roots. Some fell among thorns and was choked by them. But some seed fell on rich soil and produced a wonderful crop.

The parable shows what happens to the Word of God. Some people do not listen to it at all. Some accept the Word at first but are too weak to live by it. Some accept the Word, and then other people or things of the world kill it in their hearts. In some people, however, God's Word lives. They spread his kingdom wherever they are. To which group do you belong?

Rich Soil for the Parables

Will the parables take root in your heart? Write how a member of the kingdom would respond to these situations. Then write what might make it difficult to respond that way.

1. Your friends start teasing a classmate who is unpopular.

   Christian response: _____

   _____

   Possible difficulties: _____

   _____

2. A classmate you would like to be friends with has dared you to shoplift a CD. You realize you could be caught and arrested if you do not succeed.

   Christian response: _____

   _____

   Possible difficulties: _____

   _____

3. You and several others are at a friend's home. Your friend's parents are not there. The friend suggests drinking some liquor. There is a lot of it, and the parents will not miss it.

   Christian response: _____

   _____

   Possible difficulties: _____

   _____

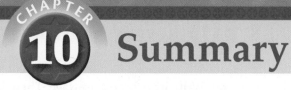

10 Summary

Remember

How do we come to know the teachings of Jesus?
We come to know the teachings of Jesus through Scripture, Tradition, and the teaching of the Church.

What is a parable of Jesus?
A parable of Jesus is a story that teaches about God and the Kingdom of God through everyday experiences.

What did Jesus say about listening to God's Word?
Jesus said, "Blessed are those who hear the word of God and observe it." (Luke 11:28)

Respond

Suppose the world were to end tonight. What would you wish to have changed about yourself to be better prepared to meet Jesus? Write it in your reflection notebook. Then list some steps you can take to make this change happen.

Reach Out

1. The message of Jesus calls us to a way of life that is very different from the way of the world. Find a newspaper story or magazine article about someone whose response to a need was Christlike. Talk about it with someone at home. Then write a paragraph about what you learned from the person's actions.

2. All the saints met opposition as they tried to live the teachings of Jesus. Sometimes they had to overcome their personal feelings. Sometimes they met criticism, ridicule, and even persecution. Research the life of a saint. Suggestions: Saint Ignatius of Antioch, Saint John Baptist de La Salle, Saint Elizabeth Ann Seton, Saint Julie Billiart, Saint Thomas More, Saint John of the Cross, Saint Isaac Jogues.

Find at least one situation in which that person followed Jesus' way even when facing opposition. Share the story with a family member.

3. The more peace, justice, and love are brought into the world, the more the kingdom is present. What can you do to further the kingdom in your family, your neighborhood, and your world? Gather with one or more family members and brainstorm for ideas. Then select one idea and create a plan for how you will carry it out.

4. Be open to God's Word today. Pay attention to a homily, read a section of the Gospel, or read an article in a Catholic periodical. Share what you learn with someone in your family.

5. Design a poster that is based on one of the parables. Ask a family member to help you create it. Then display it where it can be seen and talked about.

Words to Know

evangelization
Magisterium

Parables in Art Choose a parable about God. Write its title and message. Then draw a picture to represent it. Do the same for the Kingdom of God and for the members of the kingdom.

Title: _____

God: _____

_____

Title: _____

The Kingdom of God: _____

_____

Title: _____

Members of the Kingdom: _____

_____

True or False Write **T** if the statement is true or **F** if it is false.

_____ **1.** Scripture was written before Tradition began.

_____ **2.** The Magisterium is the teaching authority of the Church.

_____ **3.** The Church can change dogmas.

_____ **4.** The Holy Spirit leads us to new understandings of Christ's teachings.

_____ **5.** Parables are stories meant only for the people in Jesus' time.

_____ **6.** The Kingdom of God is already here.

_____ **7.** The parables urge us to listen to God's Word and to serve the kingdom.

Gather and Go Forth

Know and Proclaim

Knowing our Catholic faith helps us know God's truth. We proclaim God's truth in what we say and do.

We Know Our Faith	We Proclaim Our Faith
Jesus is the Light of the World. His teachings are the truth that lights the way to God.	Catholic young people participate in youth leadership conferences and youth ministry events to better understand how God is calling them.
Jesus taught using parables. His parables used familiar things to teach the truths about God.	Catholics pray with and meditate on sacred art that often depicts the parables of Jesus. Catholics apply the lessons of the parables to everyday life.
Jesus' teaching are known through Scripture, Tradition, and the teachings of the Church.	Catholics participate in Scripture study, whether in person or online, to come to know the teachings of Christ.

Jesus revealed truths about God through parables. By applying Jesus' parables to our own lives, we will bring light to the world.

"Knowledge of the mysteries of the kingdom of God has been granted to you; but to the rest, they are made known through parables, so that 'they may look but not see, and hear but not understand.'"

Luke 8:10

Test Your Catholic Knowledge

Fill in the circle that best answers the question.

What are all baptized Catholics responsible to do?

○ pray the Rosary each Saturday

○ attend daily Mass

○ pray after meals

○ evangelize others

A Catholic to Know

The story of Saint Stephen, deacon and martyr, is recounted in the Acts of the Apostles. (Acts 6:1—8:1) Chosen by the apostles as a man filled with faith and the Holy Spirit, Stephen became a deacon and assisted the Twelve. Stephen became known for working great wonders and signs among the people, prompting false accusations of blasphemy. During interrogation by the high priests, he proclaimed Christ and challenged their piety. Angered, they drove him from the city and stoned him to death. Saint Stephen died speaking words of forgiveness for his executioners. We honor his witness to Christ on December 26.

Saint Stephen

Witness and Share

These sentences describe what Catholics believe. Listen carefully as they are read. Ask yourself, "How strong are my Catholic beliefs?"

My Way to Faith

- I read the Gospels to learn more about Jesus' teachings.

- I look to the Church to learn the truth about Jesus.

- I believe that the invitation to the Kingdom of God is given to all people.

- I encourage my friends to do the right thing if they are tempted to act in ways contrary to the example of Jesus.

- I read about the lives of the saints to better understand what it means to be a disciple.

Share Your Faith

Think about Jesus' parables. Write your own parable on the lines below and continue it on a separate sheet of paper. What truth about God are you trying to share? What lesson are you trying to teach? Invite others to listen to your parable.

_____

_____

_____

_____

_____

Miracles: Signs Jesus Worked

Jesus the Miracle Worker

Beyond Explanation

- The pastor of a poor parish can't pay his electric bill. He prays to the Sacred Heart. The next day's mail brings a check from an anonymous donor for the exact amount of the bill.
- As Ruth picked up the newspaper, she realized she locked herself out of the house. She said a prayer asking God to help her find a solution. Just then her sister drove up to return the spare key she used when watering the plants while Ruth was on vacation.
- According to the Gospels, Jesus worked fantastic cures:

  > The crowds were amazed when they saw the mute speaking, the deformed made whole, the lame walking, and the blind able to see, and they glorified the God of Israel.

  > Matthew 15:31

Do you believe in miracles? Why or why not?

Miracles Make Sense

The universe is filled with marvelous events and mysteries. Natural wonders, such as a spectacular sunset or a newborn baby, make us aware of God's presence. In miracles, God's presence is seen in our world even more dramatically. A **miracle** is a phenomenon that seems to have no natural cause and can be explained only as a direct intervention of God. The Gospels contain many examples of miracles performed by Jesus as signs of God's love and concern for the people.

The Synoptic Gospels call miracles acts of power, but John's Gospel calls them signs. Jesus' extraordinary acts were signs that the kingdom he proclaimed is among us. Miracles were one way that Jesus taught truths about himself, the kingdom, and its members.

Acts That Teach

Jesus' miracles reveal that he is the Holy One. He is goodness, mercy, and life. The miracles show him to be Lord over nature, sin, sickness, Satan, and death.

Some people believed that suffering and death were the result of personal sin. Read John 9:1–3. How did Jesus react to this belief?

Pain, weakness, suffering, and death are the result of Original Sin. Except Jesus and Mary, each person throughout history bears its weight and suffers its effects. People longed for the Messiah who would free them from bondage to sin. The disciples of John the Baptist asked Jesus, "'Are you the one who is to come, or should we look for another?'"

(Matthew 11:3) He replied, "'Go and tell John what you hear and see: the blind regain their sight, the lame walk, lepers are cleansed, the deaf hear, the dead are raised, and the poor have the good news proclaimed to them.'" (Matthew 11:4–5) Jesus' healing of physical evils is a sign of his victory over all evil. Jesus is truly the Savior of the world.

The miracles teach lessons just as the parables do. When Jesus healed on the Sabbath and touched unclean people, he showed that God's law of love surpasses all human laws. When he worked miracles for outcasts, sinners, and Gentiles, he showed that God's kingdom is open to all. When he worked wonders for people in need, he showed God's compassion and love. The miracles also teach the importance of faith. Jesus often praised the faith of the people who came to him for help. Where there was no faith, he worked no miracles.

Miracle Stories

Many people became disciples of Jesus because they saw his miracles. They watched him heal the sick and bring the dead back to life. They saw him break Satan's hold over people. They

Julius Schnorr von Carolsfeld, *The Marriage at Cana*, 1819.

realized that in Jesus, God was with them. The following Gospel stories about miracles are rewritten as eyewitness accounts. As you read them, be open to their teachings. After each one, list the truths that it reveals to you.

Wine Overflowing
as told by Mary (John 2:1–12)

I remember the first miracle Jesus worked. My son, some of his new friends, and I were at a wedding in Cana. Everyone was having a good time, but the wine was getting low. If it ran out, the newly-wed couple and their families would be deeply embarrassed. Thinking my son could help somehow, I merely said to him, "They have no wine." Jesus answered, "Woman, how does your concern affect me? My hour has not yet come." I wasn't sure what he meant, but I knew I could depend on him. I told the servants, "Do whatever he tells you."

Sure enough, Jesus ordered the servants to fill six stone jars with water. These jars, used for ritual washings, each held about 20 to 30 gallons. When they were filled to the brim with water, Jesus told the servants to take some to the headwaiter. I watched the headwaiter sip the wine. He went to the bridegroom and said, "Everyone serves good wine first and keeps the cheaper wine until people have had plenty to drink, but you have kept the best wine until now." Jesus' new friends were also astounded. They remembered that providing in abundance for people is a sign that God was present to his people in a special way. Many of his friends came to believe in him that day.

Truths: Jesus has power over _____

_____

_____

_____

_____

_____

Rising from Paralysis and Sin
as told by a friend (Mark 2:1–12)

When we heard that Jesus the healer was home again in Capernaum, four of us decided to take our paralyzed friend to him. With great hope we carried our friend on his mat to the house where Jesus was preaching. To our dismay, people packed the house and crowded around the door. We couldn't even get near Jesus. Then we had a brilliant idea. We hoisted our friend up the side steps to the roof. We broke through the thatched roof right above Jesus and carefully lowered the mat holding our friend through the opening. You should have seen the look on the people's faces! The crowd made room for our friend.

Jesus said to him, "Child, your sins are forgiven." We knew that the religious leaders sitting there were probably horrified since only God can forgive sins. Jesus seemed to read their minds. He asked, "Which is easier to say to the paralyzed man, 'Your sins are forgiven' or 'Rise, pick up your mat and walk'? So that you may know I have authority to forgive sins,"—then he said to our friend, "Rise, pick up your mat, and go home." With that, our friend, who hadn't even been able to move his little finger, stood and picked up his mat. He passed through the crowd of people and out the door a free man.

Truths: Jesus has power over _____

_____

_____

_____

Stilling a Storm
as told by Peter (Mark 4:35–41)

One evening after a hard day of teaching, Jesus said, "Let's cross the lake." Leaving the crowd on the shore, we got in our boat and sailed off. Jesus was so exhausted that before long he was sound asleep on a cushion. Suddenly a violent storm blew up. Huge waves crashed over us, filling our boat with water. We woke Jesus, shouting, "Teacher, don't you care that we are perishing?" First, he commanded the wind to stop. Then he said to the sea, "Quiet. Be still." At his word the wind ceased and everything became very calm. With disappointment written on his face, he asked us why we were terrified. He asked, "Don't you have faith yet?" All we could do was marvel at what we had seen and wonder who he was. Never in all our years of sailing have we met someone whom the wind and sea obeyed.

Truths: Jesus has power over _____

_____

_____

_____

Laura James, *Jesus Calms the Storm*, 1995. ❯

A Burst of Miracles

Learn more about Jesus by reading the miracle stories listed below. Summarize the stories using a chart with three columns labeled "Power Over . . . ," "How Jesus Showed Compassion," and "Who Showed Faith?"

- Luke 5:1–11   Great catch of fish
- Mark 10:46–52   Blind Bartimaeus
- Luke 7:1–10   Centurion's slave
- Mark 9:14–29   Possessed boy
- Luke 7:11–17   Widow's son

A Man for Others

Compassion is sympathy for people who are suffering and a desire to reduce or relieve their pain—even to suffer in their place. It is being one with them in their suffering. Jesus showed limitless compassion for people who were poor, sick, sinners—for anyone who was suffering. His desire to help people often moved him to work miracles. Jesus has the same compassion for us today. He wants us to turn to him with faith when we are suffering. Sometimes he helps us through one another.

As followers and friends of Christ, we respond to others as he did. We reach out with compassion to people who are suffering, and we work the "miracle" of kindness. Our miracles will not be as spectacular as those of Jesus. However, with the help of his grace, we can perform miracles of love such as:

- healing someone with kind words;

- encouraging sinners by showing them forgiveness;

- going out of our way to help someone;

- doing a hidden act that brightens someone's day;

- helping a friend overcome temptation and make the right decision;

- bringing an outsider into the circle of friendship;

- persuading our family to sponsor a child in another country who is poor.

What miracles can you work today?

_____

_____

How would these miracles be wonders?

_____

_____

What would these miracles be signs of?

_____

_____

A Moment with Jesus

The practice of compassion is needed in our world. Reflect for a moment on how Jesus showed compassion for people who suffered. Then silently think about the people you see every day—family, friends, strangers. Who might need a compassionate word or deed? Decide how you will respond to that person. Then thank Jesus for the opportunity to make his compassion known in the world.

Remember

What do Jesus' miracles show him having power over?

Miracles show Jesus having power over nature, sin, sickness, Satan, and death.

What can we do if we have faith?

Jesus said, "If you have faith the size of a mustard seed, you will say to this mountain, 'Move from here to there,' and it will move. Nothing will be impossible for you."

Matthew 17:20

Word to Know

miracle

Respond

Jesus often praised the faith of the person who had asked for his help. How strong is your faith? Choose three of the questions below and answer them in your reflection notebook.

- Which actions of yours show that you believe in God?
- What do you do to strengthen your faith?
- When have you turned to Jesus for help?
- How have you given witness to your faith when it was tested by what others said and did?
- How do you thank God for the gift of faith?
- How have you tried to share your faith with others?

Reach Out

1. Jesus and Mary were welcome guests at the wedding feast of Cana. Would they have been welcome at the last party you attended? Why or why not? Do you think they would have been happy to be there, or might they have been uncomfortable? With a group of friends or with your family, set some ground rules for parties. How can you create a party environment in which Jesus and Mary would feel comfortable?

2. Reflect on these questions about miracles:
   - Why do you think that faith is important for a miracle?
   - What miracles can you pray for today?

3. Plan and present a trilogy of miracle plays. Invite another class, your family, or members of your parish. You might record your plays to show to people who cannot attend.

4. Find out about miracles that have occurred in recent times. Look for stories about miracles in magazines, newspapers, or online. Prepare a report to share with your class.

5. Friends tend to imitate each other. They often like the same music, clothes, books, movies, or sports. Sometimes they even think alike. In what ways are you like your friend Jesus? How can you be more like him? Think about those questions and write your thoughts in your reflection notebook. Begin by listing qualities or virtues of Jesus. Do you have any of those qualities? Select one quality that you would like to improve. Plan actions you will take to accomplish that.

6. Think of ways to imitate the compassion of Jesus and bring healing to others. Here are some things you might consider doing.
   - Send a card or note to someone who is ill or living alone.
   - Offer to read to an elderly person, or write letters for him or her.
   - Do something to give someone who cares for you extra rest, especially when he or she seems very tired or is not feeling well.
   - Plan to visit a nursing home. Call to find out times and rules for visiting. Ask an adult to be your advisor and to help you decide what you will do on your visit.
   - Be considerate and quiet around the house when someone is ill or has a headache.
   - Send a donation to an organization that helps people who are suffering from a war.

What Do You Think? **Use what you learned to answer these questions.**

1. Before a person is canonized (declared a saint), usually two miracles worked through the person's prayers must occur. Why are miracles a good test for sainthood?

   _____

2. When two people witness an extraordinary event, one might respond "It's a miracle," and the other, "It's just a coincidence." What makes the difference in their responses?

   _____

3. How are miracles like parables?

   _____

Miracle Mix **Unscramble the letters of the words under the lines to complete the sentences.**

1. A _____ is an act of power, a wonder through which God gives us a sign.
   crliema

2. The miracles of Jesus were a sign of the presence of the _____.
   gdimkon

3. Pain, suffering, and death are the result of _____.
   ilogarin ins

4. Jesus' miracles show his power over all _____.
   live

5. Miracles are closely linked with _____.
   tifha

6. Jesus' first miracle was in response to _____.
   ayrM

7. When Jesus healed the paralyzed man, he also _____ him his sins.
   voefgar

8. Jesus' calming the storm showed his power over _____.
   etanur

9. Jesus healed the centurion's _____ who was ill and about to die.
   vleas

10. Jesus raised to life the son of a _____.
    wwoid

11. Jesus worked miracles because he had _____.
    mssoopcnai

12. We are like Jesus when we are _____.
    dikn

Gather and Go Forth

Know and Proclaim

As Catholics, we recognize God's miracles in the large and small events of our lives, and we proclaim the miracle of our faith to others.

We Know Our Faith	We Proclaim Our Faith
A miracle is a sign or wonder that can only be explained as a direct action of God.	As Catholics, we see miracles as evidence of God's direct involvement in our everyday lives. We commonly pray for miracles and for the faith to recognize them.
Jesus' miracles reveal that he is the Holy One and more powerful than nature, sickness, sin, Satan, and death.	Catholics recognize that by performing works of mercy, others may come to recognize God's miraculous compassion and mercy in their lives.
Jesus' miracles reveal to us the presence of God's kingdom and teach us about the importance of faith.	By serving those in need, Catholics follow the examples of the saints, to whom many miracles are attributed. Miracles are a sign that God is present and active in people's lives.

Jesus' signs and miracles enabled others to witness the power of God, who sent him. In Jesus, the impossible becomes possible.

Then he asked them, "Where is your faith?" But they were filled with awe and amazed and said to one another, "Who then is this, who commands even the winds and the sea, and they obey him?"

Luke 8:25

Test Your Catholic Knowledge

Fill in the circle that best completes the sentence.

The miracle associated with Jesus that is most central to our Catholic faith is the:

○ calming of a storm at sea.

○ healing of a paralytic.

○ wedding at Cana.

○ Resurrection.

A Catholic to Know

Saint André Bessette

"I am sending you a saint," read the message from André Bessette's pastor to the Holy Cross brothers in Montreal, Canada. They were not convinced that the illiterate young man in fragile health was suitable for their teaching order, and they asked him to leave. André appealed, however, and was assigned work as a porter in a school. Brother André became known for his unwavering devotion to Saint Joseph. He spent many hours praying for people who were sick, and they reported miraculous healings. Taking no credit for these cures, Brother André gave gratitude to Saint Joseph's intervention. Brother André died on January 6, 1937.

Witness and Share

These sentences describe what Catholics believe. Listen carefully as they are read. Ask yourself, "How strong are my Catholic beliefs?"

My Way to Faith

- I look for signs of God's active presence in my life.

- I spread Jesus' miraculous love to others by performing works of mercy.

- I honor the saints of the Catholic Church and imitate their witness.

- I help my friends overcome temptations and make good decisions.

- I can name some of Jesus' miracles, such as Jesus healing a blind man.

- I recognize Jesus' miracles as signs that he is the Son of God.

Share Your Faith

Consider how the Holy Spirit may be working miracles in your life. Write your ideas on the lines. Resolve to increase your awareness of God's presence, and invite a friend or family member to share with you the miracles of God in his or her life.

_____

_____

_____

_____

CHAPTER 12

Penance and Anointing of the Sick

Jesus the Healer

When was the last time you needed healing? All people need healing in some way. It may be the healing of a sick and weakened body, or it may be the healing of a spirit wounded by sin and guilt. Jesus came to heal the world of sin and to heal us—body and soul. While on earth he healed people by word and by touch, showing God's love and mercy. Nearly one-fifth of the Gospels deals with healings. Christ's healing ministry continues today especially in the Sacraments of Penance and Reconciliation and the Anointing of the Sick. His ministry is also carried on in other sacraments, in works of charity, and in the prayer of the community. Being Christian means both being healed and healing.

Healing of Spirit

Every time Steve walked into math class, he saw the boarded-up window. The principal was still trying to find out who had broken it the night of the basketball tournament.

Every day Steve waited to get caught. He was quieter at home. The few remarks he did make to his brothers and sisters were harsh. How they all annoyed him lately! Steve and his friends found themselves tense and quick to argue. The daily reminder of the boarded-up window unnerved them.

Steve was working on his bike when his father walked up to him. Steve had always found it easy to talk to him, but now he did not even want to look at his father.

"It's a good day for fishing, Steve."

"I'm kind of busy today. Maybe some other time."

Steve's father was patient, but insistent. Soon they were at the lake. Far away from school, the broken window, and the other guys, Steve found it easier to talk. Before long the whole story poured out. Steve's father listened carefully, looking intently at his son.

Yes, it was an accident but he had been foolish to run away from it. Yes, in some way he wanted to make up for it.

Already Steve felt the relief of a burden being lifted. Together, he and his father spoke to the principal. Every day after classes, Steve would work in the school until he could pay for a new window.

What kind of healing did Steve need?

Who helped Steve become healed? How?

What were some of the effects of Steve's guilt, and who felt them?

If you had been with Steve the night the window was broken, what would you have done?

Greek icon depicting the parable of the prodigal son.

Healing of Forgiveness

Sin cripples and wounds us. Jesus showed God's mercy and love for sinners. He gave his disciples the authority to forgive others in his name. Today, in the Sacrament of Reconciliation, sins we have committed after Baptism are forgiven through Jesus' priests. We are reconciled to God and others. We are healed. Individual confession of serious sins followed by absolution is the ordinary way of celebrating the Sacrament of Reconciliation.

Jesus told three parables to show how anxious God is to forgive us after we have sinned: The Lost Sheep (Luke 15:3–7), The Lost Coin (Luke 15:8–10), and The Lost Son (Luke 15:11–32), better named The Forgiving Father. Read those parables, realizing how good it is to be forgiven, to be welcomed home with love and acceptance.

In the Sacrament of Reconciliation, sinners who are sorry for their sins and intend not to sin again can be certain of God's forgiveness. They receive the grace to change their lives and follow Christ more closely. The sacrament is also a sign that the Christian community, which has been harmed by their sin, forgives them too.

Receiving God's Forgiveness

Four elements must be present whenever the Sacrament of Reconciliation is celebrated:

Contrition

This is true sorrow for failing to love. You intend not to sin again and are ready to model your life on the life of Jesus. Conversion, turning away from sin and turning toward God, is at the heart of the sacrament.

Confession

When you tell your sins to the priest, discussing them is more helpful than just listing them. Talk about things in school, at home, and at recreation places that keep you from being the kind of person Jesus expects you to be. Ask questions.

Penance

Conversion of heart is shown by an act of penance or satisfaction. It may be a prayer, an act of self-denial, or a work of charity that makes up for damage or pain your sins have caused. It can help you begin again and live more completely for Christ.

Absolution

God, through the ministry of the Church and its priest, gives you pardon for your sins with these words:

> "God the Father of mercies,
>   through the death and resurrection
>   of his Son
> has reconciled the world to himself
> and sent the Holy Spirit among us
> for the forgiveness of sins;
> through the ministry of the Church
> may God give you pardon and peace,
> and I absolve you from your sins
> in the name of the Father, and of the Son,
> and of the Holy Spirit."

A Moment with Jesus

In the Gospels, Jesus teaches us that God the Father is always ready to forgive us. Choose one of the three parables mentioned above and reread it. Then pause for a moment to think about the ending.

Recall a time that you were in need of forgiveness and found love and acceptance in return. Ask Jesus for the grace to forgive others just as you have been forgiven. Then thank him for showing you the Father's mercy and love.

Mending Relationships

The father in the parable of the lost son had two sons. The older son, who refused to forgive his repentant brother, was refusing to love. He too was a sinner and in need of reconciliation.

When were you last called to forgive someone? Did you tell the person he or she was forgiven? Was your relationship restored? When were you last forgiven? How did you know you were forgiven? How did you feel?

Christ challenges us and gives us the grace to forgive as he forgave—freely, completely, and lovingly. God's greatest desire is that we ask forgiveness for our sins and forgive others as we have been forgiven.

Healing of Body

On a spring day, Lisa came home with a headache and a 103° fever. Her mom took her to the doctor. A physical exam and blood test showed Lisa had mononucleosis. She would need to stay home to rest for at least two weeks and not participate in school activities.

Family and friends called and wrote. They visited, brought cards and flowers, and shared news. Everyone listened as Lisa talked about her experiences and what she had learned. Day by day, Lisa became the lively girl they had known before. With loving care and rest, she would continue her summer activities and be ready for school in the fall.

Who helped Lisa regain health? How?

_____

_____

A Gift for the Suffering

The book *Old Age Isn't for Sissies* suggests the difficulty of being weakened by age. Old age and illness often bring frustration, discouragement, and even bitterness. Those who are sick may feel lonely, and wonder why God permits them to suffer. They may envy the energy

and health of others. Some elderly people fear losing their independence. People who are elderly and sick may be impatient and feel unappreciated. There can be many temptations for them at a time when they feel very weak.

Christ understands suffering. He knows the pain, the stress, and the emptiness that we endure. Through the celebration of the Sacrament of the Anointing of the Sick, he strengthens and comforts the seriously ill, grants them forgiveness, and restores their health if it is God's plan for them.

Check the attitudes that apply to you.

What is your attitude toward sickness? Do you
- ○ refuse to think about it until it happens to you personally?
- ○ complain when you are ill?
- ○ think it is a punishment from God?
- ○ pray when you are sick?
- ○ thank God for your health?

What is your attitude toward people who are sick and elderly? Do you
- ○ pray for them?
- ○ feel sorry for them, but find it difficult to be around them?
- ○ find joy in visiting them?

People who are sick and elderly can unite their sufferings with Christ and offer them for the Church. What other gifts can they bring to the community?

_____

_____

_____

_____

_____

_____

The Anointing of the Sick

The Sacrament of the Anointing of the Sick may be celebrated anywhere. At times a parish anointing service is held for all those in need of the sacrament. Usually the Church is represented by at least the priest, family, and friends who have gathered to pray for the sick person.

The priest sprinkles the sick person with holy water, recalling Baptism when he or she was given new life through Christ's passion and Resurrection. Then everyone participates in the penitential rite. The sick person may celebrate the Sacrament of Reconciliation in private at this time. Then God's Word is proclaimed, offering comfort and hope to all.

Next, just as Jesus often healed by touching, the priest lays his hands on the head of the sick person. This act signifies invoking the Holy Spirit to come upon the sick person. It also signifies the blessing and prayers of the Church and its union with the sick person. Then the priest anoints the person with oil on the forehead and hands, saying,

> "Through this holy anointing may the Lord in his love and mercy help you with the grace of the Holy Spirit. May the Lord who frees you from sin save you and raise you up."

The ancient practice of anointing with oil means healing, soothing, and strengthening. It is a sign of the presence of the Holy Spirit.

After the anointing, everyone prays for the physical and spiritual health of the one anointed. The sacrament concludes with praying the Lord's Prayer, receiving Holy Communion, and a blessing.

Food for the Journey

A person who is dying may receive Holy Communion in a special rite called *viaticum*. The word means "with you on the way." In viaticum, Jesus accompanies us through the struggles at the end of life and into the banquet of the heavenly kingdom. The rite includes a renewal of the baptismal profession of faith and may end with everyone giving the dying person the sign of peace.

Do you know someone who is seriously ill or elderly? What can you do to help that person?

The Gift of Healing

Today Christ's healing ministry is very much alive. Not only does Christ bring healing to us through the Sacraments of Penance and Reconciliation and the Anointing of the Sick but through certain people. At times, God gives people a special gift of healing for the good of others and the Church. Working through them, Jesus responds to the faith and prayers of sick people and their friends. He continues to cure people with many kinds of illnesses—physical, mental, and spiritual. Often the greatest healing is spiritual.

Each one of us, though, is called to be a healer through our words and actions, our prayers and sacrifices.

When have you been healed?

_____

How have you helped heal someone else?

_____

Remember

How do the Sacraments of Healing heal us?

In the Sacrament of Reconciliation, Christ offers forgiveness and reconciliation to those who have turned away from God and the community. In the Sacrament of the Anointing of the Sick, Christ offers forgiveness, healing, and strength to those who are weakened by age or sickness.

What are the four elements of the Sacrament of Reconciliation?

The four elements of the Sacrament of Reconciliation are contrition, confession, penance, and absolution.

What is viaticum?

Viaticum is the rite in which a dying person receives Holy Communion.

How can we bring healing to others?

We can bring healing to others by

- being willing to forgive and to ask for forgiveness;
- visiting, supporting, and caring for people who are sick or elderly;
- praying for people who suffer physically, mentally, or spiritually.

Respond

Suffering is a part of everyone's life. Recall one of your own experiences of suffering. Then read 2 Corinthians 4:7–18. In your reflection notebook, write your reflections on suffering: its mystery, its value, and what it has done for you. Include who or what gave you hope during this time.

Reach Out

1. Reconciliation begins at home. Try to recognize one good quality of every member of your family. Write a short note to each one, thanking him or her for sharing that gift with the family. Plan to celebrate with your family the Sacrament of Reconciliation or a reconciliation ceremony.

2. Read how Jesus deals with two women who were sinful: The Pardon of the Sinful Woman (Luke 7:36–50) and A Woman Caught in Adultery (John 7:53–8:11). Write a paragraph about how Jesus related to sinners.

3. Speak with people who care for people who are sick or elderly and ask them to share their experiences with you. They could be ministers of care in your parish or workers in a hospital or home for elderly people. Write your reactions and present them to the class.

4. Adopt a person in your parish who is a shut-in. Write to the person, make cards or small gifts, and do things for him or her throughout the year.

5. Make banners, design remembrances, and prepare refreshments for your parish celebration of the Anointing of the Sick.

6. Find examples in the news recently of nations, churches, companies, or individuals that have asked forgiveness. Write a paragraph about the value of forgiveness for the good of society.

Jan Sanders van Hemessen, detail from *Christ and the Woman Taken in Adultery*, 16th Century. Jesus points to an inscription that defends a persecuted woman.

Making Connections   Underline the answers that match each description.

1. Called a Sacrament of Healing:
   Reconciliation   Anointing of the Sick   Holy Orders   Penance

2. The means Christ uses to heal today:
   sacraments   works of charity   community prayer   healers

3. Parables of God's forgiveness:
   The Net   The Lost Coin   The Lost Son   The Lost Sheep

4. Necessary elements of the Sacrament of Reconciliation:
   Scripture reading   contrition   confession   absolution   penance

5. Acts of penance:
   prayer   work of charity   act of self-denial   sickness

6. Someone who pardons in the Sacrament of Reconciliation:
   God   the priest   the penitent   the community

7. Effects of the Sacrament of the Anointing of the Sick:
   strength and comfort   forgiveness   health   grace

8. Viaticum:
   Holy Communion   exorcism   strength for death   the last sacrament

The Rite Sequence   Each picture depicts a step in the Sacrament of the Anointing of the Sick.
Below each picture, write the name of the step being shown. Then in the circle, number the steps in the
order they are performed.

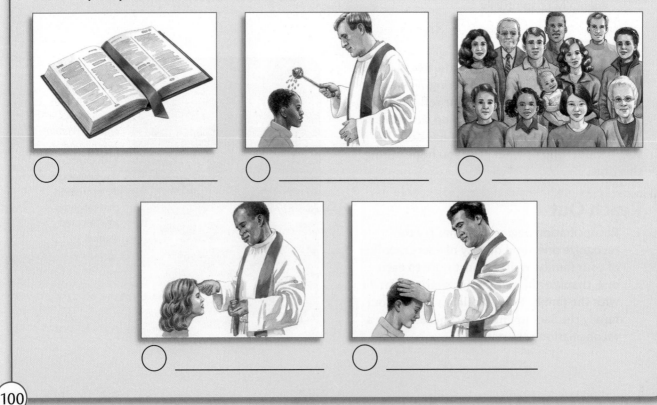

Gather and Go Forth

Know and Proclaim

God's compassion and mercy are present in our Catholic faith. We proclaim our faith by healing and comforting others.

We Know Our Faith	We Proclaim Our Faith
Christ's healing ministry continues today, especially in the Sacraments of Healing.	Catholics continue Jesus' healing ministry by operating hospitals. Catholic health care providers act in ways that respect and protect human dignity and serve the common good.
Contrition, confession, penance, and absolution must be present during the Sacrament of Reconciliation.	As Catholics, we admit our sorrow for having sinned when we pray an Act of Contrition during the Sacrament of Reconciliation. Then the priest offers absolution.
Through the Sacrament of the Anointing of the Sick, Jesus comforts and strengthens people who are seriously ill.	All Catholics are responsible for the care of those who are sick. Catholics who suffer from serious illness or the elderly in poor health celebrate the Sacrament of the Anointing of the Sick.

As ambassadors for Christ, Catholics unite themselves in friendship with God and with one another. We can follow Christ and be healers, too, by using kind words of forgiveness and understanding.

So we are ambassadors for Christ, as if God were appealing through us. We implore you on behalf of Christ, be reconciled to God.

2 Corinthians 5:20

Test Your Catholic Knowledge

Fill in the circle that best completes the sentence.

The Anointing of the Sick is a Sacrament of Healing for those:

○ with any physical ailments.

○ who are elderly or experiencing serious illness.

○ who don't attend Mass regularly.

○ who have celebrated the Sacrament of Reconciliation.

A Catholic to Know

Francis of Assisi (1182–1226) dreamed of becoming a knight. However, when he had a chance to become a soldier, he realized that his dreams of glory were not what he had expected. After experiencing hatred, fighting, and a yearlong imprisonment, he began to look for more meaning in life. One day, while praying in an old church, Francis heard a voice say, "Francis, go and repair my house which, as you can see, is falling into ruin." Francis gave up everything he had and went about rebuilding the church by hand. Eventually, Francis saw that he was not called to rebuild church buildings but the Church itself. He modeled his life after Jesus, and he spread the message of God's loving care to all creatures.

Saint Francis of Assisi

Witness and Share

These sentences describe what Catholics believe. Listen carefully as they are read. Ask yourself, "How strong are my Catholic beliefs?"

My Way to Faith

- I pray for people who are sick and suffering.

- I visit those who are sick and elderly, such as my grandparents.

- I thank God for my health and the health of others.

- I express sorrow for my sins when I pray the Act of Contrition.

- I recognize that my sins affect the whole community.

- I offer words of comfort to people who are hurting and suffering.

Share Your Faith

Consider how you are sorry for anyone you have hurt. On the lines below, write down some ways you can make up for those hurts. Invite family members or friends to discuss how they forgive others and seek forgiveness for themselves.

_____

_____

_____

_____

The Sermon on the Mount, 16th Century, Dutch.

The Message of Jesus: Choose Life

Jesus the Teacher

Fullness of Life

Complete these statements.

My favorite activity is

_____

A place in the world I especially like is

_____

A person I like to be with is

_____

I enjoy eating

_____

Life is a precious gift. It enables us to enjoy all those wonderful things and more. Out of millions of possibilities, the Father called you into being and made you the unique person you are. On top of that, Jesus gave his life that you might live forever. He taught us the secret to fullness of life: love. Read his two great commandments in Matthew 22:36–40.

To love as Jesus did means cherishing the gift of life—our own and others. It means reverencing all human beings and avoiding anything that harms them. We look on every child of God made in God's image as "another self." If we truly love, we will enjoy life, and we will enable others to enjoy it. The following stories show Christlike love in action.

A Modern Love Story

During the Vietnam War, a village orphanage was bombed. Several missionaries and children were killed. One eight-year-old girl was badly injured. Without a quick blood transfusion, she would die. An American doctor who came to help asked in halting language and sign language if anyone would be willing to donate blood. After a long silence, one boy, Heng, volunteered.

As Heng lay on a pallet with a needle in his vein, he began to sob. When the doctor asked if it hurt, Heng replied, "No," and tried to hide his crying. But something was wrong. Finally, a Vietnamese nurse arrived who was able to talk to Heng. She explained to the American, "Heng thought he was dying. He thought you had asked him to give all his blood so that the little girl would live."

"Why would you be willing to do that?" the doctor asked Heng.

"She's my friend," Heng said.

An Old Love Story

Jesus gave us a model for Christian love in the parable of the Good Samaritan. Read Luke 10:29–37, remembering that the Samaritans and the Jewish people were enemies.

Based on these two love stories, what words would you use to describe Christian love?

_____

_____

Go for It!

Christian love is not easy. It is a challenge. Jesus demands an entirely new way of thinking and acting. He admits, "How narrow the gate and constricted the road that leads to life. And those who find it are few." (Matthew 7:14) How are you at accepting challenges? How do you react when

- a group invites you to join them in an activity that would endanger your life?

- a family member, a teacher, or a classmate needs help?

- a friend experiments with cigarettes, alcohol, or drugs?

A New Understanding

Daily choices are important. They are a reflection of your attitudes and beliefs. Because human acts are done in freedom, you are responsible for your actions. You must live with the consequences of your choices. They shape both your present and future life. You can improve your ability to make good choices by reading and reflecting on Scripture, personal prayer, and the celebration of the Eucharist and the Sacrament of Reconciliation.

The Sermon on the Mount (Matthew 5–7) contains some teachings of Jesus that guide our decisions. Just as Moses climbed Mount Sinai and received the Law, Jesus climbed a hillside and gave us a new understanding of the Law. Jesus teaches us that at the heart of the Law is God's call for us to live with one another in love. With his help and the help of the Holy Spirit, we can become witnesses to God's love for the world.

Find an example in Matthew 5:21–48 of how Jesus teaches us a new understanding of the Law.

_____

_____

Letter or Spirit?

Good laws

- protect the freedom, values, and rights that people hold as important;

- protect the common good;

- help all people reach goals and live with dignity.

Jesus said he did not come to destroy the law, but to fulfill it. We are to live not so much by the letter of the law as by the spirit. To live by the spirit of the law is to live the value that the law promotes. It is to live by what the law calls us to do and be. The motives of our hearts that are behind our actions are important.

Read the Ten Commandments on page 242. They express the moral or natural law written in our hearts as a result of our being made in God's image and sharing God's wisdom and goodness. The Law is unchangeable and permanent and is the foundation of moral and civil law. Each of the Ten Commandments asks us to reverence and promote a particular value. If we live according to the truth and the spirit, we grow into the people we were meant to be. When we fail to love, that is, when we sin, we stunt our growth.

Lovers of Life

The Fifth Commandment is "You shall not kill." (Exodus 20:13) Jesus wants us to love and care for all life—physical life and the life of the spirit. We are first of all responsible for our own life.

How can you take care of your health?

_____

_____

How can you care for your spiritual life?

_____

_____

The following topics are matters of life and death. Some of these issues are debated a great deal. For each topic, the teaching of Jesus and of his Church upholds the supreme value of life.

Anger

Argue. Yell. Hit. Hurt someone's feelings. Get even. These are ways we express anger. Anger is an emotion that can work for good or evil. It can supply the energy you need to change things that are wrong. Jesus was angry with the money changers in the Temple (John 2:13–17), but his anger was motivated by love.

It is necessary to channel anger properly. When out of control, anger can lead to sin. Angry words to a friend can destroy a relationship. Letting anger build up inside can lead you to hurt others in a desire to get even.

What advice would you give a friend who has trouble controlling his or her anger?

_____

_____

Scandal

It is easy to see how fights and unkind words hurt people. **Scandal**, or bad example, can harm people just as much. We are influenced, for better or worse, by what others do. Good example encourages and inspires, but bad example damages. Younger children usually try to imitate their older brothers and sisters and friends. Not fully understanding right from wrong, they may simply follow and learn to do what is wrong. Read Matthew 18:6–7 to find out how serious an offense Jesus considers bad example.

Abortion

Abortion is the killing of an embryo or a fetus, a developing baby, before birth. A baby has the right to life, the right to know, love, and serve God as a human being in the world. A baby can't defend himself or herself. We must protect his or her right to life.

Are you less important if you have poor eyesight or get poor grades? Are you more important if you are wealthy or popular? The importance of life does not depend on such things. Human life is valuable in and of itself. Some people believe that babies who are developmentally disabled and babies whose parents can't care for them properly are better off not being born. They think that such children should be killed in an abortion. The Catholic Church rejects that belief. We must work and pray that people will see the value of all human life. Each infant deserves a chance to live despite all odds.

In some countries, abortion is legal under certain conditions. A law may make it legal, but it cannot make it right. People who abort a baby are subject to excommunication; that is, to being cut off from the Church and the sacraments.

Suicide

Life sometimes seems unbearable. Some people see **suicide** as a way to end their problems. Suicide is the deliberate taking of one's own life. It is seriously wrong. Suicide not only contradicts our natural inclination to be alive, but it also breaks the ties that bind the person to family, nation, and human society in general. The responsibility for suicide may be diminished because of psychological problems, anguish, or fear. Even though a person who commits suicide has done an act contrary to moral law, the Church recognizes that God can provide that person with an opportunity for repentance. The Church prays for people who have taken their own lives. People who speak or act in a way that encourages suicide are committing a serious moral wrong.

What would you say to a boy who wants to die because the girl he likes just ignores him?

A Moment with Jesus

Loving ourselves and others as Jesus taught us is not as easy as it might sound. It calls us to care for the life of the body and the spirit.

Take a moment to think about what that means for you at this time in your life. What challenges to living out the Fifth Commandment in its fullest sense do you face now? Ask the Holy Spirit to inspire and strengthen you. Then thank Jesus for the gift of life in all its forms.

Getting Through a Crisis

When you or someone close to you is going through a time of crisis, it is good to know some actions that can help. What makes each of these actions a wise choice?

- Recall a problem that you solved. Remember how painful it was, but how you handled it eventually. Things change with time. Give yourself time.
- Talk with someone who cares about what you are going through and can help, such as a parent, a teacher, or a counselor.
- Try to become involved in activities, sports, or hobbies. Be with people who can support you.
- Reach out to others who may be experiencing pain. It may take the weight off of your problem.
- Bring your concerns to God and ask for help and guidance. Trust that God's love for you is greater than you can ever imagine.

Euthanasia

Euthanasia, or mercy killing, is direct intervention to end life for the purpose of ending human suffering. It causes a person to die before he or she would die naturally. Although people defend it as a kind way to treat those who suffer, it is wrong. It is contrary to the respect due to a person and his or her Creator.

Consider illness and aging from a Christian point of view. First, God alone creates. He alone has the right over life and death. Second, illness and aging may help the individual and the community in many ways. Pain may call forth love and courage. Third, illness can prepare us for eternal life and help us realize that God is the important one in life. Finally, sickness and aging are part of God's plan. Many things that happen are a mystery, but we trust that God who has gifted us with life uses all things for our good.

Allowing a person to die without artificial support is not wrong if continuing such treatment is overly burdensome in prolonging the life of a dying person. The Church teaches that extraordinary means that only prolong a person's life need not be used. The decision whether or not to use life-support systems should take into consideration the sick person, the doctor's advice, and the hope of results. Under any circumstance, ordinary care should be given. Any action to kill a seriously ill person is morally wrong.

Violence and War

Followers of Christ, the Prince of Peace, work against things that destroy peace. The violence in our communities—the drive-by shootings, gang fights, muggings, and murders—is evil, creates fear, and disturbs the peace.

Peace cannot be attained without free communication between people and respect for the dignity of every human person. Peace is the work of justice. Peace is not just the absence of war nor just a balance of powers. War results in death, suffering, and destruction. It is to be avoided unless it is necessary to protect people and their rights. Over the centuries the Church has identified strict conditions that countries must meet before they enter into war.

Capital Punishment

For the common good, a government has the right to punish criminals. In 2005 the American Catholic bishops began a campaign to end the death penalty in the United States. In the document, *A Culture of Life and the Penalty of Death,* the bishops wrote, "We renew our common conviction that it is time for our nation to abandon the illusion that we can protect life by taking life. Ending the use of the death penalty would be one important step away from a culture of death toward building a culture of life."

Life-Threatening "Isms"

Prejudice, the unreasonable dislike of a particular group of people, is wrong. It is an attitude that causes harm to people and denies them their rights. Draw a line connecting each "ism" with its description.

racism   Prejudice against older people

ageism   Regarding a race as inferior

sexism   Treating members of a certain sex unfairly

Works of Mercy

In Matthew 25:31–46, Jesus reveals that we will be judged by how we have loved others at the end of the world. We who have loved him by cherishing the lives of our brothers and sisters will be rewarded. We can foster their physical life by the Corporal Works of Mercy. We can promote their spiritual life by the Spiritual Works of Mercy. The works of mercy are listed on page 243. Which one can you practice today?

Celebrating Life

Leader: The Lord our God has gifted us with life. We are called to care for that precious gift of life in ourselves and others. Let us celebrate life!

Song and Procession with Bible

Leader: God has given us life by creating us. Jesus has given us life by redeeming us. The Holy Spirit leads us to the fullness of life in the Father and the Son. Let us listen to God now as he calls us to choose life.

Reader 1: A reading from the Book of Deuteronomy 30:15–20. *(Passage is read from Bible.)*

Leader: Let us pray.

All: Let us choose life today and always. We know that those who follow you, Lord, will have the light of life.

Song or Alleluia

Leader: We know we have love for God if we show love to others. Let us listen to the Word of God calling us to show our love in practical ways.

Reader 2: A reading from the Gospel of Luke 6:27–38. *(Passage is read from Bible.)*

Leader: Let us pray.

All: We are your people, Lord, called to love as you love.

Presentation of Symbols

Leader: Let us thank the Lord for his gift of life. Our response is, "Thank you, Jesus, for life."

Reader 1: For the power I have to walk down the street, run through a park, dance, and laugh, I say . . .

For the times I've enjoyed watching a sunset, swimming at the beach, and sitting by a fire, I say . . .

For the experiences of sharing in the Eucharist, being part of a family, and gathering with friends, I say . . .

Individual prayers may be added.

Leader: Let us show gratitude for life by living with love. Our response is, "Jesus, make me fully alive."

Reader 2: Whenever I can lend a hand to help the aged or reach out to help a child . . .

Whenever I can forgive someone who hurt me . . .

Whenever I have a chance to make a friend, to say a kind word, or to think of others first . . .

Individual prayers may be added.

Leader: For all the people in our life, for all who love us and for all who do not, let us pray . . .

All: Our Father . . .

Closing Song

Remember

What did Jesus teach us in the Sermon on the Mount?

In the Sermon on the Mount, Jesus taught us the way to the Father and called us to live a life of love and holiness.

Why must life be preserved and respected?

All life is a gift from God to be loved, preserved, and respected for God's honor and glory. Human life is a special gift because we are created in God's likeness, redeemed, and destined to live forever in God's kingdom.

What are Jesus' two great commandments?

He said to him, "You shall love the Lord, your God, with all your heart, with all your soul, and with all your mind. This is the greatest and the first commandment. The second is like it: You shall love your neighbor as yourself." (Matthew 22:37–39)

Respond

God calls us to love as he loves, which is quite a challenge. Read 1 Corinthians 13:4–7. In your reflection notebook, rewrite the passage, replacing the word *love* with your own name. List one way in which you will try to live what you have written. Ask Jesus to help you grow in love.

Reach Out

1. What is meant by the statement "It is not enough to be anti-abortion; you must also be pro-life"? Write your response. Then ask a parent, a grandparent, and an older teenager to comment on the same statement.

2. Read Psalm 136 or Psalm 148. Illustrate either psalm or compose your own litany of thanksgiving or song of praise patterned after those psalms.

3. Charity begins at home! Try one of these.
    - Go to bed on time for a week.
    - Pray an original prayer at home before a meal.
    - Use your allowance in some way for your family instead of for yourself.
    - Offer to do two extra jobs at home to replace the ordinary turn of someone else in your family.

4. Find out what a national or local pro-life group is doing to fulfill Jesus' commandment of love. Write a report. Get involved in the group's activities.

5. Write a story or play about someone you know who protects and nurtures life.

Words to Know

abortion	racism	suicide
ageism	scandal	
euthanasia	sexism	

Jesus as the peacemaker, stained glass, St. Jerome Parish, Maplewood, Minnesota. ❯

Scripture Search In chapters 6 and 7 of Matthew, Jesus gives advice to people who would follow him. Read the passages and complete the summary sentences.

1. (6:1–4) Do good deeds in _____.

2. (6:19–21) Work for _____ treasures that alone give real security.

3. (6:24) Serve _____, not _____. You cannot serve them both.

4. (6:25–34) Trust in _____ for what you need.

5. (7:1–5) Avoid _____ so that you yourself receive a merciful judgment.

6. (7:6) Treat holy things with _____.

7. (7:11) Pray to the heavenly _____.

8. (7:12) Treat others _____. This is called the _____ rule.

Sentence Sense Use each of the following terms in a sentence that reveals what you have learned.

1. choices _____

2. challenge of Christ _____

3. good laws _____

4. spirit of the law _____

5. works of mercy _____

Fifth Commandment Issues Write the letter of the term for each definition.

_____ 1. Direct intervention to end life

_____ 2. Regarding a particular race as inferior

_____ 3. Bad example

_____ 4. Unreasonable dislike of a particular group of people

_____ 5. The killing of an embryo or a fetus before birth

_____ 6. The deliberate taking of one's life

_____ 7. Prejudice against older people

a. prejudice

b. scandal

c. ageism

d. euthanasia

e. suicide

f. racism

g. abortion

Gather and Go Forth

Know and Proclaim

Knowing our Catholic faith helps us love as Jesus did. We proclaim Jesus in what we say and do.

We Know Our Faith	We Proclaim Our Faith
In the Sermon on the Mount, Jesus taught that at the heart of God's Law is the call for us to live with one another in love.	As Catholics, we show our love for our neighbors by advocating for laws and policies that respect and promote human dignity.
The Fifth Commandment is "You shall not kill." Jesus wants us to live and care for both the physical and spiritual life.	As Catholics, we help our neighbors meet their emotional and spiritual needs by participating in the Spiritual Works of Mercy.
To love as Jesus loved means cherishing the gift of life. Every person is a child of God made in God's image.	As Catholics, we demonstrate our love for life by calling for legislation and policies that respect all human life beginning at conception and ending with natural death.

Test Your Catholic Knowledge

Fill in the circle that best completes the sentence.

Jesus revealed that we will be judged by:

○ where we live.

○ how well we have loved others.

○ our obedience to the letter of the law.

○ how much money we donate to charity.

God breathed into us the breath of life, which fills us with his love. In loving as Jesus loved, we encounter God. Christian love nurtures life at all times.

God created mankind in his image;
in the image of God he created them;
male and female he created them.

Genesis 1:27

A Catholic to Know

Saint Julie Billiart (1751–1816) began teaching children about God in her hometown of Picardy, France, at age seven. When she was 14, she vowed herself to chastity and performing works of mercy. Even though a mysterious illness left her paralyzed for over 20 years, Julie still lived a full life dedicated to others. Julie founded the Sisters of Notre Dame to care for orphans, educate girls from families who lived in poverty, and train Christian teachers. Julie had learned during her years of pain and sickness that "God is good." Saint Julie is called the "Smiling Saint" whose motto was "How good the good God is."

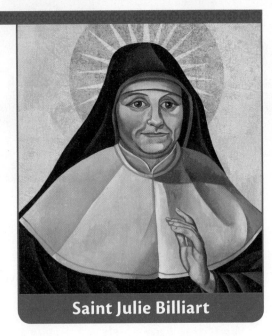

Saint Julie Billiart

Witness and Share

These sentences describe what Catholics believe. Listen carefully as they are read. Ask yourself, "How strong are my Catholic beliefs?"

My Way to Faith

- I live according to Jesus' Great Commandment to love God and to love my neighbor as myself.

- I view all human life, beginning with the unborn, as a gift from God to be cherished and protected.

- I avoid saying bad things about other people.

- I make sure that my anger does not hurt others.

- I take a stand against any form of discrimination.

Share Your Faith

How do you demonstrate the value and dignity of human life? Write your ideas on the lines. Invite family members and friends to talk with you about how the choices they make respect life.

_____

_____

_____

_____

Charles Rolt, *The Sermon on the Mount*, 1861.

The Challenge of the Beatitudes

Jesus the Light of the World

We are programmed to seek eternity. We long to live forever. People such as Spanish explorer Ponce de León have searched for a legendary fountain of youth that gave people health and eternal life.

A rich young man who obeyed the commandments asked Jesus for the secret of eternal life. Jesus did not tell him to cross an ocean, climb a high mountain, or destroy a monster in order to win eternal life. He set before the young man an even greater challenge. He looked at him, loved him, and said to him, "'Go, sell what you have, and give to [the] poor and you will have treasure in heaven; then come, follow me.'" (Mark 10:21) The man walked away sad. He had many possessions.

How to Be Happy

In Matthew's Gospel, Jesus began the Sermon on the Mount by spelling out how to follow him. He gave us the Beatitudes, guidelines for Christlike living that will make us happy and lead us to eternal life. If we live those guidelines, our lives will be blessed. Each beatitude pairs a value with a promise. People who live in the light of those values journey safely and surely. Someday they will reach the Kingdom of Heaven where they will not "need light

from lamp or sun, for the Lord God shall give them light, and they shall reign forever and ever." (Revelation 22:5)

Called to Be Happy

Read the Beatitudes in Matthew 5:3–10. List below the people who will be blessed. They are the people whose way of life will bring them happiness.

1. _____

2. _____

3. _____

4. _____

5. _____

6. _____

7. _____

8. _____

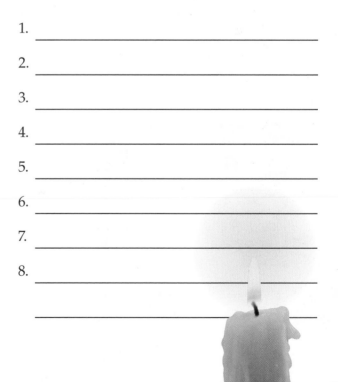

The Be-Attitudes

Jesus was poor in fact and in spirit. People who are poor are dependent on others in ways that people with money are not. People who are economically poor can be rich in other ways, such as in happiness, gratitude, and a generous spirit. Although we may not be poor financially, we can still be poor in spirit. That means having the attitudes of the poor. We remember that everything we have comes from our Creator, and so we depend on and turn to God for our needs. Rather than spending our lives collecting as much wealth as we can, we are willing to give up the things we have.

> Blessed are the poor in spirit,
>   for theirs is the kingdom of heaven.
>
> Matthew 5:3

Check your response to each question.

	Yes	No
Do I let other people help me?	○	○
Do I let God help me?	○	○
Do I share with others?	○	○
Do I thank God for what I have?	○	○
Do I regard people as more important than things?	○	○

> Blessed are they who mourn,
>   for they will be comforted.
>
> Matthew 5:4

Jesus felt sad when people suffered. He was filled with sorrow for those hurt by sin. He wept when his friend Lazarus died, and he wept for Jerusalem because it would be destroyed. When we truly love others, their failings and their sorrows make us feel sad.

Why do you confide in other people when something gives you sorrow?

_____

When do you take hurts and sorrows to Jesus?

_____

> Blessed are the meek,
>   for they will inherit the land.
>
> Matthew 5:5

A meek person is gentle and humble. Jesus was a gentle person. Cardinal Newman wrote that a gentleman is someone who never gives pain to another. A gentle person is not a wimp. On the contrary, being gentle takes great strength and courage. It is easier to be pushy, bossy, inconsiderate, stubborn, and mean. A gentle person is polite, kind, patient, and strong enough to love everyone as Jesus did.

What else do gentle people do?

_____

> Blessed are they who hunger and thirst
>   for righteousness,
>   for they will be satisfied.
>
> Matthew 5:6

When you are hungry or thirsty, you do something about it. People who hunger and thirst for what is right act to make the kingdom come in this world. They try to live by the values Jesus taught and to help others live Jesus' way. They desire to keep their friendship with God.

> Blessed are the merciful,
>   for they will be shown mercy.
>
> Matthew 5:7

Jesus is a friend of the poor, of outcasts, of sinners. He forgave sinners and people who hurt him. Jesus asked his Father to forgive his executioners. He forgives us. As imitators of Jesus, we must have a heart for others and be willing to forgive them.

> Blessed are the clean of heart,
>   for they will see God.
>
> Matthew 5:8

Think of a bicycle wheel. Every spoke is attached to the hub. Jesus' life is like a wheel. He did many things: curing, preaching, and praying. The center of all his activity was the Father's will. Being pure in heart means having God at the hub of your life. All your days, thoughts, actions, and decisions are centered on and flow from God. Your gifts are used as God wishes—for the good of all.

What can we foolishly put at the center of our life in place of God?

> Blessed are the peacemakers,
>   for they will be called children of God.
>
> Matthew 5:9

Jesus brought peace wherever he went. He reconciled us with God. Jesus brought God's love so that we could share it with everyone for the good of everyone. To be a peacemaker, we must first be at peace ourselves. Then we can spread peace to the community.

Check the statements that express true peace.

○ Peace means having everything go the way you want.

○ Peace means coming to grips with yourself— your strengths and your weaknesses.

○ Peace means going along with the crowd when there is trouble and praying you do not get caught.

○ Peace means forgiving those people who hurt you.

○ Peace can mean conflict—that you will have to stand up for what is right.

○ Peace means knowing that God made you and that you are valuable to God and others.

○ Peace means not getting involved.

> Blessed are they who are persecuted for
> the sake of righteousness,
> for theirs is the kingdom of heaven.
>
> Matthew 5:10

Persecution is the outcome for many people who live the Gospel seriously. People will hurt you by their words and actions. Because Jesus lived and spoke the truth, he was crucified. As his disciples, we are called to face the challenge of what it means to be Christian. We do it with joy when we have a personal love for Jesus.

Let Your Light Shine

The teaching of Jesus was revolutionary. It made people see themselves, others, and the world differently. Today Christian values still sometimes conflict with the world's values. When you live by the Beatitudes, you dare to be different. It will be hard, but as Jesus promised, you will be happy.

Although Jesus is "The true light, which enlightens everyone" (John 1:9), some people prefer to live in darkness. Will you turn away from Jesus like the rich young man, or will you grasp Jesus' hand and follow him?

Check the statements below that reflect Christlike thinking.

○ Get even.

○ Forgive in order to become a stronger person.

○ Be number one no matter what.

○ Welcome people who are different from you.

○ Take the easy way out.

○ Make as much money as you can.

○ Lie or cheat as long as you do not get caught.

○ Give away some of your possessions to help people who are poor.

○ Stand up for people who are homeless, imprisoned, or outcast.

○ Mind your own business.

○ Do whatever makes you feel good.

When we live like Christ, his light shines forth in us. Read Matthew 5:14–16 and fill in the missing words in the following sentence.

Jesus wants us to be

like a city on a _____

and a lamp on a _____ .

A Moment with Jesus

In the Beatitudes, Jesus tells us the way to true happiness. Take a moment to reflect on the Beatitudes. Go back to each one and read it silently.

Then choose one that most speaks to you. Pray it in rhythm with your breath. As you inhale, silently pray the first phrase, and as you exhale, pray the second. Repeat this pattern several times. Ask Jesus to help you take the beatitude to heart.

Remember

What are the Beatitudes?

The Beatitudes are guidelines for Christlike living that will make us happy and lead us to eternal life.

What did Jesus say we are to do to have eternal life?

Jesus said, "Go, sell what you have, and give to [the] poor and you will have treasure in heaven; then come, follow me." (Mark 10:21)

Respond

If you want world peace, then promote world forgiveness. Forgive people who hurt you. Saint Paul tells us the power of words in Ephesians 4:32. Look up this verse. Think it over. In your reflection notebook, write about a time you spoke words of forgiveness. Tell how your words helped you and the other person.

Reach Out

1. The Beatitudes give us ways to help others. Think about how you can help at home. Decide on one new thing you can do. You might talk to your parents about it, or you may wish to make it a "hidden caring." Write it in your reflection notebook and check every day to see if you are keeping it.

2. Read chapters 5 and 6 in the Gospel of Matthew. Pick out a favorite verse. Write it on paper, decorate it, and display it in your room. It will be a reminder to share as Jesus did.

3. Kind words heal. They promote peace and show mercy. Write a letter to an older relative or someone who is sick. Share good news with them.

4. The poor in spirit and those who hunger and thirst for justice share things with each other. Ask your parents if you can give clothes you do not need to those who need them and cannot afford them. Talk with your parents or teacher about where you can take the clothes.

5. Cut out newspaper articles about people living the Beatitudes. Glue them on paper and write a summary of each article. Share them with your class or your family.

Stained glass window depicting Jesus and the rich young man, St. Columba's Church, Ottawa, Illinois. ❯

A Blessed Change   If the people *Not Living the Beatitudes* were to change, which group of people *Living the Beatitudes* would they belong to? For each person, write the correct letter.

Not Living the Beatitudes

_____ 1. John still refuses to speak to his mother even after she apologizes.

_____ 2. José makes choices based on what makes him feel good and not on what God wants.

_____ 3. Ms. Blake never bothers to write Congress or vote on human rights issues.

_____ 4. Mr. San's goal in life is to make as much money as he can.

_____ 5. Phil is afraid to try to stop his friends from making fun of an elderly woman.

_____ 6. Jane keeps quiet when Sally is blamed for something Sue did.

_____ 7. Peter is stingy.

_____ 8. Alice goes the other way when she sees Dorothy struggling up the ramp in her wheelchair.

_____ 9. Steve always tries to get his own way.

_____ 10. Linda is secretly happy when she hears that Pam was caught stealing.

_____ 11. Bill tells a beggar that he does not have any change in order to avoid giving him money.

_____ 12. Maryann tells Sandra the nasty remark Jill made about Sandra.

Living the Beatitudes

a. the poor in spirit

b. people who mourn

c. the meek

d. people who hunger and thirst for justice

e. the merciful

f. the clean of heart

g. the peacemakers

h. people persecuted for the sake of righteousness

A Maze with a Message Solve the maze. The letters you pass through will spell an important hidden sentence. Write it below.
   Sentence:

_____

_____

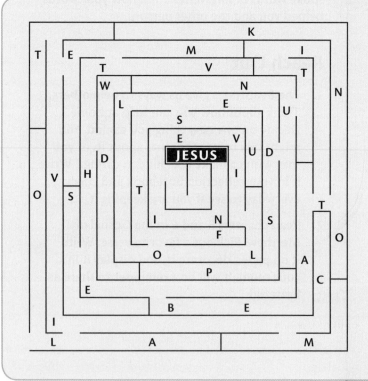

Gather and Go Forth

Know and Proclaim

We live the truths of our Catholic faith, and we proclaim that faith in the way we love one another.

We Know Our Faith	We Proclaim Our Faith
The Beatitudes are guidelines for discipleship that bring happiness and lead to eternal life.	As Catholics, we are called to be poor in spirit. We are not ruled by a desire for material goods and depend totally on God.
Jesus, as the Son of God, teaches us all we need to know about the Father's will for us. Through Christ, in the Holy Spirit, we approach the Father with all our needs.	Catholics practice solidarity with those who are poor by seeking justice and practicing charity.
Being pure of heart means having God as the center of your life. To be pure of heart, all your thoughts, actions, and decisions are centered on God.	Catholics pray the Morning Offering to center their lives in God. This prayer of self-giving reflects an openness to God's love and offers the day to God.

Test Your Catholic Knowledge

Fill in the circle that best answers the question.

In the Sermon on the Mount, Jesus taught about the meaning of true happiness. What are these teachings called?

- ◯ the Ten Commandments
- ◯ the Golden Rule
- ◯ the Beatitudes
- ◯ the New Law

Following Jesus can sometimes be a great challenge and may come at a cost, but Jesus promises us his constant presence.

What will separate us from the love of Christ? Will anguish, or distress, or persecution, or famine, or nakedness, or peril, or the sword? No, in all these things we conquer overwhelmingly through him who loved us.

Romans 8:35,37

A Catholic to Know

Born in Catalonia, Spain, in 1807, Anthony was the 5th of 11 children. He became a priest, eventually becoming archbishop of Santiago, Cuba, in 1850. At the time, the political climate in Cuba was unstable. It had not had an archbishop for 14 years. Being bishop of Santiago did not provide ideal conditions for preaching the Cross of Christ. Anthony tried to renew the priests in their vocations. He gave them an example by preaching in all the churches and spending hours hearing confessions. He made political enemies by working for updated farm methods and educating slaves. Once he was stabbed, yet when his attacker was sentenced to death, Anthony pleaded for him and obtained a prison sentence instead.

Saint Anthony Claret

Witness and Share

These sentences describe what Catholics believe. Listen carefully as they are read. Ask yourself, "How strong are my Catholic beliefs?"

My Way to Faith

- I follow Jesus' teachings in the Beatitudes.

- I am moved to action when I see other people suffering.

- I place God at the center of my life.

- I live a just life.

- I use self-control and respectful behavior when people try to insult me.

- I depend on and turn to God for all my needs.

Share Your Faith

What do the Beatitudes mean to you? Choose one and rewrite it using your own words, saying how you can live it. Invite family members and friends to share their ideas on what the Beatitudes mean to them.

_____

_____

_____

_____

Jesus' Kingdom of Justice and Truth

One day on the front page of a newspaper there was a story about John Shultz. He was a dog warden who had received a $2,500 raise. Although he had five children and did not own his home, Mr. Shultz decided to split his raise with four assistants because he thought they too deserved more pay. Why was that front-page news? What if everyone acted like Mr. Shultz?

Jesus announced, "The kingdom of God is at hand. Repent, and believe in the gospel." (Mark 1:15) It is the proclamation of God's merciful love reaching out to include everyone, especially people who are poor, rejected, and sinners. God's kingdom is a kingdom of love and peace where everyone lives in justice and truth.

All members of the Church are called to serve God's kingdom and create a just world. The Church challenges us to act on behalf of justice and serve the Kingdom of God. The Church's body of teaching on social justice issues is called **Catholic Social Teaching.** People such as Mr. Shultz serve the kingdom.

A Crucial Decision

Are you putting too much value on things that do not matter? The kingdom calls us to be sure that our values are in line with Jesus' values. Serving God's kingdom is up to us.

Jesus the King

A sinner named Zacchaeus decided to change his life when Jesus, out of love, called up to him. Zacchaeus's decision gained him the kingdom. Read his story in Luke 19:1–10.

What actions showed that Zacchaeus was ready to serve the values of the kingdom?

People First

For Christians, people are more important than things. The dignity of the human person is valued over material goods. If you love others, you will respect their right to own property. You will not steal from them or cheat them. You will support and strengthen them by participation in all that promotes their well-being. Possessions are good. They can help you grow in your friendship with God and others. Possessions, however, are to be respected as gifts from God. We care for our world and use all things as God intended.

The Seventh and Tenth Commandments help you to act on those beliefs. The Seventh Commandment, *You shall not steal,* tells you to be honest. You protect your property and the property of others. You work honestly to earn things. The dignity of work is an important way in which we participate in God's creation. Work united to Christ's actions can help redeem the world. You share what you have—not only material goods but also spiritual goods—to

Quentin Metsys, *The Moneylender and His Wife* (detail), 1514.

contribute toward the common good. The Tenth Commandment, *You shall not covet your neighbor's goods,* tells you to be honest even in your attitudes toward others and their things. An honest person avoids envy and greed.

Envy Kills

Envy is feeling deprived or sad because of another's belongings, talents, or success. When you are envious, you cannot appreciate people. An unhealthy competition grows. Sometimes competition is good because it motivates you to achieve. In unhealthy competition you look for the faults of others, compare their talents to yours, and put them down. When you see signs of envy in yourself, remember that God loves you for who you are. Thank God for the gifts given to others. Practice good will, humility, and trust in God's providence.

Greed Destroys

Greed is the desire to possess and control things. It is the root of most wars. Greedy people want more than their neighbor and may be willing to get it unfairly. People who steal and cheat do not respect the fundamental rights and responsibilities of others. They break down trust in the community.

To be forgiven for stealing and for damaging property, it is essential to pay restitution. This means that stolen property must be returned or paid for, and damaged items must be repaired or paid for. This may be done anonymously. If direct restitution is not possible, restitution can be made by contributing to a charity.

A Sinful World

Social sin is a term for situations and institutions that harm people and are opposed to the will of Christ. When a person or group of people is deprived of food, clothing, shelter,

Priorities

1. Is cheating on a test as wrong as stealing from a store? Explain.

_____

_____

2. How does not wasting food or material things help other people?

_____

_____

_____

3. If someone drops a $20 bill and does not notice it, why should you return it?

_____

_____

and security, there is an injustice. The goods of the earth belong to everyone.

As followers of Christ, we are responsible for resisting those situations and promoting justice and respect. We are called to change unjust systems and organizations. The first step is to change our own attitudes.

The Power of Words

In the Letter of James, the tongue is compared to the rudder that controls a ship. It is small but mighty. The letter also says, "Consider how small a fire can set a huge forest ablaze. The tongue is also a fire." (James 3:5–6) Followers of Christ value truth. They speak the truth to one another and about one another. When they hurt another person by untruths, half-truths, or gossip, followers of Christ repair the damage they have done.

Truth builds relationships. We depend on one another to tell the truth. Lying is saying what is not true with the intention of deceiving. It breaks down trust, causes confusion, and prevents people from knowing what is real. God gave us minds to know the truth and hearts to go to others in love. The Eighth Commandment is *You shall not bear false witness against your neighbor.* It forbids untrue words and acts and anything that damages another's good name.

Why Do People Lie?

Fear is the number one reason people lie. Some people are afraid others will not like them, so they cover up truth and exaggerate. Lying about yourself and your achievements is much easier than being real. People who lie do not have to say I'm wrong, I'm sorry, or I don't know.

To be "on top" is another reason people lie. Some people want to impress others and get their attention. They may lie to win, to be popular, to get good grades, or to get out of work or trouble. But a lie only works for the moment. In the end a person loses friends, peace, and, worst of all, friendship with God.

Kayla's Campaign

"Look who's running for student council!" remarked Jena sarcastically as she looked across the room. There stood Kayla Adams handing out campaign buttons.

"Looks decent," said Zach to Jena as he looked up from doing his homework.

"Shows what you know," answered Jena. "She really thinks she's something."

"Well, she was class treasurer last year," Alexis reminded the group around Jena. "She was captain of the cheerleaders."

"Kids like her," claimed Tyrone.

"The teachers like her!" corrected Jena. "She's so sweet to their faces. The kids don't know about her, or they wouldn't vote for her. That's for sure."

"The kids don't know what?" asked Alexis.

Jena lowered her voice, "Well, I'm only going to tell you. I heard that she took money from the class treasury last year and that she lifts stuff from stores."

"I've never heard that," said Zach.

"I don't believe it," snapped Tyrone.

"You vote for her if you want, but I'm not," said Jena firmly.

Alexis frowned and muttered, "I didn't know she was *that* kind of person."

1. What did Tyrone and Alexis first think of Kayla?

_____

_____

2. How has Jena hurt Kayla?

_____

_____

_____

3. Do you think Jena lied? Explain.

_____

_____

_____

_____

_____

Keeping Confidences and Promises

Confidences are intended to be kept private, so they are not repeated. Silence is necessary when you are tempted to spread gossip. Keep family confidences within the family and guard other promises. Priests, doctors, lawyers, secretaries, and other professional people are bound to keep information about their work private. Before revealing information that may hurt others, we should ask if it is necessary and if it is kind.

Having Troubles Being Truthful?

Use these steps to help you change.

Pray Tell Christ you desire to be truthful. Ask him to help you. Do this every morning.

Think Look at your real self. Christ loves you. He died so that you could share eternal life with him.

Reflect Catch yourself exaggerating? Lying? Spreading rumors? Decide why you do this and stop it.

When someone tells you something in confidence, it is a way of saying: I trust you, I like you, I respect you. Sharing that confidence with others would be wrong. Reading another person's private letters or journal would also be wrong.

In some circumstances, however, if you have information about a person's intent to harm oneself or others, you have the responsibility to speak to someone in legitimate authority.

Keeping promises is being true to your word. It lets others know they can rely on you.

Silence is not always good, however. When can silence be a lie?

A Moment with Jesus

Truth is a powerful thing. It builds relationships and strengthens trust and respect.

Stop for a moment now and quietly reflect on what you've read so far in this chapter. What one aspect of justice and truth stands out as most important for you right now? In your own words, share it with Jesus. Ask him to help you live the values of the Kingdom of God as Jesus did. Thank Jesus for calling you to be his disciple.

Living in Truth

Being a truthful person goes hand in hand with your strength of character. You have confidence and courage. You take responsibility and cope with consequences. You gain the trust and respect of others. Honesty also builds a better society. By being truthful, you show Christ's unselfish love and spread his peace all around you. You further God's kingdom.

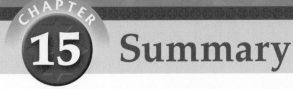

Remember

What do the Seventh and Tenth Commandments tell us?

The Seventh and Tenth Commandments tell us to be honest and to respect others' property.

What does the Eighth Commandment tell us?

The Eighth Commandment tells us to be truthful in our words.

What is Catholic Social Teaching?

Catholic Social Teaching is the Church's body of teaching on social justice issues.

Respond

Read John 14:23–27. The peace Jesus gives is not free from troubles or difficulties. It is a deep, inner peace that comes from being true to God, yourself, and others.

In your reflection notebook, write about an experience you had trying to be truthful. Was it hard? Did you ask Jesus or anyone else to help you? How did you handle it? Would you act differently in the future? Why or why not?

Reach Out

1. Jesus often spoke about riches and the kingdom. Read his parable about the rich man and Lazarus (Luke 16:19–31) and decide what the rich man's crime was. Then read these passages: Luke 12:15–21, Matthew 6:19–21, Matthew 6:24, and Matthew 19:23–24. Prepare a one-minute talk encouraging people to use the wealth of this world justly.

2. Compliment members of your family, classmates, or other people you meet whenever you can during a day. Do this for three days, keeping a tally. Share your results with the class.

3. Make up a short play about someone who stole something and how he or she made restitution.

4. Remember that everything we use is property to be respected. Take care of the things you have and use. Try cleaning your room and keeping it neat for one week.

5. Write an article for your school newspaper or bulletin on the value of honesty as opposed to stealing or cheating. Tell how honesty makes the whole school better.

Words to Know

Catholic Social Teaching
greed   social sin

"What does love look like? It has feet to go to the poor and needy. It has eyes to see misery and want. It has ears to hear the sighs and sorrows of others."

–Saint Augustine

Saint Augustine. ❯

Seven, Eight, or Ten? Check *Yes* if the person's values are in line with Jesus' values. Check *No* if the person's values are not. Record the number of the commandment (7, 8, or 10) related to the action.

	Yes	No	Number
1. Mike uses someone else's ID to buy beer.	_____	_____	_____
2. Susan copies from Tyler's test.	_____	_____	_____
3. Jerry admits he made a mistake.	_____	_____	_____
4. Eddie accepts change for $20 when he gave the cashier $10.	_____	_____	_____
5. Nita cannot eat all of her lunch. She saves it instead of throwing it away.	_____	_____	_____
6. Sam was involved in drinking after the roller-skating party. When his parents ask if he was drinking, he says, "Some of the guys were," implying that he was not.	_____	_____	_____
7. Carol says that when her sister uses her things, she takes one of her things to pay her back.	_____	_____	_____
8. Patsy says nice things to a teacher to get what she wants.	_____	_____	_____
9. Rosa knows Jean is hurting herself by taking drugs but does not say anything for fear of losing her friendship.	_____	_____	_____
10. Ken resents that Carlos has many expensive things.	_____	_____	_____
11. David broke Pete's CD by accident and offers to pay for it.	_____	_____	_____
12. Maria changes the subject when Joe starts criticizing Ann.	_____	_____	_____
13. Megan promised to be home by 10:00, but she stays out until 11:00.	_____	_____	_____
14. Abby copies her history report from the encyclopedia.	_____	_____	_____
15. Nancy reads her sister's journal.	_____	_____	_____
16. Julie refuses to tell a secret although many people are mad at her.	_____	_____	_____
17. Dan feels happy when other people win. He tries hard not to compare himself to others.	_____	_____	_____
18. George does not want to spend his allowance money on school supplies, so he always borrows supplies from others.	_____	_____	_____
19. Jeff discovers his brother got into trouble for vandalism. He keeps this knowledge within the family.	_____	_____	_____
20. John scratches words into desks and marks up walls.	_____	_____	_____
21. Mark knows Alex shoplifts but does not tell their classmates.	_____	_____	_____

Seventh Commandment	**Eighth Commandment**	**Tenth Commandment**
You shall not steal.	You shall not bear false witness against your neighbor.	You shall not covet your neighbor's goods.

Gather and Go Forth

Know and Proclaim

Catholics are people of integrity. We live in truth and justice and act to share our faith and the truth it proclaims.

We Know Our Faith	We Proclaim Our Faith
All members of the Church are called to serve God's kingdom, build a just world, and act on the behalf of justice.	As Catholics, we consider working for social justice to be an important part of our baptismal call. We work to make sure all people have a just share of the earth's resources.
Followers of Christ are called to transform situations and institutions that harm people and are opposed to God's will.	Catholics support efforts to respect the right of workers to a fair wage and safe and humane working conditions. To support workers, Catholics encourage employers to treat their employees with respect and justice.
The Eighth Commandment calls us to live in truth.	Catholic media seeks to report the news in truth and without bias.

As disciples, we show our love and respect for one another by living in justice and truth. We choose to walk in the way of justice as members of God's kingdom of peace.

"Let your 'Yes' mean 'Yes,' and your 'No' mean 'No.' Anything more is from the evil one."

Matthew 5:37

Test Your Catholic Knowledge

Fill in the circle that best answers the question.

What is Catholic Social Teaching?

○ the Church's laws that govern how parishes operate

○ the Church's body of teaching on social-justice issues

○ the Church's body of teaching on faith and morals

○ the Church's laws that govern religious orders

A Catholic to Know

Saint John of Capistrano (1386–1456) was called the "soldier saint." He began his adult life as an attorney in Naples, Italy, when the king appointed him governor of Perugia. During a war between Perugia and a neighboring town, he was betrayed and imprisoned. During his stay in prison, John realized he could serve God more directly. He became a priest and established Franciscan communities of renewal throughout Europe with the zeal that helped him drive out crime as a governor. At age 70, Pope Pius II asked John to help lead the resistance against the invading Ottoman Empire. Aided by John's preaching and enthusiasm, the Hungarian general John Hunyadi led 70,000 soldiers in defeating the Turkish attack.

Saint John of Capistrano

Witness and Share

These sentences describe what Catholics believe. Listen carefully as they are read. Ask yourself, "How strong are my Catholic beliefs?"

My Way to Faith

- I help build a more just world by respecting the property of others.

- I support the rights of workers and the dignity of work.

- I thank people for their work.

- I tell the truth, even if it will get me or my friends in trouble.

- I can be trusted with things that people tell me in confidence.

- I am happy for other people when good things happen to them.

Share Your Faith

Consider ways in which you can practice honesty in your relationships with God and with others. Write your ideas on the lines. Invite a friend or family member to discuss the value of honesty in his or her family and community.

Jesus' Kingdom of Love

Jesus the Sacred Heart

Do you know a couple who have celebrated their 50th wedding anniversary? They are probably best friends. Name some qualities of friendship that would help a man and woman stay happily married.

_____

_____

Friendship is one of the greatest gifts you can give to another person. In sharing your time, your affection, your thoughts and feelings, you are sharing yourself.

Sometimes you see the initials of two lovers inside a heart. A heart stands for a person's whole being. Jesus' love is greater than friendship. He gave his life so that we would be happy. When Jesus died on the Cross, his heart was pierced by a lance. His sacred heart has symbolized his great love ever since.

People who serve God's kingdom try to imitate Jesus' totally selfless love. In doing so, they find meaning for life and great joy. Such selfless love exists in a special way between a man and woman who are married.

Marriage: Made in Heaven

"God created man in his image; . . . male and female he created them." (Genesis 1:27) Our maleness or femaleness is our sexuality. Every cell in a man's body is marked as male, and every cell in a woman's body is marked as female. Our sexuality colors everything we do: the way we think, the way we react, the way we move, the way we talk.

God has placed within men and women an attraction for each other. They need and enjoy each other. God wanted them to grow in friendship. But more than friendship, God wanted

> a man and a woman
> to join in a love so complete, so selfless,
> that their two lives would blend into one
> like two streams blending into one river.

Their union sealed by a marriage vow would last as long as they both live.

Read Ephesians 5:25–33 and complete the following comparison:

The love of marriage is like the love of

_____ .

When God calls a Catholic man and woman to make a lifelong commitment in marriage, God blesses their union through the Sacrament of Matrimony. Throughout their lives together, the couple will rely on the strengthening grace of the sacrament. Not all people have an ideal marriage. It is something to strive for.

Married love includes

- sharing all things
- treasuring the other person as he or she is
- meeting the joy and pain of daily life together
- cherishing the children God sends
- being faithful until death.

Married couples use their good qualities to grow in love and to build a good marriage.

Prepare Now!

Carla is talking with her friends by the drinking fountain at school. Ted passes by and says, "Hi." Suddenly Carla's heart begins to beat rapidly. Her face turns red. She feels clumsy, and she cannot think of anything to say. Why do you think she is or is not in love?

If you ever feel like Carla, congratulations. It is a sign of a change going on within you. Here are other signs of change. Check the ones you notice in yourself:

- ○ I seek more privacy.
- ○ I change moods quickly.
- ○ I daydream often.
- ○ I am easily embarrassed.

These signs point to a special awakening within you. Just as there are stages in our physical, intellectual, and emotional growth, mature love requires that we pass through stages. It may be a slow process.

You can prepare yourself now for the lifetime commitment of marriage by meeting as many people as possible. At your age, it is important to learn about people and how to get along with them. Group dating will make it easier for you to find the right marriage partner if God is calling you to marriage. It will also give you knowledge and skills needed for forming a lifelong relationship and for dealing with other people.

Another way you can prepare for marriage is by practicing love in various situations. How gener-

ous are you in helping your neighbors? How loyal are you to your friends? Do you sacrifice yourself and your time for family members? Can you forgive easily? If you learn how to love now, you have a better chance of experiencing deep, lasting love in your marriage.

Check the moral qualities you most admire in people of the opposite sex who are your own age.

○ kindness	○ honesty
○ prayerfulness	○ truthfulness
○ gentleness	○ self-control
○ justice	○ friendliness
○ prudence	○ forgiveness
○ courage	○ unselfishness
○ respect	○ compassion

Sex: A Gift from God

God has given each of us special gifts that are holy. Among these gifts is sex, an ability to show and deepen love and to create new persons. In this gift, God invites married men and women to share in his own power to create life. The ability to share our deepest selves with another is so sacred that God intended it to be protected by the unbreakable bond of marriage, which is the union of one man and one woman. For people who are called to marriage, sex is a joy that God has given along with the responsibilities of raising a family.

Having sex before we are ready is asking for trouble. We are not ready until we are free to take on the responsibilities of loving someone for life and being a parent. Each person born needs to belong to a loving family and learn about love from a loving mother and father.

Priests, sisters, brothers, and single people sacrifice this joy in living their vocation. Their love is focused on Christ and all his people.

A Sign of Total Surrender

Would you wash a car with motor oil? Of course not. Harm comes from not using things for the purpose for which they were intended.

The same principle applies to the use of our sexual power. The gift of sex comes with instructions, but many people ignore them. Those people learn the hard way that our happiness in this life and in the life to come depends on using God's gifts correctly.

The gift of sex, the gift of self, is far more precious than any material object. It is a gift that must be treasured and saved for marriage. The only love that this gift can honestly express is the total surrender of a man and woman who are united together in marriage and committed to support each other, no matter what. Sex expresses the complete self-lessness and oneness of married couples. It signifies a deep, faithful love. To use it in any other way cheapens it.

Who Is Boss?

The sexual drive is very powerful. Using sex for purposes for which it was not intended is like playing with dynamite. People who have sex outside of marriage risk contracting sexually transmitted diseases. They may suffer psychological damage that marks them for life and harms their marriage. Many young people who have sex wish they had not. Why do you think young people engage in sex today?

Each person faces the challenge of learning to control his or her sexual drive. Otherwise that drive will begin to control the person. What does that mean? It is like riding a bike down a steep hill in the city and discovering that the brakes do not work. The bike is taking you right into heavy traffic! You want to be in control of your thoughts, words, and actions—your human powers. God teaches you what to do and gives you the grace to do it. Jesus was once an adolescent too. He understands the changes you are going through and sees you learning to deal with the ups and downs of life.

One way to keep your sexual drive in control is to participate in good activities such as sports, hobbies, or service. Some other ways to protect your intimate center are modesty, patience, decency, and good judgment.

A Moment with Jesus

Sex is a precious gift of love from God. Like any gift, it is a reflection of the giver. Pause and reflect for a moment on the faithful love of God for you.

Then think of the married couples you know. As you imagine each one, ask God to bless them and help them to grow in love of him and of each other.

A Double Safeguard

God gave us two commandments to safeguard the sacred gift of sex: the Sixth Commandment, *You shall not commit adultery,* and the Ninth Commandment, *You shall not covet your neighbor's wife.*

In the Sixth Commandment, God forbids any sexual act that is contrary to the sacredness of marriage. That includes **adultery,** the act of being sexually unfaithful to one's husband or wife, as well as artificial means of birth control and same-sex unions. Any violation of God's plan for the use of sex, either alone or with someone else, is wrong.

God wants us to respect sex, not only in our words and actions but also in our thoughts and desires. God tells us that in the Ninth Commandment. As all God's laws do, these two commandments protect us from hurting ourselves and others. What problems and heartaches result from not following them?

_____

_____

_____

_____

_____

IV HONOR YOUR FATHER AND YOUR MOTHER.
V YOU SHALL NOT KILL.

I I AM THE LORD YOUR GOD: YOU SHALL NOT HAVE STRANGE GODS BEFORE ME.
II YOU SHALL NOT TAKE THE NAME OF THE LORD YOUR GOD

Perfect Love

The Sixth and Ninth Commandments call us to practice the virtue of chastity. Chastity helps us to integrate our sexuality with our spiritual nature. It helps us to be completely human, able to give to others our whole life and love. A chaste person recognizes that our power to bring new life into the world should be used only by husband and wife and according to the divine plan. All people are called to practice chastity. For married people, chastity is being faithful to their partner. For unmarried people, it means forgoing the use of the power of sex completely.

Christ challenges us to become perfect as our heavenly Father is perfect. To mirror God's perfect love, we must be pure in our thoughts, words, and actions. We must be like Christ, our model of chastity.

If you really believed that God is within you, would you have sex outside of marriage?

Breaking Through Illusions

Which line segment is longer?

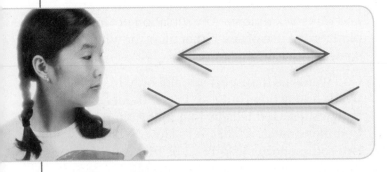

The line segments are equal. Were you fooled by this optical illusion? A design can appear to be something it is not. Illusions are not only found in designs, but also in ideas and opinions. Whenever an idea appears appealing but is contrary to God's plan, it offers only an illusion of goodness. It is a trap.

Do Not Be Fooled

Many TV shows, videos, Web sites and maybe even the lifestyle of some of your friends and neighbors show that many people do not recognize the true value of the gift of sex. They act on illusions such as the following:

- Using sexual powers can prove love and popularity.
- Sex may be used for entertainment.
- Using language that makes fun of sex is adult behavior.

Why are these ideas based on illusions?

Planning for Real Love

Here is a plan to help Christians of all ages break through illusions about the gift of sex. Use the word box to complete the plan.

chaste	loved by God	modesty
	self-control	values

1. Decide to reverence yourself and all you have been given by God. You are valuable and very precious because you are

   _____.

2. Discipline yourself. Do not always choose the easy way. Strong, unselfish people show

   _____.

3. Use common sense. Reading books, watching movies and TV programs and visiting Web sites that have a respectful attitude toward sex will help you to be _____.

4. By dressing, speaking, and acting in a way that shows you respect yourself and others, you will be practicing _____.

5. Develop healthy friendships with people who agree with your _____.

Remember

What is the purpose of the Sixth and Ninth Commandments?

The purpose of the Sixth and Ninth Commandments is to protect marriage, the family, and the sacred gift of sex.

In God's plan, when is the gift of sex to be used?

In God's plan, the gift of sex is reserved for use in marriage.

What does the virtue of chastity help us to do?

The virtue of chastity helps us to integrate our sexuality with our spiritual nature. All people are called to practice chastity.

Respond

Choose a point in the plan on page 132. In your reflection notebook, list specific actions and practical ways that you will carry out the point. Then write a note to Jesus, asking him to help you, particularly if there is a situation or a person bothering you.

Reach Out

1. Get together with one of your friends and share some ways you can support each other in practicing chastity. After your conversation, write in your reflection notebook. Make two columns. In one column, list the ways you asked your friend to support you. In the other column, list the ways your friend asked you for support.

2. Choose a popular song that you think expresses the values of Christian love. Reflect on why it shows Jesus' view of love and how living this song can make you a better person.

3. Research devotions to the Sacred Heart of Jesus. Use prayer books, Catholic encyclopedias, or the Internet to find information about where and when the devotion began, artwork associated with the Sacred Heart, religious orders dedicated to the Sacred Heart, and novenas, litanies, and other prayers to the Sacred Heart.

Word to Know

adultery

The Sacred Heart of Jesus. ❯

What Is Dangerous? When are sexually tempting situations dangerous? Rate each of the following situations. Color the traffic light RED if the situation is so dangerous you should stop it. Color it YELLOW if it is somewhat dangerous and you should proceed with caution. Color it GREEN if it is safe to go ahead without being sexually tempted.

Situation   *Rating*

1. Using drugs

2. Attending a party without adult supervision

3. Going on a group date

4. Being alone with a person of the opposite sex at your house when nobody else is home

5. Being alone with a person of the opposite sex in a movie theater

6. Going to a supervised party

7. Attending a school dance with friends

8. Going to a basketball game with a person of the opposite sex

9. Walking home after school with a person of the opposite sex

10. Meeting a person of the opposite sex at the park late at night

11. Meeting a person of the opposite sex at a restaurant

12. Drinking alcohol

Reprinted by permission from Junior High Ministry Magazine, copyright 1987, Group Publishing, Box 481, Loveland , CO 80539.

True or False Write **T** if the statement is true or **F** if it is false.

_____ **1.** Sexuality is our maleness or femaleness.

_____ **2.** If a marriage does not work out, a Catholic couple may divorce and remarry.

_____ **3.** Sex is sacred.

_____ **4.** Sex outside of marriage is wrong and harmful.

_____ **5.** Some people do not have to practice chastity.

_____ **6.** Through sex, men and women cooperate with God in the act of creation.

_____ **7.** The love between a married man and woman is a symbol of the love of Christ for us.

Gather and Go Forth

Know and Proclaim

Knowing the truths of our Catholic faith enables us to proclaim our beliefs in loving relationships.

We Know Our Faith	We Proclaim Our Faith
Marriage is the lifelong commitment between a man and a woman. God blesses their union through the Sacrament of Matrimony.	Going to Mass helps married Catholics imitate Jesus' selfless love.
Sex is a gift from God that allows a husband and wife to deepen their love for each other and to participate in God's creation of life.	Young Catholics prepare for marriage by developing healthy relationships and by practicing acts of love, such as helping their neighbors, spending time with their families, and forgiving others.
The Sixth and Ninth Commandments help people safeguard the sacred gift of sex.	Catholics practice modesty by enjoying entertainment that shows restraint and respect for the dignity of other people.

God is love. We are made to love one another and to love God. To love perfectly as God loves, we must be pure in our words, thoughts, and actions.

Let love be sincere; hate what is evil, hold on to what is good; love one another with mutual affection; anticipate one another in showing honor.

Romans 12:9–10

Test Your Catholic Knowledge

Fill in the circle that best answers the question.

Which virtue grows out of following the Sixth and Ninth Commandments?

○ prudence

○ courage

○ chastity

○ justice

A Catholic to Know

Agnes was a beautiful child who lived in Rome in the 200s. She lived during the reign of Emperor Diocletian, and his widespread persecution of Christians put everyone at risk. At only 12 years old, Agnes already had a deep faith in God. When her persecutors attempted to force her to worship at the pagan altars, she fearlessly refused. Since she had dedicated her life to God, she resisted offers to marry. Agnes showed unusual valor and inner strength. She prayed as she was threatened with punishment and cruel treatment. Finally, her persecutors ran out of patience and executed Agnes. Because the power of her faith was greater than the cruelty she suffered, Saint Ambrose, the bishop of Milan, honored her death as "a new kind of martyrdom."

Saint Agnes

Witness and Share

These sentences describe what Catholics believe. Listen carefully as they are read. Ask yourself, "How strong are my Catholic beliefs?"

My Way to Faith

- I believe that Christ raised Matrimony to the dignity of a sacrament in which a baptized man and a baptized woman make a lifelong commitment of love to one another.

- I will reserve sex for marriage because it is a gift from God.

- I look to Christ as a model for living a chaste life.

- I sacrifice my time to help others in need.

- I limit my enjoyment of entertainment to those forms that are respectful of other people.

Share Your Faith

Consider what you read, the music you listen to, and what you watch on TV. Do these forms of entertainment respect others and reflect healthy relationships? Write examples of entertainment that respect God's plan. Invite a friend to share ideas for your list.

_____

_____

_____

_____

Jesus Christ the Truth

Looking Back

In Unit 2, you have looked at some of the values and demands of Christian living. You have learned that Jesus calls you to live in his truth. He has called you to serve the kingdom. Your attitudes, thoughts, and actions should show that you know what it means to serve the kingdom. Jesus asks you to base your decisions on God's law and on his example. He challenges you to respect life, to respect people and property, to live honestly, and to cherish the gift of sex.

Ask yourself these questions. Write your answers in your reflection notebook.

1. How has this unit helped me understand what Jesus asks of those who follow him?

2. What do I need to remember when I am tempted or when others make it difficult for me to do the right thing?

3. What practical steps can I take to live the life of a disciple?

> Rather, living the truth in love, we should grow in every way into him who is the head, Christ.
>
> Ephesians 4:15

Personal Inventory

How well do you let the principles Jesus taught guide your judgments and direct your actions? Circle **u** (usually), **o** (often), or **s** (seldom).

1. Do you think of what Jesus would want you to do or say in situations?
   u   o   s

2. Do you go to people you respect for advice?
   u   o   s

3. Do you see that little things in life (at home, at school) are opportunities to show respect for others and for property?
   u   o   s

4. Do you go out of your way to serve others?
   u   o   s

Parable Truths

Which parable do the type of people listed need to hear? Write the letter of the parable on the line.

_____ 1. Envious or greedy

_____ 2. Careless about using gifts

_____ 3. Selfish, uncaring

_____ 4. Holds grudges

a. The Rich Man and Lazarus (Luke 16:19–31)

b. The Workers in the Vineyard (Matthew 20:1–16)

c. The Unforgiving Servant (Matthew 18:21–35)

d. The Talents (Matthew 25:14–30)

Change Your Attitude!

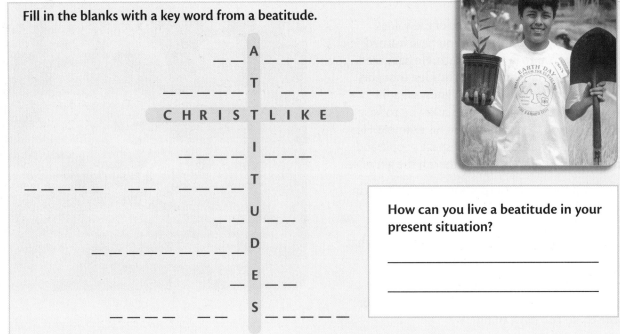

Fill in the blanks with a key word from a beatitude.

```
        _  _  A  _  _  _  _  _  _  _
     _  _  _  _  T     _  _  _    _  _  _  _  _
   C  H  R  I  S  T  L  I  K  E
        _  _  _  I  _  _  _
_  _  _  _  _     _  _     _  _  _  _  T
        _  _  U  _  _
     _  _  _  _  D  _  _  _  _  _
        _  _  E  _  _
     _  _  _  _     _  S     _  _  _  _  _  _
```

How can you live a beatitude in your present situation?

_____

_____

Help Wanted

How would you respond to the following letters? Write your answers on a sheet of paper.

Help! I was with a group of friends at the mall yesterday, and before I left I stole a calculator.

Help! My mom and I argue constantly. She never really understands and won't let me do anything.

Help! My friends and I had been sneaking beer from our parents. I decided to stop and told my parents what I had done. They have called the parents of all my friends and told them about it.

Help! I am in junior high and I have been going to many parties with Pat. I know we are getting too serious and I am really worried about this.

Now switch. Imagine yourself in one of the situations. What would you do in each situation? How do you wish you could handle such situations?

Puzzling Possibilities

Fill in the puzzle.

Across

2. What the young man had that Jesus said makes it difficult to get into heaven

3. Gift from God to create life

5. Communion for a dying person

9. Sexual unfaithfulness to a spouse

11. Who the kingdom is open to

13. The pardon of our sins in the Sacrament of Reconciliation

14. Virtue by which we respect our sexual power

17. Teaching authority of the Church

19. Mercy-killing

21. Kind of sin that is an evil in an institution or a situation and that everyone in society is responsible for changing

22. Used in the Anointing of the Sick

23. Subject of a parable that tells of the growth of the kingdom

24. Site of the Beatitudes, according to Matthew

25. What Jesus is the source of as a guide for us in life

Down

1. Subject of a parable about the kingdom's value

4. Feeling deprived or sad because of something another person has or has achieved

6. True sorrow for sin

7. Repairing or paying for property stolen or damaged

8. Place of the first miracle

10. Belief taught by the Church as true

12. Bad example

15. The evil one that Jesus overcame

16. Stories Jesus told about God and the kingdom

18. What Jesus did for people out of compassion

20. Commandment that protects marriage and the family

Celebrating

Jesus Christ the Truth

Opening Song

Leader: Let us praise God, who guides us through life.

All: Amen.

Leader: Each of us is on a journey. As we follow Jesus Christ, the Way, we discover what it means for us to live in truth. Jesus Christ, the Truth, is our model. Let us pause and reflect on how we witness to his truth.

Reader 1: A reading from the holy Gospel according to Matthew. (Matthew 13:44–46)

The kingdom of heaven is like a treasure buried in a field, which a person finds and hides again, and out of joy goes and sells all that he has and buys that field. Again, the kingdom of heaven is like a merchant searching for fine pearls. When he finds a pearl of great price, he goes and sells all that he has and buys it.

The gospel of the Lord.

All: Praise to you, Lord Jesus Christ.

Leader: Let us pause for a moment of silence and reflect on what we just heard.

What are you willing to do in order to make following Jesus a priority in your life?

Time for personal reflection

Leader: Christ Jesus, you are the Truth. You have enlightened our minds and touched our hearts.

Side 1: Thank you for the truth and mysteries you have revealed to us.

Side 2: May we grow in understanding your teachings, the teachings of the Church.

Side 1: Thank you for your parables.

Side 2: May we take their lessons to heart and serve your kingdom.

Side 1: Thank you for your miracles.

Side 2: May we always look to you for healing in our lives.

Side 1: Thank you for the Beatitudes.

Side 2: May we be numbered among the happy ones.

Side 1: Thank you for your law of love.

Side 2: May we always walk the way of justice, truth, mercy, and reverence for life.

Leader: Let us each choose one parable, miracle, or teaching of Jesus that we have learned about in this unit that has special meaning for us and make a symbol of it out of foil. Let our action be prayer. As we work silently, let us speak with Jesus about the event or teaching we have chosen, thanking him for it and applying it to our lives.

Prayer activity with background music

Leader: Let us pray a short prayer based on our symbol.

Time for reflection

Leader: Let us pray.

All: Make known to me your ways, LORD; teach me your paths.
Guide me in your truth and teach me, for you are God my savior.
For you I wait all the long day, because of your goodness, LORD.
Remember no more the sins of my youth;
remember me only in light of your love. (Psalm 25:4–5,7)

You will show me the path to life, abounding joy in your presence, the delights at your right hand forever. (Psalm 16:11)

Leader: May God our loving Father bless us and grant us the grace to follow Jesus Christ, who is our Way, our Truth, and our Life.

All: Amen.

Closing Song

A Junior High Student Puts Faith into Action

How does a young person live the message of Jesus today? For Margaret Blazunas, the 14-year-old shown here with her pastor, Father John White, S.J., following Jesus' way of love is not only fulfilling but fun.

Maggie has been volunteering at McGregor Home, a retirement community, since she was in the fifth grade. She helps the residents with crafts, takes out their curlers in the beauty shop, scoops out ice cream at the ice-cream parlor, and reads letters from their children. Maggie says that she benefits from doing these works of mercy and enjoys listening to the stories the people tell. Her life is also enriched by new friends, such as Mrs. Cooley, one of the residents.

After Maggie volunteered last summer, the director of volunteers wrote a letter to Maggie's principal. In it she expressed appreciation for the 67 hours of service that Maggie gave. She commented, "Maggie is always willing to try something new. Our residents enjoyed her enthusiastic manner. She was a joy to have here." Maggie has also worked after school at St. Patrick's Hunger Center, preparing and serving meals for people who are homeless in Cleveland, Ohio.

As the president of Student Council at Gesu School, Maggie leads the student body in service activities. The students in her school assist with doughnut Sundays at the parish and promote Red Ribbon week (a "students against drugs" program) in the school.

Why does this busy teenager make time to help others? Maggie traces her spirit of faith-in-action to her father, who is a member of the Knights of Columbus, an organization at the service of the Church. Maggie's personal convictions motivate her. She believes serving is really important. She does not see it as something she has to do in order to get service points for Confirmation. To Maggie, reaching out to others is something God wants her to do. Maggie believes that being a Catholic requires more than going to Mass. She says we have to take our faith out of the religion class and act on what we hear in the Gospels. For her, "Being a Catholic is doing what Jesus would do."

Maggie encourages other students to try volunteering now so that volunteering will become a habit they will have as adults. Besides, speaking from experience, Maggie says that when you help people in need, you feel great.

A Treasure for the Daring

Jesus promises a treasure to those who live by his truth. To discover what it is, fill in the blanks by unscrambling the letters below them. To check your answer, search John 14.

Whoever _____ me will keep my _____ and my _____ will love him,
　　　　　seovl　　　　　　　　　　　　rdwo　　　　　　　　　reahFt

and we will _____ to him and _____ our _____ with him.
　　　　　　　meco　　　　　　　　keam　　　　　　gliednlw

Gather and Go Forth

Know and Proclaim

We seek to know the truths of our Catholic faith. Then we proclaim our beliefs in truth and with respect for others.

We Know Our Faith	We Proclaim Our Faith
Jesus calls his disciples to live in his truth and to base their decisions on God's law and his own example.	Catholics imitate the lives of the saints to help them understand how to live by God's command and Jesus' example.
Jesus challenges his disciples to respect life, people, and property; to live honestly; and to cherish the gift of sex.	Catholics believe that civic virtue is a moral obligation. They exercise their civic duties by working toward legislation that promotes the life and dignity of all people.
The Fifth, Sixth, and Ninth Commandments are God's gift to his people to help them respect the dignity of themselves and others.	With the help of the Holy Spirit, Catholics develop the virtues of prudence and temperance to channel and control their desires in order to respect others.

As disciples, we are people of truth because our faith rests in Jesus. Following Christ the Way demands that we follow Christ the Truth.

"God is Spirit, and those who worship him must worship in Spirit and truth."

John 4:24

Test Your Catholic Knowledge

Fill in the circle that best completes the sentence.

The Church works to strengthen society by:

○ punishing sinners.

○ respecting all stages of life from conception to natural death.

○ making everyone happy.

○ ignoring the challenges society faces.

A Catholic to Know

Maria Goretti, the modern patron of youth, showed a
deep love of God, respect for her body, and Christlike
forgiveness. Maria was born in 1890 in Italy. When
she was twelve, Maria was attacked by a man named
Alessandro. Maria resisted, and Alessandro stabbed
her 14 times. Before Maria died from her wounds, she
forgave Alessandro and prayed for God to have mercy
on him. While in prison, Alessandro had a dream
that Maria forgave him. After his release, Alessandro
begged forgiveness of Maria's mother. She forgave him,
and the two attended Mass together the following day.
When Maria Goretti was canonized in 1950, her mother,
brothers, sisters, and Alessandro were all present.

Saint Maria Goretti

Witness and Share

**These sentences describe what Catholics believe. Listen carefully as they are read.
Ask yourself, "How strong are my Catholic beliefs?"**

My Way to Faith

- I base my decisions on Jesus' examples.

- I respect the property of other people.

- I get advice from people who are virtuous.

- I read the Gospels to help guide my decisions.

- I obey the Ninth Commandment by respecting myself and others.

- I practice chastity by respecting my sexuality.

Share Your Faith

**Consider the ways in which you let Jesus' truth guide what you say and do. How do
you decide between right and wrong? Write your ideas on the lines, and invite a family
member to discuss how Jesus helps him or her decide between right and wrong.**

_____

_____

_____

_____

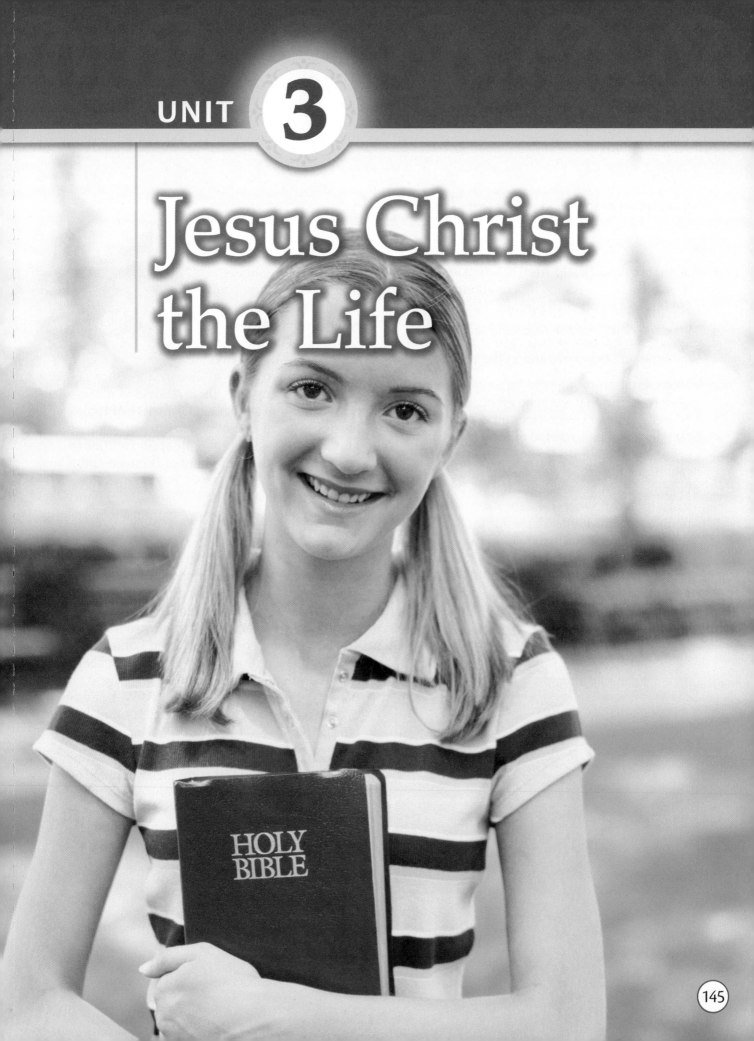

Jesus Christ the Life

Deepening Family Faith

FAITH IS NOT AN ABSTRACT IDEA. It is a reality that is rooted in a relationship with God. Like any other important relationship, our relationship with God deserves our attention. We are called to nurture our family's faith at home, in the parish, and in the world.

Home is a natural place to introduce our children to traditional Catholic practices, such as prayer, seasonal celebrations, and acts of kindness, forgiveness, and the other virtues. In the context of the family, faith is caught as well as taught. Children observe not only what we as parents say, but especially what we do. They learn their faith each time they see us welcome people into our home, share our faith around the kitchen table, or turn to God in prayer. They learn by the religious art we choose to put on our walls as well as by how we make room for the needy at our family table and in our family budget.

We are also members of a parish family. The heart of parish life is the weekly celebration of the Eucharist. Parishes offer a number of other ways for members to grow in their relationship with God. Many offer Bible study and adult faith formation sessions on a variety of topics. During Advent and Lent, parishes offer times of prayer and reflection with opportunities to participate in the Sacrament of Penance and Reconciliation. Your parish may offer events where the whole family can learn about your faith and about service opportunities to help those in need.

Lay people in the Church have the mission of bearing witness to Christ. This mission extends beyond our neighborhood to our city, our country, and our world. We have the responsibility to act in ways that promote justice, diminish oppression, and honor the dignity of each human person. You can keep informed by reading your diocesan newspaper, going to Church-sponsored Web sites, or subscribing to Catholic magazines and newspapers.

Because your example is so important to your child's development in faith, pick the practices at home, in the parish, and in the world that are calling you, and commit to them. Involve your whole family, and make sure you have fun. Our life in faith is meant to bring us joy.

Visit **www.christourlife.com** for more family resources.

CHAPTER 18

Living Faith in Jesus

Jesus the Prophet

An Incredible Life

What if a stranger came to you and told you that tomorrow you would be able to fly, or to read minds, or to be in two places at once? You probably would not believe it. Such superhuman powers are part of science fiction, not real life.

Jesus stepped into our world and told us something just as incredible. He said we could share God's life and live forever. Jesus was a prophet, someone who spoke for God. Those who accept him believe that in Baptism God offers us grace, a share in God's own life.

God gives us the gift of himself. What greater gift can you give than to give yourself? The special grace of God dwelling within us is called sanctifying grace.

Spiritual life is friendship with God present within us. Through grace, we can speak to God, respond to God, and someday enjoy fullness of life with God eternally.

Your Spiritual Life Inventory

Read the statements below about spiritual life. Check the endings that apply to you.

I think of Jesus
- often.
- rarely.
- when I am in church.
- when I am happy.
- when I am in trouble.
- when I am at home.
- often throughout the day.
- when I am with my friends.

I pray
- in the morning and evening.
- in church.
- with my friends.
- with my family.
- when I am alone.

I try
- to help others.
- to live so that others know I am a Christian.
- to be understanding and kind.
- to remember the love Jesus has shown for me.
- to make other people happy.

I celebrate Reconciliation and the Eucharist
- occasionally.
- regularly.

I think of God as
- very close.
- far away.

Life Is a Journey

Life is a journey from birth through death to eternal life. For the believer, life is the journey to the Father, through the Son, in the Spirit. Jesus came that we may have eternal life. He invites us to believe in him and to share his friendship and love. Throughout the Gospels, people respond to his invitation. The following two stories of encounters with Jesus tell us about faith.

Nicodemus: Night Class

Nicodemus, a Pharisee and probably a member of the Sanhedrin, wanted to know more about Jesus.

Read John 3:1–21.

Why do you think Nicodemus came at night?

_____

_____

Nicodemus needed faith to see that Jesus was more than a teacher or a miracle worker.

What did Jesus tell Nicodemus we must do to enter the Kingdom of God? (John 3:5)

_____

_____

What must happen to Jesus so we may have eternal life? (John 3:14)

_____

_____

_____

After Jesus died, Nicodemus brought spices for his body and helped to bury it. His encounter with Jesus transformed Nicodemus into a true believer.

The Woman at the Well

The Jewish people did not associate with Samaritans. (See page 27.) Nor did they speak to women in public. So when Jesus spoke to the Samaritan woman, she was surprised. The Samaritan woman, who had had five husbands, accepted Jesus' invitation to a life of faith. After she came to believe in Jesus, she spread the news to her entire town. At first, people believed in Jesus because of what the woman told them. Then, when they met him and heard him personally, their faith deepened.

Read John 4:4–30.

What did Jesus tell the Samaritan woman he could offer? (John 4:14)

_____

_____

_____

The Faithful Friend

To both of these people—Nicodemus and the Samaritan woman—and to many others, Jesus reached out to offer life. The same is true in your spiritual life: Jesus begins the relationship. Then he is always there, inviting, forgiving, helping, caring, loving.

A Moment with Jesus

Jesus does not wait for us to look for him. He comes to meet us where we are.

Pause for a moment to reflect on the stories of Nicodemus and the Samaritan woman. Jesus invited each of them to a deeper relationship with him. Then ask Jesus to help you recognize his invitation to greater friendship with him. Thank him for walking with you on your spiritual journey.

Dan's Difficult Day

For Dan, it had been a hard day at school. There had been a surprise quiz in history, he had forgotten his English homework, basketball practice had been canceled, he got in trouble for talking in class, and he had an argument with his friend. By the time he got home, he had had it! Dan's mother also had a difficult day. Her work at the office had brought her problems. She had already done the laundry at home and was in the midst of preparing dinner.

When Dan walked into the house, his mother greeted him with a list of jobs to do, reminded him to watch his younger brother, told him to clean his room, and not to play the radio so loud. As Dan heard all this, he felt like arguing. Instead, he thought about how his mother felt and what would be the right thing to do.

What decision would you have made if you had been in Dan's place?

_____

_____

Grace—It Is Free!

Original Sin left us with a tendency to do wrong. Dan's urge to do what is right was from the Holy Spirit. It is something that you often experience: God's invitation to deeper friendship—or grace. Grace has many meanings. You have already seen it as God's life. God's presence in you (sanctifying grace) brings about changes in your life. It prompts you to do what is good.

Grace is a free gift. You must be open to it, however, to share in God's life. Actual grace gives you the desire to lead a Christian life.

Actual grace strengthens you to make decisions and act according to the Father's will. Through actual grace, you can believe Jesus' message, choose to do good, and turn more and more to Christ.

Grace works like human friendship. When you become friends with someone, you often grow alike. You begin to see things the same way. The more you accept Christ's offer of friendship, the more influenced you are by him. You begin to see things and make decisions as he would. You avoid sin to imitate his obedience to God. You become more like Jesus.

Hints from God

God inspired Dan to do what was good. By choosing to do the right thing, he grows closer to God. However, Dan could reject God's friendship and help. If he did, he would be turning away from God and from all that could make him happy. Even then, God would call to him to think about what he had done and start anew.

Think of any way you have experienced God's grace today. It may have been a good thought. It may have been something you saw or heard that made you think of God, God's love for you, or all God has done for you. Write it below.

_____

_____

Super Strength for the Journey

You can respond to God and deepen your friendship through virtues poured into your heart at Baptism. A virtue is an attitude or a way of living that enables you to do good. Virtues grow and develop through graces received through prayer, good works, and the sacraments, especially the Eucharist. You have received Theological Virtues and cardinal virtues. You might think of them as the vitamins of your spiritual life.

Theological Virtues

Theos means "God." The **Theological Virtues**—faith, hope and charity—are gifts given by God and centered on God. They lead us to know, love, and trust God. With their help, we are capable of acting as God's children and reaching our journey's end: eternal life with God.

Faith is the virtue by which we believe God completely and accept as true all that God has revealed and teaches through the Catholic Church. Faith helps us grow in our understanding of God's goodness. We often use a creed to express the truths we believe. We are united in what we believe and in whom we believe.

We believe because we trust a person. When we really trust, we are willing to stake our life on what we believe.

Read the Act of Faith on the inside back cover of your book. What words tell why you can believe God?

_____

The virtue of hope is the trust and confidence that God will give us eternal life and all the help necessary along the way. Two sins against hope are despair and presumption. Despair is to believe God cannot or will not help and so to give up even trying to be saved. Presumption is to expect God automatically to give all you hope for even though you do not cooperate with God's grace or make any efforts to live a

Charity.

Christian life. You presume on the goodness of God. Also, presumption is to think you can find eternal life without God.

Charity (love) is that virtue that helps us to love God and to give God first place in our lives. Our model is the love shown in the life and Death of Jesus. Saint Paul wrote about the various gifts given by God. Read 1 Corinthians 13:1–13.

What is the most important gift? _____ Why? (See verse 8.)

Faith.

Cardinal Virtues

The **cardinal virtues** are fundamental to leading a moral life. They are habits that allow us to do good acts and to give the best of ourselves. The cardinal virtues order our feelings and actions according to human reason and faith. The word *cardinal* means "hinge." Our spiritual life hinges on the cardinal virtues.

Prudence is the virtue that directs us to decide what is good. Prudent people ask responsible people for advice. They think through their beliefs and choices and reflect before they act.

Justice is the virtue that guides us to respect the rights of others. It gives us the determination to protect those rights and to fulfill our responsibilities to people and to God.

Fortitude is the virtue that gives us the courage to do what is right even when it is very difficult. It may mean having patience, being generous, enduring ridicule, or not responding to peer pressure.

Temperance is the virtue that helps us to control our desire for pleasure. Temperance keeps us from overdoing it in eating, drinking, sex, money, and the way we dress, act, and speak.

Life Means Growth

You can easily see how you have grown and changed physically and intellectually over the years. How about spiritually? How much more do you know about God and your faith now than you did before? How much has your life become a reflection of your Christian values and ideals? Growing closer to Jesus is vital and takes energy and time—a lifetime. Remember that life in Christ and prayer are inseparable.

Remember

What is grace?

Grace is a free gift of God's life in us. It is friendship with God that strengthens us and makes us holy.

What are the Theological Virtues?

The Theological Virtues are powers given by God at Baptism and centered on God: faith, hope, and charity.

What are the cardinal virtues?

The cardinal virtues—prudence, justice, fortitude, and temperance—are fundamental to leading a moral life. They are habits that allow us to order our feelings and actions according to human reason and faith.

Respond

What matters in life is how you respond to Christ. Responding with love and longing will bring you eternal life. If you respond with indifference or hostility, you risk separation from God. Read Luke 9:18–21. If Jesus were to ask you the same two questions, what would you say? Write your responses in your reflection notebook.

Reach Out

1. Look at the Apostles' Creed or Nicene Creed on the inside front cover of your book. On paper, design a series of church windows based on it. Or write a creed in your own words. To get ideas, read these expressions of faith found in Scripture:
   - Mark 8:29
   - Romans 1:3–5 or 8:34
   - 1 Corinthians 15:3–8
   - 2 Timothy 2:8
   - 1 John 2:22

2. Jesus offered the Samaritan woman living water. Water has many uses. It can destroy life or save it. It can nourish, cleanse, and refresh. Find examples in the Bible and in everyday life where water is used in any of the ways mentioned above. How is it used in John 13? How did John the Baptist use it?

3. Write an autobiography of your faith life. Begin with your Baptism and name the people and events that have helped you grow in faith. Include your favorite prayers and Scripture stories. List the parishes you have been a member of and saints who have inspired you. Share your story with someone.

4. Tape three cardboard boxes end-to-end to make a kiosk, a pillar that serves as a bulletin board. On your kiosk, put pictures and captions encouraging people to live their faith, especially by helping people who are poor. Display your kiosk in your parish.

Words to Know

cardinal virtues	prudence
fortitude	temperance
justice	Theological Virtues

Joachim Patinir, *The Baptism of Christ,* 16th century, Dutch.

Hendrik Siemiradzki, *Christ and the Woman of Samaria*, 1890, oil on canvas, Poland.

Words of Life   Use each word in a sentence that reveals its meaning.

1. grace

_____

2. sanctifying grace

_____

3. virtue

_____

4. cardinal virtue

_____

People of Faith   Write yes or no in answer to each question.

_____   **1.** Did Nicodemus have more faith at the end of Jesus' life?

_____   **2.** Did Jesus tell Nicodemus that we would have eternal life because Jesus would be lifted up?

_____   **3.** Would Jesus be following a Jewish practice by speaking with a Samaritan woman?

_____   **4.** Did Jesus lead the Samaritan woman to believe in him?

_____   **5.** Did the Samaritan woman bring other people to Jesus?

_____   **6.** Did Jesus tell Nicodemus that there is nothing we can do to enter the Kingdom of God?

Gather and Go Forth

Know and Proclaim

We seek to grow in our love of the Catholic faith and proclaim our love by following the example of Jesus' life.

We Know Our Faith	We Proclaim Our Faith
Grace is a free gift from God. Sanctifying grace sustains us and compels us to preserve our relationship with God.	Catholics develop their spiritual life by praying such prayers as the Rosary and by doing penance such as fasting and giving alms.
Faith, hope, and charity are the Theological Virtues. These virtues are given by God and focus on God.	At the beginning of the Rosary, Catholics pray three Hail Marys, one for each of the Theological Virtues. These virtues help bring them closer to God.
The cardinal virtues of prudence, justice, fortitude, and temperance lead us to a moral life and allow people to do good acts.	Catholics develop the cardinal virtues by thinking before they act, considering the needs of others, being strong when facing opposition, and practicing restraint.

Test Your Catholic Knowledge

Fill in the circle that best answers the question.

What do we call our growing, loving relationship with God?

○ tradition

○ spirituality

○ sanctifying grace

○ particular judgment

Our greatest journey in life is the journey of the spirit. We grow in our faith as we grow in our ability to be more like Jesus in what we say and do.

Let no one have contempt for your youth, but set an example for those who believe, in speech, conduct, love, faith, and purity.
1 Timothy 4:12

A Catholic to Know

John was the youngest son of a peasant family. His father died when John was two, and the family became very poor. As a youngster, John taught religion to other boys and got them to go to church. Encouraged by a priest, John entered the seminary. John started gathering boys together on Sunday for a day in the country. They would begin with Mass, followed by breakfast and games. The afternoon would include a picnic, a catechism lesson, and evening prayers. John Bosco gave a father's care to rowdy, neglected boys. He opened workshops to train boys to be shoemakers and tailors. In 1859 John began a religious community of priests which is still active today, caring for boys who have been neglected.

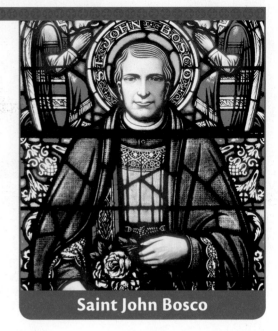

Saint John Bosco

Witness and Share

These sentences describe what Catholics believe. Listen carefully as they are read. Ask yourself, "How strong are my Catholic beliefs?"

My Way to Faith

- I rely on the virtues of faith, hope, and love to bring me closer to God.

- I devote time and energy to developing my spiritual life.

- I think before I act, consider the needs of others, show strength in the face of opposition, and show self-control.

- I let others know that I am a Christian by the way I live.

- I do good to others without expecting anything in return.

Share Your Faith

Consider ways in which you can take a more active role in developing your spirituality by exploring different forms of prayer and service. Write your ideas on the lines, and invite a family member or friend to join your exploration of faith.

_____

_____

_____

_____

Opposition to Jesus

Jesus the Suffering Servant

In moments of joy, faith helps you become aware of God's presence, his power and his goodness. Faith can fill your heart with gratitude to God. But you also have times of sorrow and disappointment. In those moments, your faith can help you to believe that God is with you and will bring good out of the sorrows. Faith can help you accept them with trust. Through sorrows, you can become the person God has called you to be.

Glory Through Suffering

Suffering was part of Jesus' life. Words from the prophet Isaiah apply to him:

> Because of his affliction
> he shall see the light in fullness of days;
> Through his suffering, my servant shall
> justify many,
> and their guilt he shall bear.
>
> Isaiah 53:11

For Jesus the road to glory was through suffering. This was difficult for the apostles to understand until the Spirit came at Pentecost. When Jesus first predicted what he must undergo as the suffering servant, Peter would not hear of it. The apostles needed stronger faith for the trials to come. So Jesus took Peter,

James, and John to a mountain (possibly Mount Tabor) where they saw him transfigured.

Jesus willingly endured suffering and death for the sake of our salvation. His choice shows his love for the Father and us. The **Transfiguration** teaches us that glory comes through the Cross. Just as the Israelites passed from death to life in the Exodus, Jesus passed from death to Resurrection. Because Jesus knew suffering, he is a willing companion on our road through suffering. He wants to share in our lives as we walk with him on the road to glory.

Faith Builders

The Father tells us how to meet joys and sorrows. He says, "Listen to my Son." Jesus speaks to us and strengthens our faith especially in Scripture, in prayer, and in the sacraments. We believe that Jesus is with us in all the events of life.

Check the events in which you have experienced the presence or guidance of Jesus.

○ being misunderstood by parents
○ taking a test
○ participating in the Sunday Eucharist
○ losing a friend
○ making a decision

How could faith help you to come closer to Jesus in one of those situations?

A Wall of Opposition

Jesus faced difficulties throughout his public life. Sometimes people did not understand him or accept him. From the beginning, the religious leaders watched his every move with suspicion. They did not like his popularity and his criticism of their rigid view of the law. Instead of being open and changing their narrow-minded attitudes, they gradually built a wall of opposition.

For each stone, look up the Scripture passage and write the form of opposition that Jesus faced. Choose the form from the Opposition Box below.

Luke 4:16–30
_____
_____

Luke 8:34–37
_____
_____

Mark 11:15–19
_____
_____

John 10:31–33
_____
_____

Matthew 12:22–24
_____
_____

John 8:54–59
_____
_____

OPPOSITION BOX
- picked up stones to throw at him
- asked him to leave town
- said he had power from the devil
- accused him of blasphemy
- attempted to throw him off a cliff
- looked for a way to put him to death

In the face of such opposition, Jesus remained true to his goal—to do the will of the Father and to proclaim the kingdom. The raising of his friend Lazarus from the dead united the forces of opposition and was the immediate cause of Jesus' Death. In the account of Jesus' suffering, Death, and glory, life and death are intertwined.

Man Dead Four Days Lives!

BETHANY—A man dead for four days was restored to life yesterday by the Galilean preacher and wonder-worker, Jesus of Nazareth.

Lazarus, a distinguished citizen of Bethany, died Monday after a brief illness. Prescribed Jewish burial rituals were performed, and the body was laid in the family tomb outside the city.

Tomb of Lazarus in Bethany, Israel.

Miracle Reported

Yesterday Jesus, a close friend of the family, arrived and requested that the tomb be opened. The deceased man's sister Martha objected, for she knew what the body would be like after four days.

Nevertheless, at Jesus' insistence, the stone was removed. Observers said that Jesus commanded Lazarus to come out. Seconds later the corpse appeared in its burial clothes at the entrance of the tomb. At the order of the Galilean, the sisters of Lazarus unwound the burial linens and found themselves face-to-face with their brother, alive and well!

Excitement runs high today as people discuss proclaiming Jesus as the Messiah. The Sanhedrin is expected to convene to address the issue and determine the action it will take. A reliable source has disclosed that the members fear Jesus' power to draw crowds will attract Rome's attention.

From Death to Life

Behind a front-page news article, there is an inside story. To find out the inside story about the raising of Lazarus, read John 11:1–53. Then answer the following questions:

1. Why didn't the apostles want Jesus to go to Lazarus?
2. What encouraging message did Jesus give Martha?
3. What were Jesus' emotions at the tomb?
4. How did Jesus show that he was following his Father's will?
5. What attitude toward death did Jesus have? Mary and Martha?

You can imagine how people flocked to Jesus after he raised Lazarus from the dead. According to the Gospels, when Jesus rode into Jerusalem on a colt near the feast of Passover, a great crowd greeted him. They waved palm branches, a sign of welcome for a conqueror. They shouted, "Hosanna! Blessed is he who comes in the name of the Lord, the king of Israel." The Pharisees were helpless to stop the demonstration. They cried, "Look, the whole world has gone after him."

Pachomian Brotherhood, detail of Lazarus from modern Byzantine-style icon, Mount Athos, Greece.

A Dead End?

If you took a poll asking "How do you view death?" you might find answers like these:

- Death is beautiful. It is coming home to God.
- Death is cruel and meaningless. It is a total end of life.
- Death is frightening. I do not want to think about it.
- Death is a mystery. I cannot understand it.
- Death means goodbye. I do not want to lose what I have.
- Death is confusing. There must be life after death, but I am not sure what kind.

Raising Lazarus was a sign that Jesus could give eternal life to those who believe in him. Not long after that miracle, Jesus freely and obediently offered his life to the Father in order to free us from our sins and give us eternal life. By offering his life, he changed death into a doorway leading to happiness with God.

The Christian Views Death

Through Baptism, you share in the life won by Jesus' Death and Resurrection. God has called you to live in friendship with him that is beyond death and lasts forever. Death can be your final yes to God. You can accept it and offer your life to the Father as Jesus did. Here are four positive ways of looking at death for a Christian:

- You are united with God in the kingdom of love forever.

- You are freed from evil's power forever.
- You deepen your relationship with all those who have already died and are united with Christ.
- You have a new relationship in love with those who have not yet died.

If death means all these good things, why are we afraid? Death, the result of sin, brings pain and suffering. It leads us into the unknown, away from all that is familiar and loved.

Even Jesus dreaded death. The night before he died, he went to the garden of Gethsemane. There he faced his coming death and was overwhelmed with fear. As he prayed, he was strengthened to accept death. Jesus willingly gave his life to the Father. Like him, we are called to accept our fear and give ourselves with trust into the hands of our Father. Our faith and our hope in eternal life strengthen us to do this.

When Someone You Love Dies

Imagine how empty and lonely life would be if your best friend moved away. A similar experience on a deeper level is the loss through death of someone you love. The emptiness and loneliness are great. At such times, remember that through your union with Christ, you remain united to the one you love and that suffering will lead to a life of glory together.

A Moment with Jesus

It takes faith to believe in eternal life. With eyes of faith, we can see beyond today and believe in God's promise of life after death.

Pause for a moment and think about your own belief in eternal life. How has it been a comfort to you in times of loss? Reflect on the gift that faith is. Then thank Jesus for your faith and for the promise of eternal life.

Remember

What is the Christian view of death?

For a Christian, death is a final chance to accept God's will and offer oneself freely to God, following the example of Jesus.

What is Jesus' promise of eternal life?

Jesus said, "I am the resurrection and the life; whoever believes in me, even if he dies, will live." (John 11:25)

What is the Transfiguration?

The Transfiguration is the glorified appearance of Jesus that was witnessed by the apostles Peter, James, and John.

Respond

The apostle Thomas had a special meeting with Jesus. Read John 20:19–29. What did Thomas say to Jesus when he met him? What did Jesus say to Thomas? Did you ever have to believe without seeing? What did you feel like? What helped you to have faith in Jesus? Answer these questions in your reflection journal.

Reach Out

1. Read Luke 7:11–17, Luke 8:49–56, and John 11:1–44. Create a front-page news story for one of the passages from Luke. Or, with a small group, make up a skit for one of the three passages.

2. Make a photo album of the main events in Jesus' life. Draw the photos and add captions. Include the times of opposition Jesus faced. Share your photo album with younger family members. Use it to teach them about Jesus.

3. When have you faced opposition for acting as a Christian? How did you respond? Reflect on the incident in your reflection notebook. Write a prayer asking to meet opposition courageously.

4. Imagine that a close relative of your friend has died. Write a sympathy note, sharing the Christian view of death. Decorate the note with Resurrection symbols.

5. Participate in the funeral for someone in your parish. Pray for him or her as a representative of the faith community. Report on what you observed that strengthened your faith.

Thomas's special meeting with Jesus, stained glass, St. Mary's Church, Killarney, Ireland. ❯

Sorting Events   If the statement refers to the Transfiguration, write **T**. If it refers to the raising of Lazarus, write **L**.

_____ **1.** Moses and Elijah spoke with Jesus.

_____ **2.** Jesus proclaimed that he was the resurrection and the life.

_____ **3.** Peter wanted to stay on the mountain with Jesus.

_____ **4.** The apostles learned that glory comes from the Cross.

_____ **5.** The Pharisees were determined to kill Jesus.

_____ **6.** The apostles' faith was confirmed.

_____ **7.** The Father told us to listen to his Son Jesus.

_____ **8.** Jesus appeared in glory.

_____ **9.** People in Jerusalem greeted Jesus as the king of Israel.

_____ **10.** Jesus showed his humanness.

Not Wanted   Give examples of how Jesus was rejected.

_____

_____

_____

Riddles   Answer these questions.

1. Why is death a comma, not a period?

_____

2. Why can we say Jesus "loved us to death"?

_____

3. Why is life after life better than life?

_____

_____

_____

4. How do you turn death into a yes?

_____

Gather and Go Forth

Know and Proclaim

We proclaim the truths of our Catholic faith in times of joy and sorrow.

We Know Our Faith	We Proclaim Our Faith
Faith helps us believe that God is with us even in times of sorrow. Faith can help us accept sorrow with trust.	Because Mary was a mother who lost her son, many Catholics pray to her under the title "Our Lady of Sorrows." The Seven Sorrows of Mary recall the challenges that Mary had as a disciple of Christ.
Jesus willingly endured suffering and death for the sake of our salvation. The Transfiguration teaches us that salvation comes through the Cross.	Catholics commemorate the suffering and Death of Jesus when they walk the Stations of the Cross. Pictures or statues depict Jesus carrying the Cross, stumbling as he walks, his crucifixion, and Death.
By offering his life to the Father, Jesus changed death into a doorway that leads to happiness with God.	The paschal candle is lit during Catholic funerals. It is also lit during Baptisms, on the Easter Vigil, and during the Easter season, connecting death with life.

Our faith allows us to trust in God with courage and confidence even in times of pain and suffering. Through Jesus, we receive the strength to hope for an eternal life in glory.

Faith is the realization of what is hoped for and evidence of things not seen.

Hebrews 11:1

Test Your Catholic Knowledge

Fill in the circle that best completes the sentence.

In his Transfiguration, Jesus teaches that:

○ Mary is his mother.

○ all sins will be forgiven.

○ glory comes through the Cross.

○ the Father, Son, and the Holy Spirit are one.

A Catholic to Know

On February 5, 1597, 26 men were crucified in Nagasaki, Japan. Among these men was a Jesuit brother named Paul Miki. When Japan first allowed foreign visitors to enter the country in 1549, Saint Francis Xavier was among the first missionaries to share the Good News of Christ with the Japanese people. Paul Miki was one of a small but committed group of Christian converts. Christianity spread rapidly until 1587, when Emperor Hideyoshi expelled all foreign missionaries, beginning an era of Christian persecution. Paul Miki and his companions met their death singing psalms of praise and joy. Their witness to the faith continues to give Christians the strength to profess their faith.

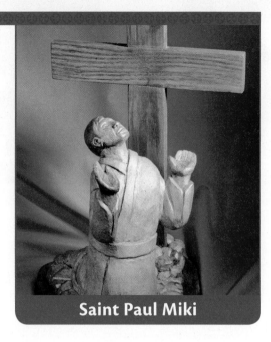

Saint Paul Miki

Witness and Share

These sentences describe what Catholics believe. Listen carefully as they are read. Ask yourself, "How strong are my Catholic beliefs?"

My Way to Faith

- I turn to Jesus when things are hard.

- I am comforted by God's presence during times of sorrow.

- I remain true to Jesus even in the face of opposition.

- I believe that as a good Christian, when I die, I will be with God in his kingdom forever.

- I thank God for the gift of eternal life.

Share Your Faith

Think about the times your faith has given comfort to you and your family during experiences of suffering and sorrow. Write your experiences on the lines. Invite a family member to share how his or her faith provided comfort in times of sorrow and distress.

_____

_____

_____

_____

_____

The Eucharist

Jesus the Bread of Life

The Way We Celebrate

- During Pope John Paul II's visit to the United States in 1995, a eucharistic celebration was held outdoors. Thousands of people in Baltimore, Maryland, participated.
- In Uganda, Father Dan, a missionary, parks his truck where Catholics gather for Mass. He sets up an altar alongside the road, and the people celebrate the Eucharist.
- Mr. and Mrs. Fields celebrated their sixtieth wedding anniversary with a Mass. Friends and relatives gathered around the altar to break bread together.

Which celebration of Mass most impressed you? Why?

_____

More Than a Memory

All Masses are special. Before Jesus died, he gave us a precious gift—a way he could remain with us. He gave us the Eucharist. In this sacrament, he is present with us under the appearances of bread and wine. Jesus acts in every eucharistic celebration. He continues to teach us by his word and example. He is our one and only Mediator making the offering of his life present to us. Jesus Christ nourishes us with his Body and Blood, and he unites us with himself and with one another in the Catholic community. The Eucharist is a sign of

Jesus' permanent love for us. It is the perfect act of worship and the heart of Christian life.

Meals That Made History

God prepared humankind for the gift of the Eucharist. Long ago, God rescued the Israelites from slavery in Egypt and brought them to freedom. To commemorate that great saving event, Jewish people celebrate a special Passover meal. Another hint of the Eucharist occurs in the story of the Israelites' journey to the Promised Land. God fed them in the desert with manna, a breadlike substance.

Preparation for the Eucharist continued when Jesus fed great crowds with bread and fish.

Read Mark 6:30–44. How is this miracle like the Eucharist?

_____

_____

_____

_____

_____

In Chapter 6 of John's Gospel, after that miracle, Jesus promised the Bread of Life. Many people could not accept it when he said, "Whoever eats my flesh and drinks my blood has eternal life." Those people no longer followed him.

The Last Supper

Jesus' last meal with the apostles was probably a Passover meal. At that meal, Jesus put a towel around his waist and washed the feet of the apostles like a servant. He told them that if he, the master and teacher, washed their feet, they ought to wash one another's feet. Then Jesus showed a greater proof of his love. He took bread, blessed it, broke it, and gave it to the apostles, saying, "This is my body which will be given for you; do this in memory of me." Then he took a cup, passed it to the apostles and said, "This is my blood of the covenant, which will be shed for many." The next day Jesus would die on the Cross for us. The sacrifice offered at the Last Supper was the sacrifice of Calvary.

Jesus now offers that same sacrifice to the Father for us and with us in the Eucharist. Each time we celebrate the Eucharist, we come in contact with the dying and rising of Jesus. Only validly ordained priests can preside at the Mass and pray the prayer of consecration over the bread and wine.

A New Covenant

Sacrifices and covenants were familiar to the Jewish people. They considered the Covenant, or agreement, God made with them at Sinai as their birthday as God's people. There God revealed the divine name to the Jewish people and gave them the Law. They agreed to live by the Law. The Covenant was sealed by a ritual in which the blood of sacrifices was sprinkled on the altar and on the people. At the Last Supper, Jesus gave us a new commandment. He said, "Love one another. As I have loved you so you also should love one another." Humankind entered a new covenant with God sealed by the blood of Jesus. All who die and rise with Christ at Baptism share in the celebration of this covenant. They offer Christ's sacrifice and grow in love.

A Thanksgiving Meal

Eucharist means "thanksgiving." This sacrament is the greatest act of praise and thanksgiving we can offer God. We are obliged to participate in the Eucharist on the Lord's Day and on every holy day of obligation. Some people celebrate Mass on other days and benefit from the grace it offers. Any time something wonderful happens and your heart is full of joy and gratitude to God, consider celebrating Mass to give God thanks.

What days might you make special by participating in the Eucharist?

_____

_____

The celebration of the Eucharist has two main parts: the Liturgy of the Word and the Liturgy of the Eucharist.

The Liturgy of the Word

During the Liturgy of the Word, God speaks to us in the readings. In the Gospel, we are assured of God's love for us. We hear Jesus teach us what the Father wants us to know and what he wants us to do to lead a new life. The homily gives us insight into what God's words mean for us. Then we ask God's help in the Prayer of the Faithful. Nourished and strengthened by God's Word, we are fed with the Bread of Life in the Liturgy of the Eucharist.

The Liturgy of the Eucharist

Jesus' words and actions of the Last Supper are repeated at every Eucharist. By them we not only call to mind the Paschal Mystery, but Jesus makes it actually present. We offer Jesus to the Father and ourselves with him. Then we receive Christ's Body and Blood under the appearances of bread and wine. By sharing this meal, we form the Church. Just as many grains of wheat make one bread and many grapes make one wine, so we are made one in Christ. Together we become more like him. Together we are sent to bring his love to the world.

Read John 15:4–7. What symbol did Jesus use to describe our relationship with him?

Use these answers for the questions in the next sections on the Liturgy of the Eucharist:

- **Amen.**
- **Lord, I am not worthy that you should enter under my roof, but only say the word and my soul shall be healed.**
- **Blessed be God for ever.**
- **Holy, holy, holy Lord God of hosts.**
- **We proclaim your Death, O Lord, and profess your Resurrection until you come again.**

He Takes Bread

The Liturgy of the Eucharist begins with the Presentation and Preparation of the Gifts. We take bread and wine to the priest. He says a prayer over each gift. These prayers remind us that the bread and wine symbolize the gifts of God and the work of our hands. They symbolize each one of us and our offering with Jesus. What do we respond to each of these prayers?

He Gives Thanks

Then the priest says a prayer of thanks called the Preface. With him, we offer thanks and praise through Jesus to the Father. We thank the Father for his Son Jesus who became man and redeemed us through his Cross and Resurrection. Then we join the angels and saints in a song of praise. What is its first line?

He Offers Himself

The Preface is at the beginning of the Eucharistic Prayer, the high point of our act of worship. The priest stretches his hands over the gifts and calls on the Holy Spirit to make them holy. Then he prays the words of the Institution Narrative at the Last Supper, and Jesus Christ's Body and Blood become present on the altar under the appearances of bread and wine. This change in substance is called **transubstantiation.** Jesus Christ is present, living and glorious, soul and divinity.

The Eucharistic Prayers are found in the *Roman Missal*, the official book of prayers and directions for Mass. Here are the words of the Institution Narrative.

Over the bread the priest says,

> Take this, all of you, and eat of it,
> for this is my Body,
> which will be given up for you.

Over the wine he says,

> Take this, all of you, and drink from it,
> for this is the chalice of my Blood,
> the Blood of the new and eternal covenant,
> which will be poured out for you and for many
> for the forgiveness of sins.
>
> Do this in memory of me.

The priest then invites us to proclaim the Mystery of Faith that we celebrate. What is one of the memorial acclamations?

As the priest continues the Eucharistic Prayer, united with Jesus we give praise to the Father. We pray for the Church on earth, for those who have died, and we remember Mary and the saints. The priest concludes this prayer with a hymn of praise (a doxology):

> Through him, and with him, and in him,
> O God, almighty Father,
> in the unity of the Holy Spirit,
> all glory and honor is yours,
> for ever and ever.

What is our response to voice our agreement with all that is taking place?

_____

Jesus Gives Himself to Us

In the Communion Rite of the Mass, Jesus gives us himself as food and drink. We prepare to receive him by praying together the prayer Jesus taught us, the Lord's Prayer. We are called to reconciliation and to unity in faith and love, so we exchange a sign of Christ's peace. While the priest breaks the bread, we pray that Jesus, the Lamb of God, will have mercy on us and grant us his peace. Before receiving Jesus Christ in Holy Communion, we pray together a prayer that expresses both our weakness and our trust in God. What is it?

_____

_____

_____

The Church encourages us to receive Holy Communion at every Mass. When we receive Jesus, we praise and thank and love him. We tell him of our needs, confident that he will help us. All who share the Body and Blood of Jesus Christ are drawn into union with the Father and the Holy Spirit and with one another. Here is a mystery. As we accept Christ in Holy Communion, we also agree to accept and support one another in the Christian community and others in the world. If we

permit him, Jesus will gradually change us into the people he calls us to be.

A Moment with Jesus

In the Eucharist, Jesus gives himself to us as real food. We are fed and nourished by the Body and Blood of Christ.

Pause for a moment and imagine yourself at Mass preparing to receive Communion. Reflect on what this means for you as a follower of Christ. In your own words, share with Jesus your hopes about growing into the person he wants you to be. Then thank Jesus for the gift of himself to you in the Eucharist.

He Sends Us to Announce the Gospel

Having been reminded of and renewed by Jesus' love, we are more aware of others' needs and more able to serve them. With Jesus, we go forth to announce the Gospel to all.

A Feast Without End

In the Eucharist, we share in the communion of saints. We are united with all the members of the Church in heaven and on earth. We can pray for those in purgatory. At Mass, we carry out the same liturgy or praise of God's glory that echoes through heaven. Our thanks and praise are preparation for the time when we will give God glory forever. The Eucharist is a sign and pledge of the banquet of God's kingdom. There people who have been faithful to the covenant will share life with God forever.

Remember

What is the Eucharist?

The Eucharist is the sacrament in which the Paschal Mystery of Jesus is both called to mind and made present under the appearances of bread and wine. We offer Jesus with ourselves to the Father, and we are united through eucharistic communion with Jesus, the Father, and the Holy Spirit, and with one another.

What is the new commandment of Jesus?

I give you a new commandment: love one another. As I have loved you, so you also should love one another. This is how all will know that you are my disciples, if you have love for one another.

John 13:34–35

What are the two main parts of the eucharistic celebration?

The two main parts of the eucharistic celebration are the Liturgy of the Word and the Liturgy of the Eucharist.

What is transubstantiation?

Transubstantiation is the change of the substances of bread and wine into the Body and Blood of Christ.

Respond

Think of a symbol that represents you. Maybe it is an eagle to show your interest in the environment, or a football, or a computer. Draw your symbol in your reflection notebook and write a prayer offering yourself to the Father.

Reach Out

1. Make next Sunday a day to share a meal—spiritual and physical. Invite a relative or friend to celebrate the Eucharist with you. Then eat together afterwards, either at home or in a restaurant. Discuss thoughts or feelings that occurred to you during the liturgy.

2. Think of someone you can offer loving service to this week. Write three things you will do for that person and then do them. Afterward, spend some time reflecting on your experience. How did your acts of loving service affect the person? How did they affect you?

3. Participate in the Eucharist at an Eastern Catholic Church or at another parish. Write a short paragraph about the similarities and differences you noticed.

4. Pay close attention to the readings and homilies of the next eucharistic celebration you attend. Write a paragraph explaining what God was saying to you that day. Then share your reflections with someone in your family.

5. Compile quotations about the Eucharist from John 6 and 1 Corinthians 10 and 11. Use one quotation to design a card for someone celebrating his or her First Holy Communion.

Word to Know

transubstantiation

Matching   Match each definition with the correct term. One term is used twice.

a. *transubstantiation*   **d.** *mediator*
b. *Roman Missal*   **e.** *Passover*
c. *covenant*   **f.** *Eucharist*

_____ **1.** A meal that makes the sacrifice of Calvary present again

_____ **2.** The official book of prayers and directions for eucharistic worship

_____ **3.** A go-between for two opposing parties

_____ **4.** An agreement between God and human beings

_____ **5.** An act of worship that means thanksgiving

_____ **6.** The change in substance from bread and wine to the Body and Blood of Jesus

_____ **7.** The Jewish meal that commemorates God's saving actions

Ordering Meals   Number these special meals in the order of occurrence.

_____ the Last Supper

_____ the manna in the desert

_____ the heavenly banquet

_____ the Passover

_____ the last Mass you celebrated

_____ the multiplication of loaves

_____ the Eucharist of the early Christian community

Liturgy in Outline   Complete the outline.

Liturgy of the (1) _____

   Old or New Testament reading(s)

   The (2) _____

   Homily

   Prayer of the (3) _____

Liturgy of the Eucharist

   Presentation and Preparation of the (4) _____

   Eucharistic Prayer

      The (5) _____

      Holy, Holy, Holy

      (6) _____

      Mystery of Faith

      The (7) _____

   Communion Rite

      The (8) Prayer _____

      Sign of (9) _____

      (10) of God _____

❮ Mosaic depicting Jesus' multiplication of loaves and fish. Copy of fourth-century Byzantine original in Tagbha, Israel.

Gather and Go Forth

Know and Proclaim

As Catholics, we are people of the Eucharist. We proclaim our belief in Jesus' Body and Blood in all that we say and do.

We Know Our Faith	We Proclaim Our Faith
At the Last Supper, Jesus gave his disciples a new commandment to love one another.	Catholics consider the Eucharist to be the most appropriate way to express joy and gratitude for God's blessings.
During the Liturgy of the Word, we are nourished and strengthened by God's Word revealed to us in Scripture.	During the Liturgy of the Word, the priest or deacon gives a homily in which he explains how the Scripture readings relate to the lives of Catholics.
During the Liturgy of the Eucharist, we offer Jesus and ourselves to the Father and then receive Christ's Body and Blood.	Catholics proclaim the Mystery of Faith during the Liturgy of the Eucharist. In the Mystery of Faith, Catholics proclaim Jesus' Death and Resurrection until he comes again.

The Eucharist is spiritual food that nourishes us on our journey of faith. We go forth from the Eucharist in peace to love and serve the Father and one another.

"For my flesh is true food, and my blood is true drink. Whoever eats my flesh and drinks my blood remains in me and I in him."

John 6:55–56

Test Your Catholic Knowledge

Fill in the circle that best answers the question.

What do we call the change in substance from bread and wine to the Body and Blood of Christ in the Eucharist?

○ transubstantiation

○ metamorphosis

○ transfiguration

○ reformation

A Catholic to Know

Isidore had three great loves in his life: God, his family, and the soil he farmed. Isidore was born in Spain more than 900 years ago. As soon as he was old enough, he began to work as a farmer. He worked all his life for a wealthy landowner named John de Vargas. Isidore prayed continuously as he worked the fields. He and his wife, Maria, were well-known for their generosity to people who were poorer than themselves. Isidore was gifted with miracles. More than once he fed hungry people with food that multiplied in response to those in need. Isidore died in 1130 following a peaceful life of manual labor. He and his wife prove that poverty, hard work, and sorrow (their only child died as a little boy) cannot destroy human happiness.

Saint Isidore the Farmer

Witness and Share

These sentences describe what Catholics believe. Listen carefully as they are read. Ask yourself, "How strong are my Catholic beliefs?"

My Way to Faith

- I receive strength and nourishment in the Eucharist.

- I believe that the Body and Blood of Jesus is truly present under the forms of bread and wine.

- I offer acts of loving kindness to others.

- I thank Jesus for the gift of the Eucharist.

- I receive guidance from God when I listen to the Scripture readings at Mass.

Share Your Faith

Consider ways in which you can thank God for the Eucharist. Write a prayer of thanks on the lines, and invite a friend or family member to attend eucharistic adoration with you. Pray a prayer of thanksgiving for the gift of the Eucharist before you go to bed tonight.

_____

_____

_____

_____

Jesus' Final Hours

Jesus the Lamb of God

The Good in Goodbye

Emma covered her face with her hands and sobbed. "I can't move again. I just can't! Not another town and school! Just when I find friends! Just when I make the team! We always move just when I finally *belong*!"

Moving can be painful. Being separated from familiar places and people can seem like dying. Every person meets "little deaths," as a part of life. Through these "deaths" a person gains new opportunities for life.

Write one good thing that may come from moving.

_____

What "little death" have you suffered that resulted in something good?

_____

What good result came from it?

_____

> [U]nless a grain of wheat falls to the ground and dies, it remains just a grain of wheat; but if it dies, it produces much fruit.
>
> John 12:24

Jesus' Passion

Like the grain of wheat, Jesus had to suffer and die in order to enter into his glory. He died as a result of sin. By his obedience and love, he brought all humankind back to God. He won for us forgiveness, salvation, and eternal life. The Jewish people sacrificed animals and the first fruits of their crops to God. Jesus offered himself to the Father for us. Like other sacrifices, his was to make up for sins and to gain benefits. Jesus was the Lamb of God—the perfect sacrifice. The events from the Last Supper to Jesus' Death on the cross are called his passion. The word *passion* means "a powerful emotion such as love, joy, hatred, or anger." We use the word *passion* to express how Jesus showed his love for us.

His Source of Strength

Under the pressure of exhaustion, rejection, loneliness, and evil, where did Jesus find the strength to go on? How could he keep loving and forgiving?

The answer lies in his union with his Father. Jesus knew the depth of his Father's love. Through prayer, he received strength to suffer and die for us. He prayed,

> "My Father, if it is possible, let this cup pass from me; yet, not as I will, but as you will."
>
> Matthew 26:39

Our Response

Suffering will always be a mystery, something we cannot fully understand. Only when we, like Jesus, trust in the Father's love and accept the suffering he permits does suffering have any meaning. As Jesus' followers, we can

- work to eliminate the evil around us
- try to relieve the pain of others
- unite our suffering with his in love
- accept suffering without self-pity or anger
- offer our sufferings for other people
- gain strength as Jesus did, through prayer and union with our Father.

Obituary

JESUS OF NAZARETH died about 3:00 P.M. Friday as a result of crucifixion at the hands of Roman soldiers.

Jesus, a former carpenter, was a controversial Jewish figure. He was popular in Galilee and Judea for his teachings and his healings.

On Thursday, Judas Iscariot, one of Jesus' followers, led soldiers to him. They arrested him in a garden and brought him to the Jewish leaders. The Sanhedrin accused him of blasphemy because he claimed to be the Son of God. The high priest Caiaphas sent him to Pontius Pilate for execution.

Finding him innocent, Pilate offered to release him, but most of the people demanded that Barabbas, a revolutionary, be freed instead. After having Jesus scourged, Pilate ordered him crucified on the charge that he had declared himself a king.

At Jesus' Death, his mother, Mary, a disciple named John, and some women were present.

Burial was immediate since the next day was the Sabbath. Soldiers guarded the tomb because Jesus had predicted he would be raised in three days.

Free to Love

Jesus wants you to share his glory, his joy. The best response you can give is to love him freely—not because you are afraid, or because you have to, or because others do, but because he is so good and you really *want* to love him.

How can you tell if you really love God?

Read 1 John 4:20–21. Compare your answer to that passage.

A Lifetime Project

> . . . that he may grant you in accord with the riches of his glory to be strengthened with power through his Spirit in the inner self, . . .
>
> Ephesians 3:16

On your journey to the Father, you have many chances to love him and others. Your choices make you who you are. How does that happen? Each time you choose to be honest, it is easier to be honest in the future. You are becoming a more honest person. On the other hand, each time you choose to be unkind, you make it easier to be unkind again. Gradually you could become a cruel person.

The change is so gradual that you and others may not be aware of it. With every decision, however, you grow stronger or weaker in the Lord. As you respond to God's grace or reject it, you set a pattern for your life.

After Death, Then What?

At the moment of death, you will see your hidden self and realize how much you have become like Jesus. Then, based on that likeness, you will realize before God how you fit or do not fit into the kingdom of love. That moment is called the **particular judgment.**

After death, there are three possibilities:

- People who have become like Jesus by loving perfectly can enter God's presence, see God face to face, and know a boundless joy. This is called heaven.

- People may need to be purified of remaining selfishness, because only those totally transformed by love can enter the kingdom. This purification is called purgatory.

- People who have freely refused in serious ways to follow God's command to love are in the state of mortal sin. Anyone in this state cannot enter heaven but will be outside of it forever. This eternal separation from God for whom we long is called hell.

The Last Things

Can you answer these questions?

1. What will you learn about yourself from God at the moment of your death?
2. What is the moment called when a person finds out about his or her eternal destiny?
3. Describe the three alternatives for a person at the moment of death.
4. What is the Parousia and its purpose?
5. What is the Last Judgment?

A Thief Enters Heaven

Read Luke 23:39–43.

How did the penitent thief show his faith in Jesus?

_____

_____

Write Jesus' response to the penitent thief.

_____

_____

No matter what the penitent thief had done in the past, Jesus welcomed him into the kingdom because the thief reached out in love. The same Jesus is always ready to forgive you and offer you his love, even to the moment of death.

The End of the World

At the end of time, Jesus will return in glory to judge the living and the dead. At that Second Coming, or Parousia, the resurrection from the dead will take place. God will reveal the plan of salvation in all its glory. The eternal destiny of the human race and of every person will be revealed in the **Last Judgment.** The souls of the just will be reunited with their glorified bodies. The universe will be transformed, and God will be "all in all." Christians long for the Parousia when God "will wipe every tear from their eyes." (Revelation 21:4) We pray, "Come, Lord Jesus!" (Revelation 22:20) If you knew Christ would return next week, how would you live differently?

Remember

What is the supreme act of God's love for all people?

> The supreme act of God's love for all people is Jesus' Death on the cross. In obedience to the Father, Jesus offered his life for our sins so that all could have eternal life.

How does the Gospel explain this act of love?

> For God so loved the world that he gave his only Son, so that everyone who believes in him might not perish but might have eternal life.

> John 3:16

Respond

Imagine that you are standing on Calvary while Jesus is dying. Experience the sights and sounds around you. Now focus your attention on Jesus in his suffering. Realize that your sins are part of the burden he is carrying. Be with him now, supporting him with your love, knowing that your love can ease his burden. Record your thoughts and feelings in your reflection notebook.

Reach Out

1. Find the traditional "Seven Last Words of Christ" in Scripture. See Mark 15:34; Luke 23:34,43,46; and John 19:26,28,30. Make a mobile to display the words, or compose a prayer based on the meaning of Jesus' words for today.

2. The mystery of Jesus passing through death to glory is the core of Christian belief. Using a missalette, list references to the Death and Resurrection of Christ in each of the four Eucharistic prayers.

3. Take a survey of five people of various ages. Ask each one to complete these statements:
   - When I was younger, I thought heaven was like . . .
   - Now I think heaven is . . .
   - I look forward to heaven because . . .

4. Read about the Last Judgment in Matthew 25:31–46. Imagine you are one of the sheep or the goats. How would you feel?

Words to Know

Last Judgment　　　**particular judgment**

Fra Angelico, *Last Judgment*, 15th century. Detail showing the separation of the saved (left) and the damned (right). ❯

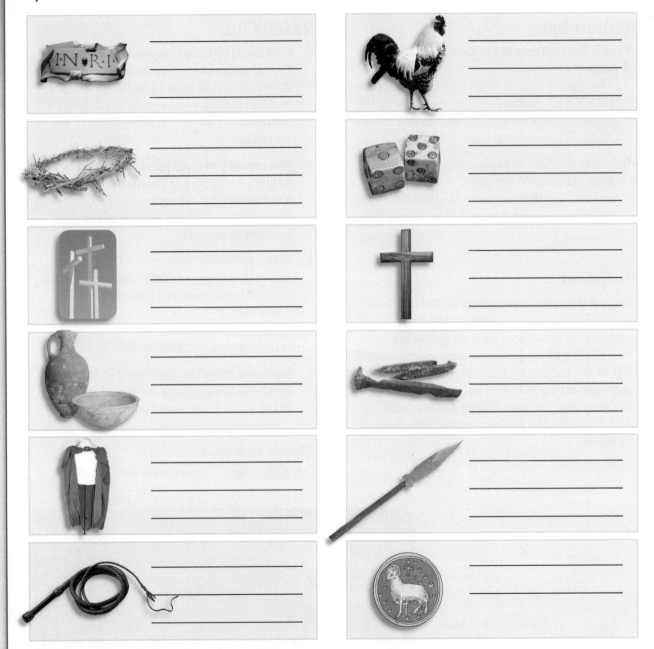

Symbols of the Passion   Write how each symbol is related to the Jesus' passion.

(answer lines for each symbol image)

Jeopardy   On a separate sheet of paper write a question each term answers.

1. Judas Iscariot
2. particular judgment
3. Jesus' passion
4. Last Judgment
5. Pontius Pilate

6. Parousia
7. purgatory
8. Mary
9. John
10. Barabbas

❮ Nikolai Ge, *What is the truth? (Christ before Pilate)*, Russia.

Gather and Go Forth

Know and Proclaim

As we seek to know our Catholic faith, our hearts burn with the desire to proclaim our beliefs in what we say and do.

We Know Our Faith	We Proclaim Our Faith
Jesus died for our sins. By his obedience and love, he reconciled us with God.	Catholics place crucifixes in their homes and places of gathering to recall Jesus' passion, Death, and Resurrection.
After death, only people who have loved like Jesus can enter God's presence. Those in need of purification experience purgatory. The eternal separation from God is called hell.	Catholics are united with the saints when they celebrate the Eucharist, and they ask the saints to intercede on their behalf and for the whole world.
Jesus will return to reveal the eternal destiny of every person in the Last Judgment.	Catholics learn about the Kingdom of Heaven by reading the Gospels.

Jesus transformed death through his Resurrection. As Catholics, we expect to be transformed with him by the mystery of his Cross and Resurrection. We walk the way of Jesus to eternal life with him.

The way we came to know love was that he laid down his life for us; so we ought to lay down our lives for our brothers.

1 John 3:16

Test Your Catholic Knowledge

Fill in the circle that best answers the question.

What is the Last Judgment?

○ the eternal separation from God

○ the period of purification of the soul of any remaining selfishness

○ the revelation of the destiny of the human race and of every person

○ the moment where you realize before God how you fit into the kingdom of love

A Catholic to Know

The Catholic faith came to Vietnam in 1615 when the Jesuits opened the first mission in Da Nang. Eventually, foreign missionaries were banned and persecution began. Catholics went into hiding. Many people opened their homes and offered a place to hide. Persecutions continued. Between 1820 and 1862, a total of 117 Vietnamese martyrs died. Among them was Andrew Dũng-Lạc, a parish priest. In 1988, Pope John Paul II canonized Saint Andrew and the others—brave bishops, priests, and lay Catholics. Today the Church in Vietnam is strong. Catholics honor Saint Andrew's witness for Christ on November 24.

Saint Andrew Dũng-Lạc

Witness and Share

These sentences describe what Catholics believe. Listen carefully as they are read. Ask yourself, "How strong are my Catholic beliefs?"

My Way to Faith

- I recall Jesus' passion and Death by reflecting on the crucifix.

- I believe that I will be reunited with God after my death.

- I pray for the souls in purgatory, that they may be united with God.

- I find strength in prayer during times of suffering.

- I do not inflict pain and suffering upon others.

Share Your Faith

Consider how you respond to difficult times. Write how Jesus comforts and helps you in your trials. Invite a trusted adult to discuss how faith comforts him or her at difficult times in life.

_____

_____

_____

_____

The Victory of Jesus

Jesus the Risen Lord

I Believe

What do you believe about eternal life? Circle *T* if you believe the statement is true or *F* if you believe it is false.

For everyone who believes in Jesus and listens to his words, eternal life has already begun.	T	F
You must have faith to believe in the Resurrection.	T	F
Christ's Resurrection is a promise of our future glory.	T	F
No one saw the Resurrection take place.	T	F
After we die, we come back to earth as other persons (reincarnated).	T	F
The Resurrection was the greatest event in human history.	T	F

No one saw the Resurrection happen. The Gospel accounts of it vary. However, they agree on two facts: there was an open, empty tomb, and the disciples had the experience of seeing Jesus risen! In the Gospel Easter stories, the early Christians convey something that is beyond human experience.

As you read the following Scripture passages, imagine you are a reporter in Jerusalem at the time of the Resurrection. Write one thing you learn from these witnesses:

Guards and women (Matthew 28:1–10)

_____

Mary of Magdala, Peter, John (John 20:1–18)

_____

Thomas (John 20:24–29)

_____

He Is Risen

Jesus lives! The **apostles**, those who accompanied Jesus in his ministry, were stunned to hear those words. Jesus of Nazareth, who died by crucifixion and was buried in a borrowed tomb, now was alive. He was still with them, appearing to his friends. Jesus was in Galilee. He was in Judea. He was eating fish. He was in the upper room. He was hiking to Emmaus.

Now pretend you are a follower of Jesus at the time of the Resurrection. What meaning would one of these stories have for you?

_____

_____

Jesus Glorified

After Jesus died, his human soul united to his divine person went to the realm of the dead and opened the gates of heaven for the holy ones there. Then he appeared on earth with his risen, glorious body. Jesus' appearances astounded the disciples and changed them forever. He had lived among them and had died. Now they saw him glorified. Death had no more power over him. As Saint Paul wrote:

> "Death is swallowed up in victory.
>   Where, O death, is your victory?
>   Where, O death, is your sting?"
>
> 1 Corinthians 15:54–55

Jesus was doing the same things he did before: teaching, forgiving, consoling, eating, and talking with his disciples. However, now they

saw him full of power, mystery, and glory. Jesus was the risen Lord who had passed beyond death. Unlike Lazarus, he would not die again. His words and his teachings were the authentic Word of God and would never pass away. Jesus had brought a totally new way of living—a way to share in eternal life, God's life. Looking at the risen Jesus, the disciples began to realize that they, too, would live as he did! Not until Pentecost, though, would they really understand who Jesus was and be empowered for their mission.

The Risen Jesus

Read Luke 24:1–11. In first-century Jewish society, women could not serve as public witnesses. Luke writes that "their story seemed like nonsense and they did not believe them." Imagine what it must have been like to be one of these women.

What led the disciples to believe that Jesus had been raised from the dead? The angels at the tomb told them so: "Why do you seek the living one among the dead? He is not here, but he has been raised." (Luke 24:5–6) The angels also reminded the women that Jesus had predicted that he would be put to death by sinners and rise on the third day.

Then Jesus appeared to his disciples. Luke tells us about Jesus' appearance to two disciples on the road to Emmaus, a village near Jerusalem. The two disciples talked with someone they believed to be a stranger. As they talked, the stranger explained and interpreted for them all that Scripture predicted about Jesus. Finally, while together at a meal, Jesus took bread, said the blessing, broke it, and gave it to them. With the breaking of the bread, the disciples recognized the stranger as Jesus.

Amazed, the two disciples returned to share the news with the other disciples. However, they arrived in Jerusalem to hear the reports from the disciples there: "The Lord has truly been raised and has appeared to Simon!" (Luke 24:34)

‹ Jesus and disciples on the way to Emmaus.

The Risen Jesus and Believers

The Resurrection was for believers. Those who believed in Jesus saw him as the risen Lord. To recognize the risen Jesus required faith, because the Resurrection is a mystery of faith. The Gospels emphasize the doubt of some disciples when they heard about Jesus' Resurrection. In each instance, Jesus took the initiative and revealed himself to them, and by his grace the disciples believed.

What if Jesus had not been raised? Read 1 Corinthians 15:12–19. What do you conclude?

_____

_____

_____

What kind of bodies will we have when we are raised? In 1 Corinthians 15:36–49, Saint Paul says that our risen body will be as different from our present body as a seed buried in the ground is from the wheat that grows from it.

We Experience the Risen Jesus

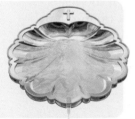

By our Baptism, we share in the life, Death, and Resurrection of Jesus and witness to him. Through his Death and Resurrection, Jesus gives us the power to die to selfishness.

We are an Easter people. There is a contagious enthusiasm about the way we live and a freedom about the way we speak and act. Jesus' Death and Resurrection give meaning to our lives. We have the hope of eternal life. Our goal is to live as companions to the risen Jesus. By following his way, we shall one day rise with him in glory.

Today we encounter the risen Lord in the sacraments, especially in the Eucharist, in the Scriptures, and in the faith community of the Church.

A Moment with Jesus

Just as Jesus appeared to the disciples after the Resurrection, Jesus comes to meet us. We might experience Jesus' presence at Mass, in Scripture, in prayer alone or with others. Perhaps you have experienced Jesus present with you in other ways.

Pause for a moment and reflect on a time when you felt the presence of Jesus. How did you recognize his presence? Thank Jesus for being always with you and for revealing himself to you.

Signs That He Is with Us

All seven sacraments are an opportunity to meet and grow closer to Jesus. Through them, Jesus acts in us and cares for us. They were instituted by him and help us live as God wants us to. Other sacred signs called sacramentals have been given to us by the Church to remind us of God. The Church's prayers and the way we use sacramentals empower them to make us holy. Sacramentals may be blessings, blessed objects such as medals and palms, or actions such as the Sign of the Cross. They prepare us for the sacraments. The risen Lord is with us no less now than he was with the first disciples.

Ascension: Jesus Is Lord

Goodbyes can be sad. People who love each other find it hard to be separated. When have you experienced such a goodbye?

_____

The **Ascension** is Jesus' return to his Father. In the person of Jesus, humanity is already with God. The early Christians believed that Jesus would come again soon in glory. As time went on, however, they realized that the Second Coming might be in the far distant future. While they waited, Jesus' invisible but very real presence remained with them.

Read Acts of the Apostles 1:6–11. Name two unusual things that happened at Christ's leave-taking.

_____

_____

_____

_____

In the Nicene Creed, we pray, "He ascended into heaven and is seated at the right hand of the Father." The Ascension was more than just a goodbye. It completed the glorification of Jesus. Being seated at the right hand of the Father showed he was Lord of the universe. Before, Jesus had limited his activity to

Palestine. Now his influence extends to the ends of the universe. When we say Jesus is Lord, we say we believe he reigns over heaven and earth, the living and the dead. We see all things as subject to him—including ourselves. We believe his teachings are God's words.

Missioned to Make a Difference!

Jesus, filled with the Holy Spirit, promised that Spirit to his disciples. His Spirit would make them "other Christs." What did Jesus predict about them? See Acts of the Apostles 1:8.

_____

_____

_____

We, too, witness to Christ Jesus and make the world aware of his justice and love. Our call to be his witnesses is a call to action! We are "givers" in a world of "takers." We are responsible for our acts and selfless in serving. We are not afraid to take risks for love of Jesus and to do the right things. We wait for Jesus to return and to change our bodies "to correspond in form to his glorified body." (adapted from Philippians 3:21)

CHAPTER 22 Summary

Remember

Why is the Resurrection of Jesus significant?
The Resurrection of Jesus is significant because it shows that Jesus is the Son of God and that we will rise someday.

What does the Ascension tell us?
The Ascension tells us that, by returning to his Father in heaven, Jesus is Lord of the universe.

How do we encounter the risen Lord today?
We encounter the risen Lord today in the sacraments, especially in the Eucharist, in the Scriptures, and in the faith community.

Respond

How exciting it must have been for the disciples on the road to Emmaus to learn from Jesus himself the meaning of his passion, Death, and Resurrection. Their hearts were "burning within them" at his words. He gave them more than words. With the breaking of the bread, he was made known to them and their hearts were opened.

Write in your reflection notebook what you would have said to Jesus if you had been on the Emmaus journey (Luke 24:13–35). Then write a prayer telling how and where you will be a witness.

Reach Out

1. Read 1 Corinthians 15:1–58. This letter of Saint Paul contains the earliest written statement about the Resurrection. It was probably written sometime between A.D. 54 and 56. Some Christians in Corinth had weakened in the faith, and Paul wanted them to know that the Resurrection was our greatest hope.

   With your family and friends, discuss how the Corinthians may have reacted to Paul's letter. Imagine that you are a member of their community and write a response to Paul expressing your belief.

2. Pray to become a peaceful person who brings the joy of the risen Jesus to others.

3. Jesus is life. Find Scripture verses from the Gospel of Saint John and make holy cards to give away. Write a cheerful message on the back of each card.

   Here are some verses you could use.

John 1:3–4	John 5:26	John 6:51
John 3:16	John 6:27	John 6:58
John 3:36	John 6:35	John 6:63
John 4:14	John 6:40	John 8:12
John 5:21	John 6:47	John 10:17–18
John 5:24	John 6:48	

4. Bring to class a newspaper article that reports a need in the world. Give the article to your teacher for posting, and then remember these needs in prayer.

5. Make a booklet of drawings and explanations of sacramentals. You could divide it into three sections: in the home, in church, and in your own life; or sacred objects, sacred actions, and sacred words.

Words to Know

apostle   Ascension

Who Am I?   Answer these riddles.

1. I am the first person Jesus appeared to according to the Gospel of John.

_____

2. I explained Scripture to two disciples on the road to Emmaus.

_____

3. I was invited to touch Jesus' wounds when I did not believe the apostles had seen him.

_____

4. I was the first disciple to recognize that the stranger who helped us fish was Jesus.

_____

5. I was the first apostle to go into the tomb.

_____

6. I am the Lord of the universe.

_____

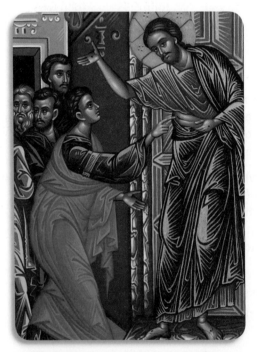

Which apostle touched Jesus' wounds?

What Am I?   Answer these riddles.

1. I am what Jesus ate to prove he was alive.

_____

2. When Jesus broke me, the disciples recognized him.

_____

3. I am what you need to believe in the Resurrection.

_____

4. I was Jesus' first words to his apostles.

_____

5. I am Jesus' return to the Father in glory.

_____

6. I was conquered by Jesus.

_____

7. I am the great miracle that made all Jesus' words believable.

_____

8. I am a blessed object or action that has power to make you holy by the prayers of the Church.

_____

Meeting Jesus   Name four ways that we can encounter the risen Lord today.

1. _____

2. _____

3. _____

4. _____

Gather and Go Forth

Know and Proclaim

We learn the truths of our Catholic faith to proclaim our belief in the risen Lord.

We Know Our Faith	We Proclaim Our Faith
The Resurrection is a mystery of faith. To recognize the risen Lord requires faith.	Catholics encounter the risen Lord in the sacraments, especially the Eucharist. Catholics also encounter the risen Lord in the Scriptures and in the Church.
The Ascension is Jesus' return to his Father. It completed the glorification of Jesus.	As Catholics, we use sacramentals, such as medals, or prayers, such as the Sign of the Cross, to remind us of the presence of the risen Christ, to prepare us for the sacraments, and to help us grow in holiness.
Jesus promised to send the Holy Spirit to his disciples. His Spirit would enable them to bear witness to him.	Catholics rely on the Gifts of the Holy Spirit to act with justice and love in the world.

As Catholics, we share in the suffering of Jesus Christ, knowing we will share in his glory. We direct our hope toward Christ's Resurrection.

For if we have grown into union with him through a death like this, we shall also be united with him in the resurrection.

Romans 6:5

Test Your Catholic Knowledge

Fill in the circle that best completes the sentence.

Grace enters our lives in the celebration of the sacraments by the power of the:

○ Holy Spirit.

○ Magisterium.

○ Acts of the Apostles.

○ Communion of Saints.

A Catholic to Know

Thérèse was born into a middle-class family in France in 1873. She thought seriously about God and prayed that her love of God would grow. Thérèse entered a Carmelite convent at Lisieux at age 15. She prayed often and did the most ordinary tasks in the convent: scrubbing floors, washing dishes, setting the tables, sewing, dusting, and cooking. Thérèse proved that we can become saints by doing ordinary things extraordinarily well. She explained it in her biography: "I want to seek a way to heaven, a new way, very short, very straight—the way of trust and self-surrender . . . I am a very little soul, who can offer only little things to Our Lord." Thérèse called her path to holiness "The Little Way." Like Thérèse, we can do every act, even small things, for the love of God.

Saint Thérèse of Lisieux

Witness and Share

These sentences describe what Catholics believe. Listen carefully as they are read. Ask yourself, "How strong are my Catholic beliefs?"

My Way to Faith

- I will live as a disciple so I can share in the glory of Christ's Resurrection.

- I am aware that the risen Christ dwells in me when I pray the Sign of the Cross.

- I recognize the true presence of Christ in the Eucharist.

- I bear witness to the risen Lord in my words and deeds.

- I use sacramentals to help me live a life of holiness.

Share Your Faith

Consider how you can practice the "Little Way." What are some little actions you do every day, and how can you do them for the love of God? Write your ideas on the lines and invite a friend to practice the "Little Way" too.

_____

_____

_____

_____

Alive with the Spirit

Jesus the Head of the Church

Turning Points

Many people have experienced turning points: events that changed them and turned their lives around. Helen Keller was one of these people. An illness as an infant left her blind and deaf. By the time she was seven, she had become uncontrollable. Helen's family hired Anne Sullivan to teach her sign language, to reach somehow into the darkness of her life. It seemed an impossible task, until one day Anne held one of Helen's hands under a pump and spelled "w-a-t-e-r" into her other hand. As Helen explained later:

> Somehow the mystery of language was revealed to me. I knew then that "w-a-t-e-r" meant the wonderful cool something that was flowing over my hand. That living word awakened my soul, gave it light, hope, joy, set it free! . . . Everything had a name, and each name gave birth to a new thought. As we returned to the house every object which I touched seemed to quiver with life. That was because I saw everything with the strange, new sight that had come to me.
>
> from *The Story of My Life* by Helen Keller

That was Helen's turning point. Although she would continue to struggle as she learned to cope in the world, her whole life had changed. She had been transformed.

Helen Keller.

Write about a turning point in your life or in the life of someone you know about.

_____

_____

_____

Pentecost: Touched by the Spirit

A turning point occurred for all humanity the day the Holy Spirit came to the Church. It was the harvest feast of Pentecost in Jerusalem, a time for pilgrims to gather in the holy city and praise God for fields of grain. Mary and the disciples were all gathered in the upper room of a house. They were waiting. They had been commissioned by Christ to go and baptize, to bring the good news of salvation and love to all people. They knew what they were to do, but they needed help. They needed confidence and guidance. They needed Christ. So they put all their trust in Christ and waited, praying. Suddenly there was a tremendous sound— as if a powerful wind was filling the house. Something like tongues of fire appeared and rested on each person. The disciples were filled with the Holy Spirit. The Spirit of God touched and transformed them.

Acts of the Apostles 2:4,11

_____

_____

Acts of the Apostles 2:14

_____

Acts of the Apostles 2:41

_____

_____

Acts of the Apostles 2:43

_____

_____

Acts of the Apostles 2:44–45

_____

_____

Spirit Alive

What the disciples experienced on Pentecost was beyond description. However, the two elements associated with the coming of the Spirit can help us understand how the Spirit changed their lives. In Scripture, wind and fire are signs of God's presence.

Name a characteristic of wind.

_____

How is the Holy Spirit's activity like wind?

_____

Name a characteristic of fire.

_____

How is the Holy Spirit's activity like fire?

_____

The Holy Spirit was present at the baptism of Jesus when he was anointed for his mission. The same Spirit empowered the disciples to fulfill their mission. Here is the mission Christ gave to the disciples and to us.

"Go, therefore, and make disciples of all nations, baptizing them in the name of the Father, and of the Son, and of the holy Spirit, teaching them to observe all that I have commanded you."

Matthew 28:19–20

Out of Hiding

How did the coming of the Spirit affect the disciples in the upper room? Read the verses listed. Then write what happened through the power of the Holy Spirit.

The most important change the disciples experienced was deep within their hearts. With the continuing presence of the Spirit, they became enthusiastic, courageous witnesses to Christ.

Fearless Followers

The Holy Spirit's power is not limited to the early Christians or to great saints and leaders. Through Baptism, you and all the faithful are gifted with the Spirit. Our encounter with the Spirit usually does not involve drastic changes, roaring winds, and tongues of fire. Instead, we grow a little each day through struggles and moments of love and understanding. In time, we become true followers of Jesus, living the way he taught us to live.

One of the most effective ways to spread the Good News is to live caring lives. People are attracted to Christ when they see Christians living his message. That kind of living, however, takes courage: courage to say no to the evil spirit, courage to say yes to the Spirit of Christ. When have you shown Christian courage?

Community of Love: The Church

At Pentecost, the Church was born with the Spirit as its strength and guiding force. All that had been foretold by the prophets was accomplished, and a new era in salvation history was begun.

After the Spirit had come upon the disciples, they did not just walk off to the farthest limits of the earth, preaching the Good News. Their first response was to form a community of believers. The community was a gift of God. In many ways, it was also a miracle because persecution and hardships surrounded the disciples.

The Christians had a common vision—a deep devotion to Jesus Christ, his way of life, and the Kingdom of God. As they sought to love Christ more, they showed a real concern for people who were poor and needy, and a thirst to spread the Good News. They also loved one another in Christ. They were bonded to one another more closely than a club or a team. They were the family of believers, the Mystical Body of Christ. In Christ, the head of the Church, they were a new people reconciled to God. They shared his ministry. They celebrated his saving mysteries.

The unity among Christians echoes the unity among the Persons of the Trinity. Four actions that bonded the community together are named in Acts of the Apostles 2:42. They are

- devotion to the teaching of the apostles
- communal life
- the breaking of bread
- prayers.

Church Bonds

Read about these bonds and the growth of the early Christian community in Acts of the Apostles 2:42–47; 4:32–35; and 5:12–16. With those passages in mind, check possible endings to the following statement.

The description of the early Church in the Acts of the Apostles

- ❍ seems impossible.
- ❍ is something I would like to experience.
- ❍ makes me want to try to be a better member of the community of believers.
- ❍ could never happen again.

Check the ways the people in the early Christian community were like people in your parish.

- ❍ The Eucharist was the center of the community's life.
- ❍ Not everyone agreed on what the Church and its practices should be.

- ❍ The people prayed together often.
- ❍ They showed concern for those in need and went out of their way to help them.
- ❍ They gathered in one another's homes for meals and sharing.
- ❍ They willingly gave money and possessions to others in the community.
- ❍ They spoke openly about their love for Christ and the Church.
- ❍ They attracted more and more people to their community.
- ❍ Some members seriously failed to live up to the ideals of Christian life.

You and the Community of Believers

You are a part of the community, the Church that was born on Pentecost. Like the apostles, you have a mission from Christ. You are to be a courageous witness to the Good News for the whole world and a loving, enthusiastic member of the community of believers, the Church.

Your role as a witness and disciple may not extend to all the world, but you are important and vital wherever you are. The Holy Spirit is at work in you this very moment. Remember, however, it may take a lifetime to be totally open to the transforming power of the Spirit.

Fruits of the Holy Spirit

How can you tell you are open to the Spirit? What will your life be like? Galatians 5:22–23 contains a list of the qualities that we call the **Fruits of the Holy Spirit** found in the life of a true disciple: love, joy, peace, patience, kindness, generosity, faithfulness, gentleness, and self-control. Church tradition has added three more: modesty, goodness, and chastity.

Choose three Fruits of the Holy Spirit. Describe how they show the presence of the Spirit in your life.

_____

_____

_____

_____

_____

_____

A Moment with Jesus

Each of us has been given a mission from Christ. It does not often reveal itself all at once. Pause for a moment and think about a time when you have taken a stand for your faith. What was the situation? How did you respond? What was the result for you? for others involved? What might that situation teach you about your call to be a witness to the Good News of Christ?

Spend a moment thanking Jesus for the gift of the Spirit at work in your life.

Remember

What is the significance of Pentecost?

At Pentecost, the Holy Spirit was poured out upon Mary, the apostles, and other believers, empowering them to proclaim the Good News as courageous witnesses and to form a community of love, the Church. At Pentecost, the Church was born, and a new era of salvation history began.

How is the Church a community?

As a community, we are bonded by love for Christ and for one another, and by service to the world with the guidance and strength of the Holy Spirit. Like the early Christian community, we share in the teaching of the apostles (expressed in the Apostles' Creed and the Nicene Creed), community life, the breaking of the bread, and prayers (especially the sacraments).

What are the Fruits of the Holy Spirit as listed in Galatians 5:22–23?

The Fruits of the Holy Spirit are love, joy, peace, patience, kindness, generosity, faithfulness, gentleness, and self-control.

Respond

The Holy Spirit empowers you to be a courageous witness to the Good News of Christ. There are times when you are called to stand up for what is right. Think of a time when you did what you knew to be right, even when it was difficult. Record the incident in your reflection notebook. Include how you felt before, during, and after making your decision. Then compose your own prayer to the Holy Spirit to use at times in the future when you will need strength and support.

Reach Out

1. Read a biography of Saint Paul, Saint Ignatius of Loyola, Saint Bernadette Soubirous, or one of your favorite saints. Find out about the turning points in his or her life and report your findings to the class.

2. The Spirit, the gift and power of God, directs the growth of the Christian community and enables its members to carry out the ministry of Christ through various gifts. Read 1 Corinthians, Chapters 12, 13, and 14, which list many of the gifts and tell how they can be used for the Church. Then think of your own community—your parish. How evident are these gifts in the parish? Be ready to explain.

3. There is much you can do right now as a member of the family of believers. Read these Scripture passages. Write a summary of each and two or three ways you can put Christ's message into action today.

   Romans 12:9–13   Colossians 3:16–17

   1 Corinthians 10:31   1 Peter 4:10–11

Word to Know

Fruits of the Holy Spirit

Saint Bernadette Soubirous. ❯

Pentecost Acrostic   Use these clues to solve the puzzle.

1. They were in the upper room with Mary when the Holy Spirit came.

2. A visible sign of the Spirit's power to enlighten

3. A sign of the Spirit's invisible action

4. What the apostles spoke in after the Spirit came

5. The city where Pentecost took place

6. The community the followers became on Pentecost

7. What the Spirit gave the apostles

8. Qualities that are signs of the Spirit's presence in us

9. How many thousands of people were baptized on Pentecost

1. _ P _ _ _ _ _
2. _ _ _ E _
3. _ _ _ N _
4. T _ _ _ _ _ _
5. _ E _ _ _ _ _ _
6. C _ _ _ _ _
7. _ O _ _ _
8. _ _ _ _ _ S
9. _ _ T _ _ _

The Church: Ever Ancient, Ever New   Match each action you might do with a characteristic of the early Church.

a. devotion to the apostles' instruction

b. communal life

c. the breaking of bread

d. prayers

_____ 1. Celebrate the Eucharist.

_____ 2. Donate to Catholic Charities.

_____ 3. Attend religion classes.

_____ 4. Participate in parish liturgies and devotions.

Your Mission   How can you follow Christ's command to baptize all nations and teach the Good News?

_____

_____

_____

_____

PHOTO: Young Catholic pilgrims from Pennsylvania attend Mass at World Youth Day, Germany, 2005.

Gather and Go Forth

Know and Proclaim

As Catholics, we see the Church as a sign of God's grace. The Holy Spirit inspires us to proclaim our Church to the world.

We Know Our Faith	We Proclaim Our Faith
On the feast of Pentecost, the disciples were filled with the Holy Spirit. The Spirit empowered them to fulfill Jesus' mission.	Many Catholics pray the Prayer to the Holy Spirit, which begins with the words "Come, Holy Spirit, fill the hearts of your faithful."
The Church was born on Pentecost with the Holy Spirit as its strength and guiding force.	Catholics believe that the unity of all Christians reflects the unity of the Trinity. Catholics work with other Christians on social justice projects.
Through Baptism, all the faithful are gifted with the Holy Spirit. Through Confirmation, the faithful are sealed with the Spirit.	Catholics recognize seven gifts of the Holy Spirit: wisdom, understanding, counsel, piety, knowledge, and fear of the Lord. Catholics refer to the Holy Spirit as the "Spirit of Truth."

Christ sent his Spirit so that a community of love would grow in his name. As Catholics, we recognize the Holy Spirit at work in the Church, which is a sacrament of unity and salvation for the world.

If we live in the Spirit, let us also follow the Spirit.

Galatians 5:25

Test Your Catholic Knowledge

Fill in the circle that best answers the question.

In which of the following books of the Bible can we learn the most about the role of the Holy Spirit in guiding the Church?

○ the Song of Songs

○ the Gospel of John

○ the Book of Wisdom

○ the Acts of the Apostles

A Catholic to Know

Saint Peter

"And so I say to you, you are Peter, and upon this rock I will build my church . . . " (Matthew 16:18) From the time he was introduced to Jesus by his brother Andrew, Peter was a leader and spokesperson among the apostles. When Jesus asked his disciples, "Who do you say I am?" Peter replied, "You are the Christ, the Son of the living God." When Jesus said he was going to suffer and die, it was Peter who objected. When Jesus was arrested, it was Peter who drew his sword to protect him. Peter was the first to preach at Pentecost, and he arranged for the election of Matthias to replace Judas. He worked the first public miracle: curing the lame man at the Temple gate. By his example, Saint Peter reminds us what it means to be a disciple.

Witness and Share

These sentences describe what Catholics believe. Listen carefully as they are read. Ask yourself, "How strong are my Catholic beliefs?"

My Way to Faith

- I recognize the Holy Spirit at work in my life and the lives of others.

- I participate in events organized by the community of faithful, including Christians of other churches.

- I pray for the Gifts of the Holy Spirit to guide me and help me make decisions.

- I rely on the Holy Spirit to help me understand and proclaim the Gospel.

- I experience a sense of community in my parish.

Share Your Faith

Consider ways in which you can be more enthusiastic or Spirit-filled in sharing your faith with others. Write your ideas on the lines, and invite a family member or friend to participate in a faith-sharing experience with you.

_____

_____

_____

_____

Matrimony and Holy Orders

Jesus Emmanuel

What Do I Do?

The activities of your everyday life are a part of God's plan for you at this time. Your life is like a puzzle, but God will help you to put all the pieces together. He calls you through the ordinary events of your life to become like his Son, Jesus. God calls you to a particular vocation in life and is preparing you for it now.

Your Life Call

You and every Christian have received one universal call from God at Baptism. You can find it in 1 Thessalonians 4:3.

Your call to holiness is a call to develop your talents so you can serve God and others better. It is a call to witness to God's love within your family and parish, among your friends and classmates. In the future, God may call you to remain a member of the laity as a single or married person. God may call you to be a member of a secular institute, a sister or brother in a religious order, a deacon, a religious or diocesan priest, or a bishop. God may even call you to several vocations.

In all of these lifestyles, Jesus accompanies us on our journey. He is Emmanuel—God with us. He supports us with his grace. Every vocation is meant to lead us to be holy and to share in Jesus' mission. The best way of life for you is the one to which God calls you.

Call to Single Life

God calls some people to the single life. Unmarried people can be involved in a wide range of activities and can spend their lives in service to others. They become signs of God's love. They may make private vows. Some single people choose to live a vowed life as members of secular institutes. They live consecrated lives of prayer and service, while keeping their jobs in the world.

Think of an unmarried person you admire. How does he or she serve others?

_____

What qualities make him or her like Christ?

_____

Why can an unmarried person serve in a way that others cannot serve?

_____

Call to Married Life

God calls most people to a lifelong commitment as husband or wife in marriage. By their generous love for each other and for the children God sends them, husbands and wives support and encourage each other to grow in holiness and to lead their children to holiness.

How can a couple help each other to be holy?

_____

_____

_____

_____

A Covenant of Love

When 6:30 P.M. rolls around, Mrs. Rufo expects Kim to come over and babysit for her. Kim promised that she would come, and Mrs. Rufo trusts that Kim will be faithful to her promise.

To make a promise to someone can be a sign of love. If you love a person deeply, you might make a covenant. A covenant is a binding and solemn promise, a vow.

On their wedding day, Catholic couples make a covenant of love with each other before God. Jesus raised the natural reality of marriage to the level of a sacrament, the Sacrament of Matrimony. The Church celebrates marriage as something holy. The priest represents Jesus as he witnesses the couple's vows in the presence of the believing community. The man and woman act as ministers of the sacrament to each other. They bestow and receive the sacrament in the essential part of the ceremony: the exchange of vows. These vows bind them in a lifelong partnership. In the following version of the marriage vows, underline what Robert and Ann promise to do.

I, Robert (Ann), take you, Ann (Robert), to be my wife (husband). I promise to be true to you in good times and in bad, in sickness and in health. I will love you and honor you all the days of my life.

Covenant Fidelity

The love of Robert and Ann is a sign of Jesus' love for and union with the Church. Through the Sacrament of Matrimony, Jesus enables married couples to remain faithful to their wedding promises. Their faithfulness, or fidelity, is symbolized by the rings they give each other. Christian marriage is founded on the sacredness of human life and the family. Children are the supreme gift God offers married people—a sign of their love.

Before marrying, a person has to ask:

- Am I ready to share my life with another person for life?

- Am I aware what living with another person day after day really means?

- Do I really want to have children—with all that raising children involves?

Mission to Love

Throughout their married life, a husband and wife experience the effects of the sacrament. Jesus unites them and their children in a community of life and love. The family participates in the life and mission of Jesus by being king, priest, and prophet. The family builds up the Church and upholds the rights of all.

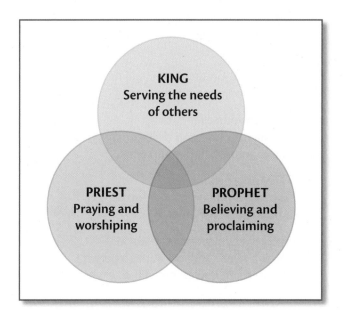

KING
Serving the needs of others

PRIEST
Praying and worshiping

PROPHET
Believing and proclaiming

Call to Priesthood and Diaconate

God calls some men through the Church to an ordained ministry of service for the life and growth of the community. Through the Sacrament of Holy Orders, they become deacons, priests, or bishops forever.

A deacon assists the bishops and priests in teaching, preaching, celebrating the liturgy, and caring for those in need. Every priest is first a deacon. Some men are called to be permanent deacons. They must be at least 35 years old, and many of them are married.

A priest works with the bishop to bring Jesus to the world through word, sacrament, and service. His life is deeply rooted in the Christian community. He is committed to being a leader, a mediator, and a servant in God's family.

A bishop is ordained by another bishop with the laying on of hands. As successor to the apostles, he has the fullness of the priesthood. With his brother bishops, he is responsible for the People of God. In addition to exercising his priestly duties, he shepherds the people in a diocese, teaching, sanctifying, and governing them.

A Leader in Proclaiming God's Word

A main role of the priest is to preach and teach the Gospel. He helps us understand the teachings of Jesus and the Church. To do this well, a priest reflects on the Word of God and studies what the Church teaches. He tries to proclaim the Word by his life as well as by his words.

A Mediator Through Sacraments

Jesus was the perfect priest because he was the perfect mediator between God and all people. By Baptism, all Christians share in his priesthood (the universal or common priesthood). We participate in the Eucharist and in other sacraments, but bishops and priests have a special share in Christ's priesthood (the ministerial priesthood). The greatest responsibility of a priest is to preside at the Eucharist when we offer Jesus and ourselves to the Father. The priest also calls us to be reconciled to God and to others, forgives sins, and administers other sacraments.

A Servant of the Church

Jesus ministered to sinners and to people who were sick, troubled, and poor He offered his life on the cross out of love. Ordained men have different gifts for different works, but they all minister to us as Jesus did. Some priests are diocesan priests who serve in a diocese under the local bishop. Together these priests and the bishop are responsible for the pastoral care of a diocese. Other priests, such as the Jesuits, the Dominicans, and the Franciscans, belong to religious orders. They may serve in a diocese or in the special activities of their order.

Call to Religious Life

God calls some people to dedicate their lives to his service as members of religious communities. Religious come from a variety of backgrounds and can be found serving in many different ways and in all parts of the world. There are certain things that all religious have in common. All are called to be signs of Christ's love and his kingdom in a special way. Their life of prayer, which unites them to Christ, enables them to follow him more closely. Their life in community provides them with the love and support of other religious. Their vows free them to love and serve God and others and to belong more completely to him. They share in a particular way in the mission of the Church.

Religious usually make three vows:

- chastity—being unmarried and chaste for the sake of the kingdom

- poverty—living a simple lifestyle and giving up control of material possessions

- obedience—listening to God particularly as he speaks through superiors.

Listen

You probably will not receive a text message from God telling you your vocation. The process of figuring out your vocation is slow but can be exciting. To hear God's call, develop the skill of listening.

LISTEN to God.
Pray in quiet. Gradually you will hear God's gentle but persistent call.

LISTEN to yourself.
Find out your likes and dislikes, strengths and weaknesses, hopes and fears.

LISTEN to others.
Talk over your plans for the future with a counselor, coach, parent, priest, or teacher.

LISTEN to the needs of the world.
Choose a need that you want to help fill. Do something now to help fill it.

A Moment with Jesus

Figuring out our call in life takes time. It requires that we pay attention to what goes on around us and how we respond to it. Pause now and silently pray the Prayer to Discern My Life Call.

Lord Jesus,
Help me to become a good listener.
Show me your plan for my life.
Bind me so close to you in friendship
    that I will be filled with your love.
Then I will bring your love to those
    who are struggling, confused, or lonely.
Show me the way I can best use my life
    to serve people in your name.
                              Amen.

Take some time to share with Jesus, in your own words, any thoughts you have about your calling in life. Then spend a moment in silence, and listen to what Jesus wants to share with you. Thank him for his friendship and his help.

Remember

What is the universal call that all Christians receive from God?

All Christians receive the universal call to holiness.

What is meant by a vocation?

A vocation is a call from God to a particular way of life in which a person can share Christ's mission and reach holiness.

What is the love between a married couple a sign of?

The love between a married couple is a sign of Christ's love for his Church and his union with it.

What is the mission of bishops, priests, and deacons?

The mission of bishops, priests, and deacons is to give Jesus Christ to the world through word, sacrament, and service.

What are the three vows that most religious make?

Religious usually make vows of chastity, poverty, and obedience.

Respond

The basis for every vocation is the call to be holy, the call to love. In your reflection notebook, write the important events of yesterday. Do any of them show that you are aware of your call to be holy and to love others? Were there specific times when you blocked this call by refusing to show God's love to your parents? to your brothers and sisters? to your friends? to others? Read John 13:34 and evaluate how you responded to this message today.

Reach Out

1. Pray daily that you will recognize the special life call that God has for you. Pray for your friends too.

2. Write a newspaper article about the service given by lay Christians, religious, or priests in your parish. Give specific examples to show how they bring Christ to others.

3. List ways that people can be involved in your parish and diocese. Ask your parents to add to the list.

4. Read the life of a founder of a religious order. Find out what led him or her to start a religious community. Share your research with the class.

5. With a partner, create a colorful, appealing poster inviting young people to consider entering religious life or becoming a priest.

6. Interview a priest. Ask him to share how he experienced God's call to the priesthood and what it has meant to him.

Pope Francis. ❯

Word Scramble   Unscramble the letters of the words under the lines to complete the sentences.

1. God calls all Christians to be _____.
   oylh

2. Single people who live a vowed life belong to _____ _____.
   rucleas   utttiissen

3. The _____ is the minister of the Sacrament of Matrimony for the bride.
   omgor

4. The marriage vows bind a couple to each other in lifelong _____.
   lidityef

5. By the vow of _____, religious promise to remain unmarried
   and chaste.   thiscyat

6. A _____ has the fullness of priesthood.
   spoibh

7. An ordained man who assists the bishop and priests is a _____.
   noedac

8. A priest's greatest privilege is to preside at the _____.
   hsiuEctar

9. The power of priesthood is passed on from a bishop by the laying on of _____.
   nasdh

10. Christians must be Christ for the world in whatever _____ they follow.
    anitcovo

First Letters   Fill in the missing words.

Three things all religious have in common:

1. p _____   2. c _____   3. v _____

Two things Christian marriage is founded on: the sacredness of

4. h _____   5. f _____

Three things a bishop does:

6. t _____   7. g _____   8. s _____

Three roles of a priest:

9. l _____   10. m _____   11. s _____

Gather and Go Forth

Know and Proclaim

We learn the truths of our Catholic faith, and we proclaim them through our vocations in life.

We Know Our Faith	We Proclaim Our Faith
God calls us to a particular vocation through the ordinary events of our lives.	Many Catholics reflect on their day by thinking about God's presence and movement in ordinary events.
God calls some people to be a sign of Christ's love for his Church through the vocation of marriage.	The Catholic family is the domestic church, or a Church in miniature. Catholics consider it their social responsibility to care for and protect the institution of the family.
Matrimony and Holy Orders are the two Sacraments at the Service of Communion.	Catholics pray for an increase in vocations to the priesthood and religious life.

Through the Sacraments of Matrimony and Holy Orders, Catholics proclaim Christ's holiness with lives of service to others.

As he who called you is holy, be holy yourselves in every aspect of your conduct, for it is written, "Be holy, because I [am] holy."

1 Peter 1:15–16

Test Your Catholic Knowledge

Fill in the circle that best answers the question.

Which of the following are the Sacraments at the Service of Communion?

○ Matrimony and Holy Orders

○ Rite of Christian Initiation of Adults

○ Baptism, Eucharist, and Confirmation

○ Reconciliation and Anointing of the Sick

A Catholic to Know

Born in Italy in 1541, John studied pharmacy. He used his knowledge while working in hospitals and prisons. But when he realized that God was calling him to serve his people, John became a priest. John entered the priesthood at a very confusing time. Many people were insecure about what to believe. Despite facing many hardships and opposition, John worked hard to strengthen people's faith through religious education and other pastoral works. John began to train lay leaders and lay catechists. In 1573, John founded a religious order of men. He later published a summary of Christian doctrine. John Leonardi proved by his life that with God, even one person can make many good things happen.

Saint John Leonardi

Witness and Share

These sentences describe what Catholics believe. Listen carefully as they are read. Ask yourself, "How strong are my Catholic beliefs?".

My Way to Faith

- I recognize Jesus' presence with me during the ordinary events of my life.

- I answer the call to be holy and to love others.

- I give witness to God's love in my family, in my school, in my parish, and among my friends.

- I open myself to the calling of the priesthood or religious life.

- I pray with my family regularly.

Share Your Faith

Consider ways in which you can contribute to the prayer life of your family. Write your ideas on the lines, and invite your family to pray with you often.

_____

_____

_____

_____

Jesus Christ the Life

Looking Back

In Unit 3, you studied the life, Death, and Resurrection of our Lord. You know that before he ascended into heaven, he commanded you to witness to his teachings and to follow the example of his life. He sent the Holy Spirit to strengthen and guide you to love one another and form a community.

Not only have you learned about Jesus' life, but you understand your own life better. You know that Jesus offers you eternal life. Your spiritual life grows through daily prayer, frequent prayerful celebration of the sacraments (especially the Eucharist), reflection on the Scriptures, and the love and support of the faith community, the Church. As a disciple, you reach out to serve your family, school, parish, and even the world. You prepare to use your gifts in the vocation to which God calls you. Following Jesus' way and living his truth will bring you his life!

As you complete this book, ask yourself these questions:

1. **How has learning about Jesus Christ, the Life, helped me become more loving and supportive in my family community, school community, and parish community?**

2. **How is my life like the life of Jesus in prayer, in helping people who are poor, and in forgiving others?**

3. **What practical steps can I take to deepen my friendship with Jesus?**

Personal Inventory

Take a close look at your spiritual life. Put a check by the statements that indicate where you have grown.

My Life and God: Do I

○ pay more attention at Sunday Mass?

○ celebrate the Sacrament of Reconciliation more frequently?

○ think of Jesus at times during the day?

○ have greater self-respect because I believe God loves me?

My Life and Other People: Do I

○ keep calm when my parents and I disagree?

○ talk kindly to people I dislike?

○ have the courage to decide as Jesus would want me to and stick to my decision?

○ forgive others when they hurt me?

My Life and Situations: Do I

○ try harder in my schoolwork?

○ remain content with what I have?

○ volunteer to help where there is a need?

○ take care of my health by eating nutritious foods, exercising, and getting enough sleep?

○ admit I make mistakes?

○ take good care of the earth?

Coin Flick

grace 1	raising of Lazarus 5	Liturgy of the Word 1	Last Supper 1	Parousia 5	priest 2
virtues 3	Eucharist 2	Paschal Mystery 4	particular judgment 5	sacramental 3	Liturgy of the Eucharist 4
Trans-figuration 4	purgatory 3	Pentecost 3	suffering 2	Ascension 2	Jesus' passion 2
multi-plication of loaves 2	sacrament 4	vocation 2	Resurrection 2	early Church 5	Sacrament of Matrimony 5
Sacramen-tary 2	Last Judgment 1	bishop 3	Fruits of the Holy Spirit 4	deacon 1	Transubstan-tiation 3

START

Put a coin on START. Flick it with your index finger onto the chart. Then tell about the words in all the squares the coin touches and win the points in the squares. If the coin lands off the chart, deduct five points. See who can reach 50 points first.

Find the Misfit

Put an X on the word in each group that does not match the rest. Write how the remaining words are alike.

All are . . .

1. prudence   hope   justice   fortitude

   _____

2. Eucharist   Jesus' Death   Last Supper Transfiguration

   _____

3. Baptism   Death   Resurrection Ascension

   _____

4. memorial   meal   vocation   sacrifice

   _____

5. heaven   Parousia   Last Judgment Passover

   _____

6. Mary of Magdala   apostle disciples on way to Emmaus   Judas

   _____

7. suffering   speaking in tongues baptisms   birth of Church community

   _____

8. breaking of bread   careers   prayer possessions in common

   _____

9. poverty   chastity   fidelity   obedience

   _____

10. teach   sanctify   govern   write

    _____

Giovanni Girolamo Savoldo, *St. Mary Magdalene Approaching the Sepulchre*, 16th century. ❯

Celebrating

Our Journey in Life

Leader: The Father calls to us with love. The glory of the Son shines on us. The love of the Spirit fills us with life. Let us celebrate our journey of life by signing ourselves with the Sign of the Cross.

All: In the name of the Father and of the Son and of the Holy Spirit. Amen.

Leader: Come, faithful pilgrims, and celebrate life.

Song

Leader: Jesus has told us "I am the Way, and the Truth, and the Life. I have come that you may have life and life to the full." Jesus taught people how to make the pilgrimage to eternal life.

Reader 1: A reading from the Gospel of John. (adapted from John 3:1–5,16)

All: Glory to you, Lord.

Reader 1: A Pharisee named Nicodemus, a leading Jew, came to Jesus at night and said,

Nicodemus: Rabbi, we know that you are a teacher who has come from God; for no one can do these signs that you are doing unless God is with him.

Jesus: Amen, Amen, I say to you no one can see the kingdom of God without being born from above.

Nicodemus: How can a person once grown old be born again?

Jesus: Amen, I say to you, no one can enter the kingdom of God without being born of water and Spirit. . . . God so loved the world that he gave his only Son, so that everyone who believes in him might not perish but might have eternal life.

All: You will show me the path of life and guide me to joy forever.

Reader 2: A reading from the Gospel of John. (adapted from John 4:47–53)

All: Glory to you, Lord.

Reader 2: Now there was a royal official whose son was ill at Capernaum. Hearing that Jesus had arrived in Galilee from Judea, he went and asked him to come and cure his son who was near death.

Nobleman: Sir, come down before my child dies.

Jesus: You may go; your son will live.

Reader 2: The man believed what Jesus had said and left. While he was on his way back, his servants met him and told him that his boy would live.

Nobleman: When did my son begin to recover?

Servants: The fever left him yesterday about one in the afternoon.

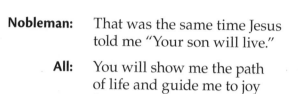

Nobleman: That was the same time Jesus told me "Your son will live."

All: You will show me the path of life and guide me to joy forever.

Prayer

Leader: Jesus is with us on our journey. In each sacrament, he acts to bring us to fullness of life.

Side 1: In you we have been baptized. We have put on Christ.

All: We are your people, Lord. Make us holy.

Side 2: We have been given the gift of the Spirit. We are to witness to you by lives of faith and love.

All: May we live the Gospel with courage, eager to proclaim the Good News to all.

Side 1: We have been nourished by the one bread and one cup and have been made one in you.

All: We are strengthened in love and promise to serve you, Lord, in one another.

Side 2: You have given us forgiveness and peace.

All: We are ready to change our lives by acts of charity, good example, and prayer.

Side 1: You have healed us. You conquered death and opened for us the way to eternal life.

All: Help us to imitate you, who went about doing good, healing and serving the sick.

Side 2: You have shown us the value of love and faithfulness by blessing marriage.

All: We will try to support our families by generous love and service.

Side 1: You have given us bishops, priests, and deacons to witness to the Gospel and celebrate the sacraments.

All: We pray that they draw close to you. Give many others the grace to devote themselves to your service.

Leader: As a sign of Christ's presence among us, let us offer one another a sign of peace.

Sign of Peace

Come, faithful pilgrims, let us continue to travel the path of the Gospel that Jesus has shown. Let us go now to love and serve the Lord.

All: Thanks be to God.

Closing Song

Life Savers

Tell how each of these situations has hurt the community and what can be done to rebuild it.

1. Peggy missed play rehearsal because she was too tired to go.

   _____

2. Rick was grouchy, so he started an argument during dinner.

   _____

3. Tom keeps borrowing money from different members of the class,
   but never gets around to paying it back.

   _____

4. Ellen was playing in the classroom with others and accidentally broke the pencil sharpener.
   The teacher does not know who did it.

   _____

5. Jessica and her friends wrote a note to one of the girls in the room, telling her she was weird
   and they hated her.

   _____

6. When Miguel does not have enough time to study, his parents write a note to the teacher
   so he will be excused from tests. Then Miguel asks other students what was on the test
   so he knows what to study.

   _____

Words to Ponder

The bread you do not use is the bread of the hungry;

the garment hanging in your wardrobe is the garment of him who is naked;

the shoes that you do not wear are the shoes of one who is barefoot;

the money that you keep locked away is the money of the poor;

the acts of charity that you do not perform are so many
   injustices that you commit.

—*Saint Basil*

Gather and Go Forth

CHAPTER 25

Know and Proclaim

Jesus came to bring light into the world. As we proclaim our Catholic faith, we reflect Jesus' light when we act with love toward one another.

We Know Our Faith	We Proclaim Our Faith
Jesus commanded his followers to give witness to his teachings and to follow the example of his life.	Catholics celebrate the Ascension of Jesus 40 days after Easter or on the following Sunday that follows, depending on their local diocese.
Through Christ, we are offered eternal life. Following his way and living his truth will bring us life everlasting.	Catholics believe that death is not the end but the beginning of eternal life. At a Catholic funeral, the baptismal candle is lit to represent our birth into eternal life through Baptism.
Disciples of Jesus reach out to serve their families, schools, parishes, and the world.	Many Catholics support their parishes and local communities by offering their time, talent, and treasure in service to others.

Test Your Catholic Knowledge

Fill in the circle that best completes the sentence.

By serving the needs of others, we participate in Christ's ministry of:

○ prophet.

○ priest.

○ king.

○ laity.

We have received the gifts of Jesus and the call to discipleship from God who loves us. Our response is to follow Jesus Christ to eternal life with God.

"For God so loved the world that he gave his only Son, so that everyone who believes in him might not perish but might have eternal life."

John 3:16

A Catholic to Know

John and his brother James, both fishermen, left everything to follow Jesus. John was with Jesus at critical times. Jesus permitted John to watch the miracle of bringing Jairus's daughter back to life, and he witnessed Jesus' Transfiguration. John was the "beloved disciple" and stayed with Jesus throughout his Passion. There is a story that when Saint John was very old, the people had to carry him to where the Christians assembled to worship. Each time he preached, his homily contained the same message: "Little children, love one another." He said that if they really did this, they would be doing what Jesus taught. John's Gospel continues to teach Christians how to love as Jesus loved.

Saint John the Evangelist

Witness and Share

These sentences describe what Catholics believe. Listen carefully as they are read. Ask yourself, "How strong are my Catholic beliefs?"

My Way to Faith

- I believe that following Jesus Christ faithfully holds the promise of eternal life.

- I pray for the courage to make the decisions that Jesus would want me to make.

- I use my gifts to serve the needs of my parish.

- I seek ways to develop and deepen my relationship with Jesus.

- I respect myself and others because I believe all human beings are made in God's image.

Share Your Faith

Consider ways in which you can seek to develop and deepen your relationship with Jesus. Write your ideas on the lines, and invite a family member or friend to talk with you about his or her own relationship with Jesus.

_____

_____

_____

_____

SACRAMENTS OF INITIATION

	Baptism	Confirmation	Eucharist
Minister	Priest Deacon (in emergency, anyone)	Bishop Abbot (by delegation) Priest (by delegation)	*For consecration:* Bishop or priest *For distributing:* Bishop, priest, deacon, acolyte and, in need, extraordinary minister of Holy Communion
Recipient	*In general:* Any unbaptized person *In particular:* • Infants or persons not yet at the age of reason • Adults and those of the age of reason who desire Baptism	Roman rite: Baptized persons not yet confirmed who are of the age of reason and wish to be confirmed	Baptized persons in the state of grace who are of the age of reason, believe in the real presence, and are properly disposed
Essentials of the Rite	Pouring of water or immersion into water with the words "(Name), I baptize you in the name of the Father, and of the Son, and of the Holy Spirit."	Laying on of hands and anointing with chrism on the forehead with the words "(Name), be sealed with the gift of the Holy Spirit."	Celebration of the Eucharistic Liturgy with its two main parts: the Liturgy of the Word (Scripture readings, homily, and Prayer of the Faithful) and the Liturgy of the Eucharist (thanksgiving, consecration of bread and wine, and communion)
Effects	• cleanses the soul of sin: original and personal • brings about new birth in the Holy Spirit • incorporates one into the Body of Christ (Church) • bestows the Gifts of the Holy Spirit • gives a share in God's life (sanctifying grace), in faith, hope, and love • indelibly marks the person • admits one into Christ's roles of priest, prophet, and king	• increases and deepens baptismal grace through the outpouring of the Holy Spirit • indelibly marks the person • unites one more firmly with Christ • empowers one to witness to Christ courageously • increases the Gifts of the Holy Spirit	• nourishes the life of grace • deepens our union with Christ and his Church • commits us to those who are poor • obtains forgiveness of venial sin and preserves us from grave sin • strengthens the bonds of charity
Some Responsibilities	• respond to the vocation to holiness • reject Satan and sin • follow the teachings of Christ and his Church • participate in the liturgical and the sacramental life of the Church • serve others by sharing the faith and witnessing to it	• grow in faith and witness courageously to the Gospel • develop the ability to lead others to Christ • be willing to suffer for Christ and his Church • participate wholeheartedly in spreading God's kingdom	• celebrate the Eucharist for every Sunday and holy day of obligation • receive Holy Communion at each Mass • show devotion to Jesus in the Eucharist • grow in love for Christ and one another • sacrifice self in service to God and to others

	SACRAMENTS OF HEALING		SACRAMENTS AT THE SERVICE OF COMMUNION	
	Penance and Reconciliation	**Anointing of the Sick**	**Matrimony**	**Holy Orders**
Minister	Bishop Priest	Bishop Priest	Bride and groom (A priest or deacon is a witness in the name of the Church.)	Bishop
Recipient	Baptized persons who have committed sin and are sincerely sorry for having offended God	Baptized persons whose health is seriously impaired by sickness or old age	Any baptized man and woman who are free to marry and are willing to enter into a lifelong marriage agreement	Mature males who have completed Christian initiation who knowingly and willingly wish to be ordained, and who have been accepted as candidates by the authority
Essentials of the Rite	Contrition, confession, act of penance, and the words of absolution prayed by the priest	Anointing of the forehead and hands with the oil of the sick and the prayer of anointing prayed by the priest	The marriage covenant of the bride and groom consenting to give themselves permanently to each other in the presence of the priest or deacon and the Church community	Laying on of hands and the words of ordination prayed by the bishop
Effects	• forgives sin • reconciles one with God and the Church • increases grace and the virtue of charity • increases self-knowledge and strengthens the will	• strengthens one to overcome the difficulties of physical illness • through the grace of the Holy Spirit, encourages trust in God • unites one with the sufferings of Christ • brings spiritual and sometimes physical healing	• entitles the married man and woman to special graces that enable them to fulfill their duties • unites husband and wife indissolubly with each other and in Christ • makes the couple a sign of God's love for his people	• configures the recipient to Christ • confers the special graces of the order received: the diaconate, the priesthood, or the episcopate (bishop) • indelibly marks the recipient • enables the recipient to lead, teach, and sanctify the people
Some Responsibilities	• celebrate the Sacrament of Reconciliation regularly • be a reconciler in the faith community • strive for greater holiness by conversion of life	• accept suffering with patience and trust in union with Christ • look toward eternity with hope in God's mercy • offer suffering for the Church on earth and for the souls in purgatory	• grow in love, care, and willingness to endure hardships for each other • share a common life • grow in faith and practice the works of mercy • provide for the physical, emotional, and spiritual needs of their children • give an example of unselfish love	• Deacon: baptize, distribute Communion, bless marriages, conduct funeral services, minister to those who are needy, preach • Priest: preach, be a spiritual leader, celebrate the Eucharist, forgive sins, celebrate other sacraments • Bishop: provide pastoral teaching, fulfill priestly duties, ordain priests, lead diocese

Special Seasons and Lessons

The Year in Our Church

Ordinary Time
Lent
Christmas
Ash Wednesday
Holy Week
Palm Sunday
Holy Thursday
Good Friday
Holy Saturday
Easter Sunday
Epiphany
Christmas
Advent
Easter
First Sunday
of Advent
Winter
Spring
Fall
Summer
Ascension
Pentecost
All Souls Day
All Saints Day
Ordinary Time

Liturgical Calendar

The liturgical calendar highlights the
seasons of the Church year. Various colors
symbolize the different seasons.

1 | Feast of All Saints

In the Gospel for the Feast of All Saints, we hear Jesus teach

> Blessed are the poor in spirit,
> for theirs is the kingdom of heaven.
>
> Blessed are they who mourn,
> for they will be comforted.
>
> Blessed are the meek,
> for they will inherit the land.
>
> Blessed are they who hunger and thirst
> for righteousness,
> for they will be satisfied.
>
> Blessed are the merciful,
> for they will be shown mercy.
>
> Blessed are the clean of heart,
> for they will see God.
>
> Blessed are the peacemakers,
> for they will be called children of God.
>
> Blessed are they who are persecuted
> for the sake of righteousness,
> for theirs is the kingdom of heaven.

Matthew 5:3–10

Saint Joan of Arc.

On the feast of All Saints, we honor all of the saints. They lived their lives in the spirit of the Beatitudes and in the spirit of Jesus. Through the grace of God, these saints share eternal happiness with God in heaven.

The saints are people who have led lives of heroic virtue that set an example for all Christians. They have witnessed to their faith in ordinary and extraordinary ways. In their lives, we see God's grace at work. This does not mean that the saints were perfect. Instead, it means that they trusted in God's love and mercy. God was able to work through them in powerful ways. This is what we try to follow in our lives. When we imitate the saints, we are also acting like Christ.

Left to right: Saint Francis of Assisi, Archbishop Oscar Romero (1917–1980), and Saint Thérèse of Lisieux (at age 13).

215

Saint Rose of Lima.

Qualities of the Saints

- **Saints Are Big Dreamers.** They make the impossible seem possible. They do not let their weaknesses or those of others hold them back from doing good. They believe that with God's grace, nothing can stop them.

- **Saints Are Go-Getters.** They believe that what is written in the Gospel is to be lived every day: turning the other cheek, loving God above all, feeding the hungry, clothing the naked, and following Jesus. When it comes to doing what is right and good, they don't wait for someone else to act first. They jump right in.

- **Saints Are Love-Bringers.** They try to see Christ in every person and in every situation. They continue to show love to us through their intercession with God on our behalf. Saint Thérèse of Lisieux spoke this belief when she said, "I will spend my heaven doing good on earth."

Saint Martin de Porres.

Today we celebrate all the saints together—the ones we know and the ones we don't know. These are the people who help us believe that love is the most important thing in the world. Their lives tell us that what matters most in life is not what we earn or own, not our status or our popularity. What really matters is how much we love God, others, and ourselves and how well we show that love.

Perhaps you know someone who is a big dreamer, a go-getter, and a love-bringer. Perhaps you are one of those special people who want to make this world a better place. Perhaps you are someone following the Good News with joy. Remember, holiness begins with little things: a smile, a helping hand, or a prayer. This is the road to sainthood. The world is waiting for St. You!

Following Their Example

The Collect Prayer of the Common of Holy Men and Women says well what we believe:

> Almighty and eternal God,
> who by glorifying the Saints,
> bestow on us fresh proofs of your love,
> graciously grant
> that, commended by their intercession and
>   spurred on by their example,
> we may be faithful in imitating your Only
>   Begotten Son.

What are examples of simple things you can do every day to imitate the holiness of the saints?

_____

_____

_____

_____

_____

2 | Advent

We wait with hopeful anticipation for many things: a relative or friend's visit, an airplane's arrival, a vacation's beginning. Think of a time you waited for a special person to arrive or a time you waited for a special event. How did you feel?

_____

_____

_____

The Coming of Jesus

Every year for four weeks the Church prepares to celebrate the mystery of Christmas when God sent his Son to be born among us. We call this time the season of Advent. The word _Advent_ means "coming". During Advent, we

- remember Jesus' coming in _history,_

- prepare for his coming in _mystery,_ and

- hope for his coming in _majesty._

Advent Word Scramble

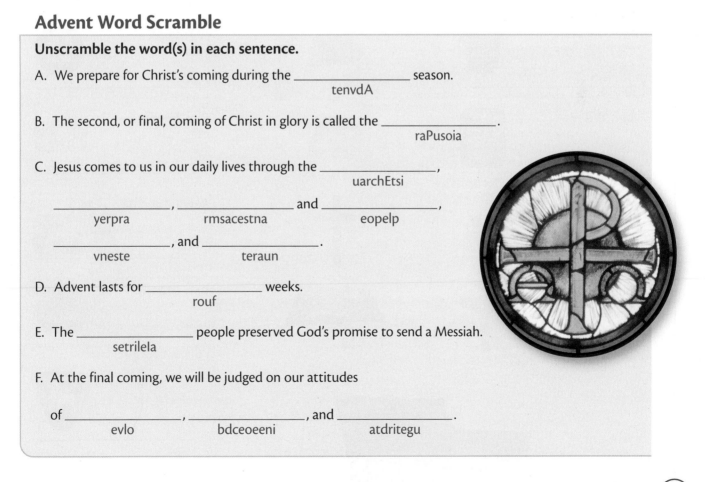

Unscramble the word(s) in each sentence.

A. We prepare for Christ's coming during the _____ season.
   tenvdA

B. The second, or final, coming of Christ in glory is called the _____.
   raPusoia

C. Jesus comes to us in our daily lives through the _____,
   uarchEtsi

   _____, _____ and _____,
   yerpra   rmsacestna   eopelp

   _____, and _____.
   vneste   teraun

D. Advent lasts for _____ weeks.
   rouf

E. The _____ people preserved God's promise to send a Messiah.
   setrilela

F. At the final coming, we will be judged on our attitudes

   of _____, _____, and _____.
   evlo   bdceoeeni   atdritegu

Preparing for Jesus

How will you prepare for Jesus during the season of Advent? Write about one practice that you will do during the Advent season to strengthen your Christian attitude.

_____

_____

Symbols of Christ

Christians use many different symbols to represent our faith. On the left are four common symbols for Christ.

Other symbols remind us of the ways that Christ comes to us. Look up the Scripture references in the first and third columns and write the names of the symbols on the lines. Discuss the meaning of the symbols listed in the second column, which identify ways that Christ comes to us today.

HISTORY

John 9:5
_____

John 10:1–7
_____

Matthew 21:5–9
_____

John 19:18–19
_____

MYSTERY

bread and wine, wheat, grapes

shell, water

cross

Lectionary, Bible

MAJESTY

Rev. 22:13
_____

Rev. 1:5–6
_____

Rev. 1:7 and Rev. 14:14
_____

Rev. 1:12–16
_____

Rev. 5:6
_____

3 | Christmas

The Incarnation

On Christmas, we celebrate God's great gift of love given to us when God sent his Son, Jesus, to be our Savior. We call this the mystery of the Incarnation.

As on many of our Church holy days, there are several opportunities to attend Mass either on Christmas Eve or Christmas Day. The Church designates a different set of readings for each of these Masses. For example, the readings for the Vigil Mass on Christmas Eve are different from the first Mass celebrated on Christmas morning. If we attend the same Christmas Mass every year, we are likely to hear the same Gospel proclaimed.

The different readings are found in the Lectionary, the book that contains the Scripture readings that are proclaimed at each Mass throughout the year.

Let's look carefully at all of these readings from the Masses for Christmas. By doing this, we will learn more about the mystery of the Incarnation that we celebrate at Christmas because each reading teaches us something different about Jesus' birth.

The Gospels of Christmas

Read and summarize each of the Gospel readings for the following Christmas Masses.

Gospel for the Vigil Mass: Matthew 1:18–25 (longer form: Matthew 1:1–25) The Vigil Mass for Christmas is celebrated on the evening of December 24.

_____

_____

_____

Gospel for Christmas Mass at Midnight: Luke 2:1–14

_____

_____

_____

Gospel for Christmas Mass at Dawn: Luke 2:15–20 This is the first Mass celebrated on Christmas morning. It is sometimes called the Shepherd's Mass.

_____

_____

_____

Gospel for Christmas Mass During the Day:
John 1:1–5, 9–14 (longer form: John 1:1–18)

_____

_____

_____

After discussing the summaries with your group, identify what these Gospel readings teach us about the Incarnation.

_____

_____

_____

The Nicene Creed and the Incarnation

Each of the Gospels proclaimed at the Masses on Christmas Day contributes to our understanding of the mystery of the Incarnation. We profess our belief in the Incarnation when we pray the Nicene Creed at Mass. The second stanza of the Creed focuses on our beliefs about Jesus. Highlight any words or phrases that remind you of the Gospels that you have read during this lesson.

> I believe in one Lord Jesus Christ,
> the Only Begotten Son of God,
> born of the Father before all ages.
> God from God, Light from Light,
> true God from true God,
> begotten, not made, consubstantial with
>   the Father;
> through him all things were made.
> For us men and for our salvation
> he came down from heaven,
> and by the Holy Spirit was incarnate of
>   the Virgin Mary,
> and became man.

Reflection on Emmanuel

The Gospel of Matthew describes Jesus as *Emmanuel*, God-with-us. When do you recognize God's presence in your life?

_____

_____

_____

Leo Cartwright, detail of the nativity, St. Paul Episcopal Cathedral, Detroit, Michigan.

4 | Lent

Our Lenten Journey

Jesus' journey led to his passion and Death in Jerusalem before he tasted the victory of the Resurrection. Each year we recall his journey during the season of Lent. In Lent, we are on a journey as well, moving closer toward our final destination: eternal life with God.

Our Lenten journey has much in common with a family trip. Complete the chart below, using the Scripture references to help you.

A FAMILY EXCURSION	OUR LENTEN JOURNEY
Discussion with family • destination or goal • length of trip • route or plan • side trips and stopovers	**Discussion (Matthew 6:5–6)** • _____ • _____ • _____ • _____
Preparation • light packing • car checkup	**Preparation (Matthew 6:1–4)** • _____ • _____
Journey • observing speed limits • obeying traffic signs and signals • following a map	**Journey (Matthew 6:16–18)** • _____ • _____ • _____ _____

Pillars of the Spiritual Life

Write examples of things you could do during Lent to practice the disciplines of prayer, fasting, and almsgiving.

prayer: _____

fasting: _____

almsgiving: _____

My Lenten Journey

Each Friday in Lent, I will read and reflect on the upcoming Sunday Gospel, writing my thoughts in my reflection notebook. Each morning, I will write a resolution for that day (see examples below). At the end of each week, in my reflection notebook, I will evaluate how well I accomplished my resolutions for that week.

SUNDAY	MONDAY	TUESDAY	WEDNESDAY	THURSDAY	FRIDAY	SATURDAY
1 A. Matthew 4:1–11 B. Mark 1:12–15 C. Luke 4:1–13				*I'll try to be kind to someone who isn't a close friend.*		
2 A. Matthew 17:1–9 B. Mark 9:2–9 C. Luke 9:28–36						*I'll do an extra chore at home.*
3 A. John 4:5–42 B. John 2:13–25 C. Luke 13:1–9						
4 A. John 9:1–41 B. John 3:14–21 C. Luke 15:1–3,11–32		*I'll avoid wasting food.*				
5 A. John 11:1–45 B. John 12:20–33 C. John 8:1–11				*I'll limit the amount of time I watch TV or play video games.*		
6 A. Matthew 21:1–11 B. Mark 11:1–10 C. Luke 19:29–40						*I'll send a note to someone who is sick.*

CYCLE A: 2014, 2017, 2020 • CYCLE B: 2015, 2018, 2021 • CYCLE C: 2016, 2019, 2022

❰ Operation Rice Bowl, a Lenten program of Catholic Relief Services, includes praying, fasting, and almsgiving. The program provides aid to people in over 40 countries.

5 | Holy Week

The Easter Triduum—Holy Thursday, Good Friday and Holy Saturday (Easter)—is the high point of the Church year. It is our great three-day celebration that begins on the evening of Holy Thursday and ends on the evening of Easter Sunday. The word *Triduum* means "three days." On these three days, counted from sundown to sundown, we journey with Christ from his Last Supper, through his Death on the cross, to his Resurrection on Easter.

Rituals of the Easter Triduum

Read the Gospel for each liturgy of the Easter Triduum. First, identify the key events from the life of Jesus that are commemorated at each liturgy. Then work with your classmates to identify the liturgical rituals specific to each night of the Easter Triduum.

Holy Thursday
Gospel: John 13:1–15

Events:

- _____
- _____
- _____
  _____
  _____

Ritual:

- _____
- _____
  _____

Good Friday
Gospel: John 18:1—19:42 (John 18:1–40 and John 19:1–42)

Events:

- _____
- _____
- _____
- _____
- _____

Ritual:

- _____
- _____

Holy Saturday: the Easter Vigil
Gospel: Matthew 28:1–10 or Mark 16:1–8 or Luke 24:1–12 (choose one)

Events:

- _____
- _____

Ritual:

- _____
- _____

The Easter Triduum

Fill in the blanks.

Resurrection	cross
alleluia	Baptism
Holy Thursday	Easter Sunday
salvation	Good Friday
service	

At his Last Supper, Jesus washed the feet of his disciples to give us an example of loving _____. We remember this event on _____.

Because it is the day of our redemption, the day of Christ's Death is called _____.

When we venerate the cross on Good Friday, we adore Christ and thank him for our _____.

The sign of Christ's victory over sin and death is the _____.

Holy Saturday is spent waiting for the feast of the _____.

The elect, former catechumens, pray and, as far as possible, fast on Holy Saturday to prepare for their _____.

We celebrate Christ's Resurrection with prayers of praise and joy on _____.

The Easter word is _____.

6 | Easter

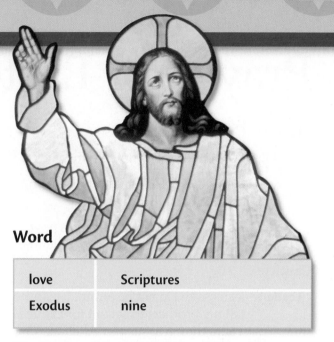

Easter Symbols

Light

fire	Promised Land
paschal candle	Christ

In the history of our faith, fire and light have been symbols of God's presence. At the beginning of the Easter Vigil, the church is in darkness. The priest lights and blesses a new fire. A large candle symbolizing _____ called the _____ is carried into the church. It reminds us of the Exodus when the Chosen People were led by a pillar of _____ into the _____.

Dirck Bouts, detail from *Altarpiece of the Last Supper*, 15th century. Israelites collecting manna in the desert during the Exodus.

Word

love	Scriptures
Exodus	nine

The stories of our Christian roots are in the _____. The _____ readings of the Easter Vigil remind us of God's powerful and faithful _____. The story of the _____ is always read at this Mass.

Water

promises	life
Baptism	Resurrection

In the Easter Vigil, water is a sign of our _____. By this sacrament, we share in the Death and _____ of Jesus. Baptism is the "new Passover" from death to _____. That is why Catholics renew their baptismal _____ at the Easter Vigil.

Prayer for Easter

Leader: God, come to my assistance.

All: Lord, make haste to help me.

Leader: Glory to the Father, and to the Son, and to the Holy Spirit:

All: As it was in the beginning, is now, and will be forever. Amen. Alleluia.

Canticle

Leader: Jesus said: Do not be afraid. Go and tell my brothers to set out for Galilee. There they will see me. Alleluia.

(Alleluias may be sung.)

Side 1: Alleluia. Sing praise to our God, all you his servants, all who worship him reverently, great and small.

Side 2: Alleluia. The Lord our all-powerful God is King; let us rejoice, sing praise, and give him glory.

Side 1: Glory to the Father, and to the Son, and to the Holy Spirit:

Side 2: As it was in the beginning, is now, and will be forever. Amen.

Reader: A reading from Hebrews 10:12–14. *(Passage is read aloud.)*

All: This is the day the Lord has made; let us rejoice and be glad, alleluia.

Canticle of Mary (Luke 1:46–55)

Intercessions

Leader: With joy in our hearts, let us call upon Christ the Lord, who died and rose again, and lives always to intercede for us:

All: Victorious King, hear our prayer.

Leader: Light and salvation of all peoples, send into our hearts the fire of your Spirit, as we proclaim your Resurrection.

All: Victorious King, hear our prayer.

Leader: You have triumphed over death, your enemy; destroy in us the power of death, that we may live only for you, victorious and immortal Lord.

All: Victorious King, hear our prayer.

Leader: We pattern our prayer on the prayer of Christ our Lord and say:

All: Our Father . . .

Concluding Prayer

Leader: God our Father,
by raising Christ your Son
you conquered the power of death
and opened for us the way to
  eternal life.
Let our celebration today
raise us up and renew our lives
by the Spirit that is within us.
Grant this through our
  Lord Jesus Christ, your Son,
who lives and reigns with you and
  the Holy Spirit,
one God, for ever and ever.

*Liturgy of the Hours:
Easter Sunday
Evening Prayer*

All: Amen.

Dismissal

Leader: Go in peace. Alleluia, alleluia.

All: Thanks be to God. Alleluia, alleluia.

Closing Song

7 | Pentecost

Sending of the Advocate

Jesus promised to send the Holy Spirit to his disciples. This promise was fulfilled on the Jewish feast of Pentecost when the Spirit descended upon the disciples gathered in the room in Jerusalem. On the feast of Pentecost, 50 days after Easter, we offer praise and thanksgiving to God for the gift of the Holy Spirit given to the first disciples and given to us as well.

Read each of the Scripture passages from the Gospel of John and answer the questions that follow. In each passage, Jesus is speaking about the Holy Spirit that he will send to his disciples.

"If you love me, you will keep my commandments. And I will ask the Father, and he will give you another Advocate to be with you always, the Spirit of truth, which the world cannot accept, because it neither sees nor knows it. But you know it, because it remains with you, and will be in you. I will not leave you orphans; I will come to you. In a little while the world will no longer see me, but you will see me, because I live and you will live. On that day you will realize that I am in my Father and you are in me and I in you."

John 14:15–20

Saint John the Evangelist

"When the Advocate comes whom I will send you from the Father, the Spirit of truth that proceeds from the Father, he will testify to me. And you also testify, because you have been with me from the beginning."

John 15:26–27

"I have much more to tell you, but you cannot bear it now. But when he comes, the Spirit of truth, he will guide you to all truth. He will not speak on his own, but he will speak what he hears, and will declare to you the things that are coming."

John 16:12–13

What names did Jesus use when he spoke of the Holy Spirit?

_____

List at least three ways that Jesus says the Holy Spirit will help the disciples.

_____

_____

_____

_____

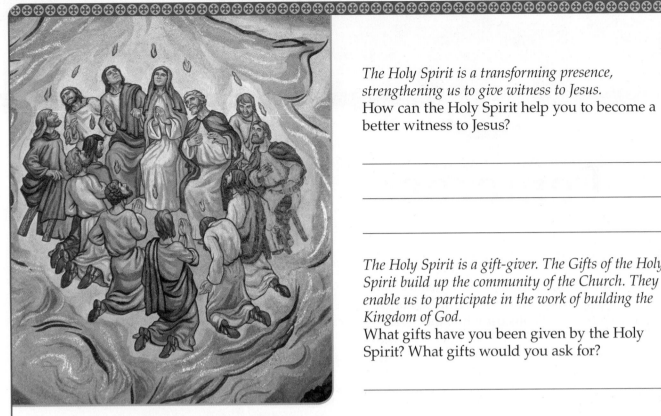

Pentecost mural, St. Louis Cathedral, St. Louis, Missouri.

The Holy Spirit is a transforming presence, strengthening us to give witness to Jesus.
How can the Holy Spirit help you to become a better witness to Jesus?

_____

_____

_____

The Holy Spirit is a gift-giver. The Gifts of the Holy Spirit build up the community of the Church. They enable us to participate in the work of building the Kingdom of God.
What gifts have you been given by the Holy Spirit? What gifts would you ask for?

_____

_____

_____

The Holy Spirit

As our Advocate, the Holy Spirit helps us and prepares us to be Christ's disciples today. The action of the Holy Spirit in our lives prepares us to be advocates for Christ and the Kingdom of God in our world. In a letter to the Church titled *Catechesis in Our Time,* Pope John Paul II summarized how the Holy Spirit helps each of us, and all members of the Church, today. Read these summaries and then answer the questions that follow.

The Holy Spirit is our teacher, helping us to grasp more fully all that Jesus taught.
What would you like to understand better about Jesus?

_____

_____

_____

_____

The Holy Spirit also helps us to pray. Saint Paul wrote in the Letter to the Romans:

. . . the Spirit too comes to the aid of our weakness; for we do not know how to pray as we ought, but the Spirit itself intercedes with inexpressible groanings. And the one who searches hearts knows what is the intention of the Spirit, because it intercedes for the holy ones according to God's will.

Romans 8:26–27

We pray on Pentecost and every day:

Lord, send out your Spirit, and renew the face of the earth.

Responsorial Psalm Pentecost
Psalm 104:30

What Catholics Should Know

(continued on next page)

(continued from previous page)

Prayer and How We Pray

God is always with us. He wants us to talk to him and listen to him. In prayer we raise our hearts and minds to God. We are able to speak and listen to God because through the Holy Spirit, God teaches us how to pray.

What Is Prayer?

Being a Christian requires that we believe all that God has revealed to us, that we celebrate it in the liturgy and the sacraments, and that we live what we believe. All this depends on a vital and personal relationship with the living and true God. This relationship is rooted in prayer. Prayer is a gift from God. We can pray because God seeks us out first and calls us to meet him. We become aware of our thirst for God because God thirsts for us. Prayer arises from our heart, beyond the grasp of reason. Only the Spirit of God can understand the human heart and know it fully. Prayer is the habit of being with God—Father, Son and Holy Spirit. This communion with God is always possible because through our Baptism we are united with Christ. By being united with Christ, we are united with others. Christian prayer is communion with Christ that branches out to all the members of his body, the Church.

Many Forms of Christian Prayer

The Holy Spirit, who teaches us to pray, leads us to pray in a number of ways. This conversation with God can take the form of adoration, blessing, contrition, petition, intercession, thanksgiving, or praise.

Adoration

In a prayer of adoration, we acknowledge God as Creator and Savior. In adoration we recognize how little we are in respect to God's greatness. Like Mary in the *Magnificat*, we confess with gratitude that God has done great things and holy is his name.

Blessing

To bless someone is to acknowledge the goodness of that person. The prayer of blessing is our response to God's goodness because of all the gifts he has given us. In the prayer of blessing, God's gifts and our acceptance of them come together.

Contrition

Contrition is the prayer of sorrow for sin along with a resolution not to sin again. If contrition is motivated by love of God alone, it is called perfect contrition. If contrition is motivated by fear of just punishment, it is called imperfect contrition.

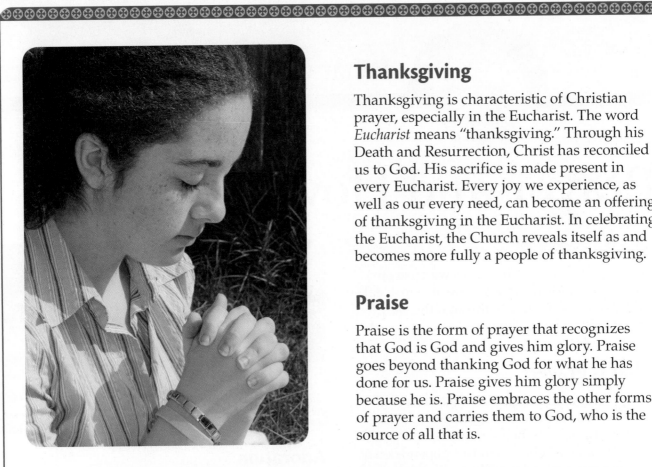

Thanksgiving

Thanksgiving is characteristic of Christian prayer, especially in the Eucharist. The word *Eucharist* means "thanksgiving." Through his Death and Resurrection, Christ has reconciled us to God. His sacrifice is made present in every Eucharist. Every joy we experience, as well as our every need, can become an offering of thanksgiving in the Eucharist. In celebrating the Eucharist, the Church reveals itself as and becomes more fully a people of thanksgiving.

Praise

Praise is the form of prayer that recognizes that God is God and gives him glory. Praise goes beyond thanking God for what he has done for us. Praise gives him glory simply because he is. Praise embraces the other forms of prayer and carries them to God, who is the source of all that is.

We Meditate and Contemplate

To meditate is to think about God. We keep our attention and focus on God, using Scripture, prayer books, or religious images to help us concentrate and spark our imagination. To contemplate means that we rest quietly in God's presence.

We Get Ready to Pray

We can get ready for meditation by resting our bodies in a comfortable position, sitting with our backs straight and both feet on the floor. We can close our eyes, fold our hands in front of us, take a deep breath, and then slowly let it out. We can establish a rhythm by slowly counting to three while breathing in and slowly counting to three while breathing out. Concentrating on our breathing helps us quiet our thoughts.

Petition

Petition is much more than asking God for things we want or need. By prayers of petition, we express our relationship with God as our Creator. We depend on him, and we ask him for something for ourselves. Sometimes we sin and turn away from God. The first step in the prayer of petition is turning back toward him and asking for forgiveness. We can then ask God for what we need, confident that he knows what we need before we ask.

Intercession

In prayers of intercession, we ask something on behalf of another. As a prayer form, intercession is a prayer of petition that leads us to pray as Jesus did. Throughout his life on earth, Jesus interceded with the Father on behalf of all people. To pray in this way means that our hearts are turned outward, focused on the needs around us.

Prayers We Pray as Catholics

We can pray with any words that come to mind. Sometimes when we find that choosing our own words is difficult, we can use traditional prayers. Memorizing traditional prayers such as the following can be very helpful. When we memorize prayers, we take them to heart, meaning that we not only learn the words but also try to understand and live them. See the inside front and back covers of your book for the most frequently used prayers.

Act of Contrition

O my God, I am heartily sorry for having offended Thee, and I detest all my sins because of thy just punishments, but most of all because they offend Thee, my God, who art all good and deserving of all my love. I firmly resolve with the help of Thy grace to sin no more and to avoid the near occasion of sin.
Amen.

Act of Contrition (Prayer of the Penitent)

My God,
I am sorry for my sins with all my heart.
In choosing to do wrong
and failing to do good,
I have sinned against you
whom I should love above all things.
I firmly intend, with your help,
to do penance,
to sin no more,
and to avoid whatever leads me to sin.
Our Savior Jesus Christ
suffered and died for us.
In his name, my God, have mercy.
Amen.

Jesus Prayer

Lord Jesus Christ, Son of God, have mercy on us sinners.

Prayer for Generosity

Eternal Word, only begotten Son of God,
Teach me true generosity.
Teach me to serve you as you deserve,
To give without counting the cost,
To fight heedless of wounds,
To labor without seeking rest,
To sacrifice myself without thought of any
    reward
Save the knowledge that I have done your will.
Amen.

Peace Prayer of Saint Francis

Lord, make me an instrument of your peace.
Where there is hatred, let me sow love; where
   there is injury, pardon;
where there is doubt, faith; where there is
   despair, hope;
where there is darkness, light; and where there
   is sadness, joy.
Grant that I may not so much seek to be
   consoled as to console,
to be understood as to understand, to be
   loved as to love;
for it is in giving that we receive, it is in
   pardoning that we are pardoned,
And it is in dying that we are born to eternal
   life.

Memorare

Remember, O most gracious Virgin Mary,
that never was it known
that anyone who fled to thy protection,
Implored thy help,
or sought thy intercession,
was left unaided.
Inspired by this confidence
I fly unto thee,
O Virgin of virgins, my Mother.
To thee do I come,
before thee I stand,
sinful and sorrowful.
O Mother of the Word Incarnate,
despise not my petitions,
But in thy mercy hear and answer me.
Amen.

Nicene Creed

I believe in one God,
the Father almighty,
maker of heaven and earth,
of all things visible and invisible.

I believe in one Lord Jesus Christ,
the Only Begotten Son of God,
born of the Father before all ages.
God from God, Light from Light,
true God from true God,
begotten, not made, consubstantial with
   the Father;
through him all things were made.
For us men and for our salvation
he came down from heaven,
and by the Holy Spirit was incarnate of the
   Virgin Mary,
and became man.

For our sake he was crucified under Pontius
   Pilate,
he suffered death and was buried,
and rose again on the third day
in accordance with the Scriptures.
He ascended into heaven
and is seated at the right hand of the Father.
He will come again in glory
to judge the living and the dead
and his kingdom will have no end.

I believe in the Holy Spirit, the Lord, the giver
   of life,
who proceeds from the Father and the Son,
who with the Father and the Son is adored
   and glorified,
who has spoken through the prophets.

I believe in one, holy, catholic and apostolic
   Church.
I confess one Baptism for the forgiveness
   of sins
and I look forward to the resurrection of
   the dead
and the life of the world to come.
Amen.

An Ancient Language of Prayer

From the beginning of the Church until the Second Vatican Council in the 1960s, the Church in the West used Latin as its common language. The Latin language was used in prayer, worship, documents, administration, and all areas of Church life. We have a rich and long tradition of hymns and prayers in Latin.

Even today there are parts of the Mass such as the Holy, Holy, Holy (*Sanctus*) and the Lamb of God (*Agnus Dei*) that are occasionally sung in Latin. Certain prayers that are shared by the universal Church can be learned in Latin and prayed as a sign of the universal nature of the Church.

Signum Crucis (Sign of the Cross)

In nomine Patris
et Filii
et Spiritus Sancti.
Amen.

Gloria Patri* (Glory Be to the Father)

Gloria Patri
et Filio
et Spiritui Sancto.
Sicut erat in principio,
et nunc et semper
et in sae cula saeculorum.
Amen.

Pater Noster* (Our Father)

Pater noster, qui es in caelis:
sanctificetur Nomen Tuum;
adveniat Regnum Tuum;
fiat voluntas Tua,
sicut in caelo et in terra.
Panem nostrum
cotidianum da nobis hodie;
et dimitte nobis debita nostra,
sicut et nos dimittimus
debitoribus nostris;
et ne nos inducas in tentationem;
sed libera nos a Malo.
Amen.

Ave, Maria* (Hail Mary)

Ave, Maria, gratia plena,
Dominus tecum.
Benedicta tu in mulieribus,
et benedictus fructus ventris tui, Iesus.
Sancta Maria, Mater Dei,
ora pro nobis peccatoribus,
nunc et in hora mortis nostrae.
Amen.

Agnus Dei (Lamb of God)

Agnus Dei, qui tollis peccáta mundi:
miserére nobis. (Lamb of God, you take away the sins of the world: have mercy on us.)

Agnus Dei, qui tollis peccáta mundi:
miserére nobis. (Lamb of God, you take away the sins of the world: have mercy on us.)

Agnus Dei, qui tollis peccáta mundi:
dona nobis pacem. (Lamb of God, you take away the sins of the world: Grant us peace.)

Sanctus (Holy, Holy, Holy)

Sanctus, Sanctus, Sanctus, Dóminus Deus Sábaoth. (Holy, Holy, Holy Lord, God of hosts.)

Pleni sunt caeli et terra glória tua. (Heaven and earth are full of your glory.)

Hósanna in excélsis. (Hosanna in the highest.)

Benedíctus qui venit in nómine Dómini. (Blessed is he who comes in the name of the Lord.)

Hosánna in excélsis. (Hosanna in the highest.)

*The English versions of these prayers are found on the inside front cover of this book.

PRAYERS WE PRAY AS CATHOLICS 235

The Rosary

The Rosary helps us pray to Jesus through Mary. When we pray the Rosary, we think about the special events, or mysteries, in the lives of Jesus and Mary.

The Rosary is made up of a string of beads and a crucifix. We hold the crucifix in our hands as we pray the Sign of the Cross. Then we pray the Apostles' Creed. Next to the crucifix, there is a single bead, followed by a set of three beads and another single bead. We pray the Lord's Prayer as we hold the first single bead and a Hail Mary at each bead in the set of three that follows. Then we pray the Glory Be to the Father. On the next single bead, we think about the first mystery and pray the Lord's Prayer.

There are five sets of 10 beads; each set is called a decade. We pray a Hail Mary on each bead of a decade as we reflect on a particular mystery in the lives of Jesus and Mary. The Glory Be to the Father is prayed at the end of each set. Between sets is a single bead on which we think about one of the mysteries and pray the Lord's Prayer.

In his apostolic letter *Rosary of the Virgin Mary*, Pope John Paul II wrote that the Rosary could take on a variety of legitimate forms as it adapts to different spiritual traditions and different Christian communities. "What is really important," he said, "is that the Rosary should always be seen and experienced as a path of contemplation." It is traditional in some places to pray the Hail, Holy Queen after the last decade.

We end by holding the crucifix in our hands as we pray the Sign of the Cross.

Hail Holy Queen (*Salve Regina*)

Hail, Holy Queen, Mother of Mercy,
our life, our sweetness, and our hope.
To you do we cry,
poor children of Eve.
To you do we send up our sighs,
mourning and weeping in this valley of tears.
Turn, then, most gracious advocate,
your eyes of mercy toward us,
and after this exile
show unto us the blessed fruit of thy womb,
Jesus.
O clement, O loving,
O sweet Virgin Mary.

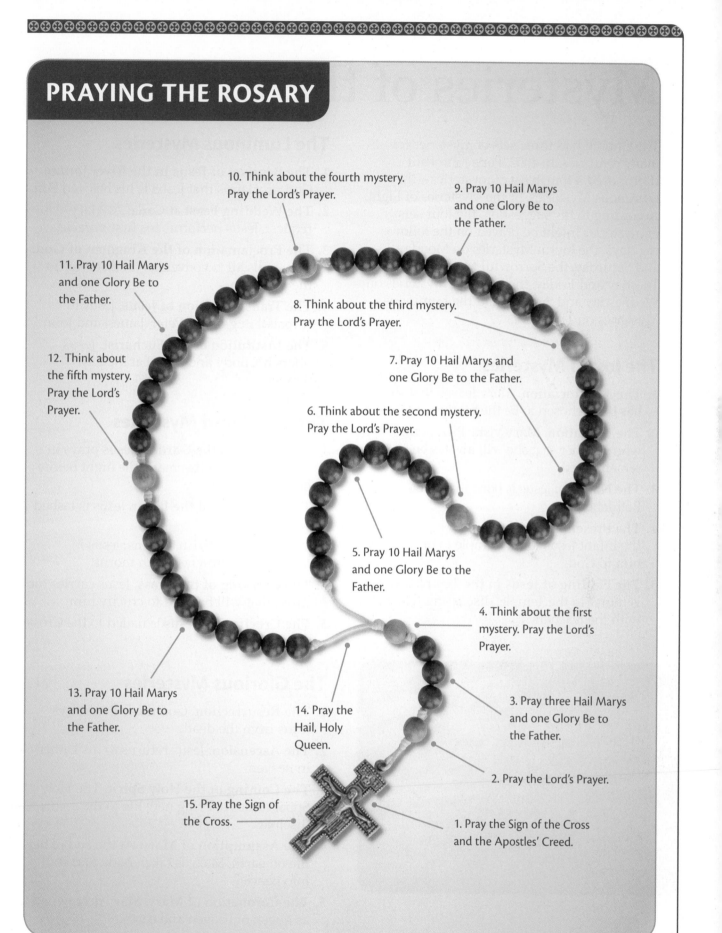

10. Think about the fourth mystery. Pray the Lord's Prayer.

9. Pray 10 Hail Marys and one Glory Be to the Father.

11. Pray 10 Hail Marys and one Glory Be to the Father.

8. Think about the third mystery. Pray the Lord's Prayer.

12. Think about the fifth mystery. Pray the Lord's Prayer.

7. Pray 10 Hail Marys and one Glory Be to the Father.

6. Think about the second mystery. Pray the Lord's Prayer.

5. Pray 10 Hail Marys and one Glory Be to the Father.

4. Think about the first mystery. Pray the Lord's Prayer.

13. Pray 10 Hail Marys and one Glory Be to the Father.

14. Pray the Hail, Holy Queen.

3. Pray three Hail Marys and one Glory Be to the Father.

2. Pray the Lord's Prayer.

15. Pray the Sign of the Cross.

1. Pray the Sign of the Cross and the Apostles' Creed.

Mysteries of the Rosary

The Church had three sets of mysteries for many centuries. In 2002, Pope John Paul II proposed a fourth set of mysteries—the Luminous Mysteries, or the Mysteries of Light. According to his suggestion, the four sets of mysteries might be prayed on the following days: the Joyful Mysteries on Monday and Saturday, the Sorrowful Mysteries on Tuesday and Friday, the Glorious Mysteries on Wednesday and Sunday, and the Luminous Mysteries on Thursday.

The Joyful Mysteries

1. **The Annunciation.** Mary learns that she has been chosen to be the mother of Jesus.
2. **The Visitation.** Mary visits Elizabeth, who tells her that she will always be remembered.
3. **The Nativity.** Jesus is born in a stable in Bethlehem.
4. **The Presentation.** Mary and Joseph take the infant Jesus to the Temple to present him to God.
5. **The Finding of Jesus in the Temple.** Jesus is found in the Temple, discussing his faith with the teachers.

The Luminous Mysteries

1. **The Baptism of Jesus in the River Jordan.** God proclaims that Jesus is his beloved Son.
2. **The Wedding Feast at Cana.** At Mary's request, Jesus performs his first miracle.
3. **The Proclamation of the Kingdom of God.** Jesus calls all to conversion and service to the kingdom.
4. **The Transfiguration of Jesus.** Jesus is revealed in glory to Peter, James, and John.
5. **The Institution of the Eucharist.** Jesus offers his Body and Blood at the Last Supper.

The Sorrowful Mysteries

1. **The Agony in the Garden.** Jesus prays in the garden of Gethsemane the night before he dies.
2. **The Scourging at the Pillar.** Jesus is lashed with whips.
3. **The Crowning with Thorns.** Jesus is mocked and crowned with thorns.
4. **The Carrying of the Cross.** Jesus carries the Cross that will be used to crucify him.
5. **The Crucifixion.** Jesus is nailed to the Cross and dies.

The Glorious Mysteries

1. **The Resurrection.** God the Father raises Jesus from the dead.
2. **The Ascension.** Jesus returns to his Father in heaven.
3. **The Coming of the Holy Spirit.** The Holy Spirit comes to bring new life to the disciples.
4. **The Assumption of Mary.** At the end of her life on earth, Mary is taken body and soul into heaven.
5. **The Coronation of Mary.** Mary is crowned as queen of heaven and earth.

Stations of the Cross

The 14 Stations of the Cross represent events from Jesus' passion and Death. Even before the Gospels were written down, the followers of Jesus told the story of his passion, Death, and Resurrection. When people went on pilgrimage to Jerusalem, they were anxious to see the sites where Jesus lived and died. Eventually, following in the footsteps of the Lord on the way to his Death became an important part of the pilgrimage.

The stations as we know them today came about when it was no longer easy or even possible to visit the holy sites in Palestine. In the 1500s, villages all over Europe started creating replicas of the way of the Cross, with small shrines commemorating the places along the

route in Jerusalem. Eventually, these shrines became the set of 14 stations we now know.

The important point to remember about the stations is that they are a prayer. They are not an exercise in remembering events from the past. They are an invitation to make present the final hours of Jesus' life and to experience who Jesus is. It becomes a prayer when we open our hearts to be touched, and it leads us to express our response in prayer. Jesus wants to use any means available to move our hearts so that we know his love for us.

At each station we use our senses and our imagination to reflect prayerfully upon Jesus' suffering, Death, and Resurrection. The stations can allow us to visualize the meaning of his passion and Death and lead us to gratitude. They can also lead us to a sense of solidarity with all our brothers and sisters, especially those who suffer, who are unjustly accused or victimized, who are on death row, who carry difficult burdens, or who face terminal illnesses.

1. Jesus Is Condemned to Death.
Pontius Pilate condemns Jesus to Death.

2. Jesus Takes Up His Cross.
Jesus willingly accepts and patiently bears his Cross.

3. Jesus Falls the First Time.
Weakened by torments and loss of blood, Jesus falls beneath his Cross.

4. Jesus Meets His Sorrowful Mother.
Jesus meets his mother, Mary, who is filled with grief.

5. Simon of Cyrene Helps Jesus Carry the Cross.
Soldiers force Simon of Cyrene to carry the Cross.

6. Veronica Wipes the Face of Jesus.
Veronica steps through the crowd to wipe the face of Jesus.

7. Jesus Falls a Second Time.
Jesus falls beneath the weight of the Cross a second time.

8. Jesus Meets the Women of Jerusalem.
Jesus tells the women to weep not for him, but for themselves and for their children.

9. Jesus Falls the Third Time.
Weakened almost to the point of death, Jesus falls a third time.

10. Jesus Is Stripped of His Garments.
The soldiers strip Jesus of his garments, treating him as a common criminal.

11. Jesus Is Nailed to the Cross.
Jesus' hands and feet are nailed to the Cross.

12. Jesus Dies on the Cross.
After suffering greatly on the Cross, Jesus bows his head and dies.

13. Jesus Is Taken Down from the Cross.
The lifeless body of Jesus is tenderly placed in the arms of Mary, his mother.

14. Jesus Is Laid in the Tomb.
Jesus' disciples place his body in the tomb.

The closing prayer—sometimes included as a 15th station—reflects on the Resurrection of Jesus.

Formulas of Catholic Doctrine

The following formulas present the basic teachings of the Catholic Church. These are core teachings every Catholic should know.

The Great Commandment

The Ten Commandments are fulfilled in Jesus' Great Commandment: "You shall love God with all your heart, with all your soul, with all your mind, and with all your strength. You shall love your neighbor as yourself." (adapted from Mark 12:30–31)

The New Commandment

Before his Death on the Cross, Jesus gave his disciples a new commandment: "I give you a new commandment: love one another. As I have loved you, so you also should love one another." (John 13:34)

The Golden Rule

"Do to others whatever you would have them do to you." (Matthew 7:12)

The Beatitudes

The Beatitudes are the teachings of Jesus in the Sermon on the Mount. They can be found in Matthew 5:1–10. Jesus teaches us that if we live according to the Beatitudes, we will live a happy Christian life. The Beatitudes fulfill God's promises made to Abraham and to his descendants and describe the rewards that will be ours as loyal followers of Christ.

Blessed are the poor in spirit,
for theirs is the kingdom of heaven.
Blessed are they who mourn,
for they will be comforted.
Blessed are the meek,
for they will inherit the land.
Blessed are they who hunger and thirst
    for righteousness,
for they will be satisfied.
Blessed are the merciful,
for they will be shown mercy.
Blessed are the clean in heart,
for they will see God.
Blessed are the peacemakers,
for they will be called children of God.
Blessed are they who are persecuted
    for the sake of righteousness,
for theirs is the kingdom of heaven.

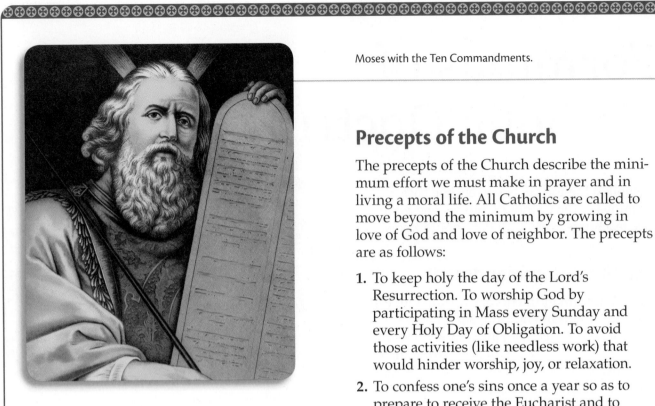

Moses with the Ten Commandments.

The Ten Commandments

As believers in Jesus Christ, we are called to a new life and are asked to make moral choices that keep us united with God. With the help and grace of the Holy Spirit, we can choose ways to act that keep us close to God, help other people, and be witnesses to Jesus.

The Ten Commandments guide us in making choices that help us live as God wants us to live. The first three commandments tell us how to love God; the other seven tell us how to love our neighbor.

1. I am the Lord your God: you shall not have strange gods before me.
2. You shall not take the name of the Lord your God in vain.
3. Remember to keep holy the Lord's Day.
4. Honor your father and your mother.
5. You shall not kill.
6. You shall not commit adultery.
7. You shall not steal.
8. You shall not bear false witness against your neighbor.
9. You shall not covet your neighbor's wife.
10. You shall not covet your neighbor's goods.

Precepts of the Church

The precepts of the Church describe the minimum effort we must make in prayer and in living a moral life. All Catholics are called to move beyond the minimum by growing in love of God and love of neighbor. The precepts are as follows:

1. To keep holy the day of the Lord's Resurrection. To worship God by participating in Mass every Sunday and every Holy Day of Obligation. To avoid those activities (like needless work) that would hinder worship, joy, or relaxation.
2. To confess one's sins once a year so as to prepare to receive the Eucharist and to continue a life of conversion.
3. To lead a sacramental life. To receive Holy Communion at least once during the Easter season.
4. To do penance, including abstaining from meat and fasting from food on the appointed days.
5. To strengthen and support the Church—assist with the material needs of the Church according to one's ability.

The Four Last Things

There are four things that describe the end of all human life.

death   judgment   heaven   hell

First is the death of the individual. Then immediately after death is the judgment by Christ. The result of this judgment is either heaven (perhaps with a time in purgatory) or hell.

Virtues

Virtues are gifts from God that lead us to live in a close relationship with him. Virtues are like habits. They need to be practiced; they can be lost if they are neglected.

Theological Virtues

The three most important virtues are called *Theological Virtues* because they come from God and lead to God.

faith   hope   charity

Cardinal Virtues

The cardinal virtues are human virtues, acquired by education and good actions. *Cardinal* comes from *cardo,* the Latin word for "hinge," meaning "that on which other things depend."

prudence   justice   fortitude   temperance

Gifts and Fruits of the Holy Spirit

The Holy Spirit makes it possible for us to do what God asks by giving us these gifts.

wisdom   understanding   counsel   piety

fortitude   knowledge   fear of the Lord

The Fruits of the Holy Spirit are signs of the Holy Spirit's action in our lives.

love	kindness	faithfulness
joy	goodness	modesty
peace	generosity	self-control
patience	gentleness	chastity
self-control	modesty	

Works of Mercy

The Corporal and Spiritual Works of Mercy are actions we can perform that extend God's compassion and mercy to those in need.

Corporal Works of Mercy

The Corporal Works of Mercy are the kind acts by which we help our neighbors with their material and physical needs:

- Feed the hungry.
- Give drink to the thirsty.
- Clothe the naked.
- Shelter the homeless.
- Visit the sick.
- Visit the imprisoned.
- Bury the dead.

Spiritual Works of Mercy

The Spiritual Works of Mercy are acts of compassion by which we help our neighbors with their emotional and spiritual needs:

- Counsel the doubtful.
- Instruct the ignorant.
- Admonish the sinner.
- Comfort the afflicted.
- Forgive offenses.
- Bear wrongs patiently.
- Pray for the living and the dead.

When we help others, we are performing works of mercy.

Celebrating and Living Our Catholic Faith

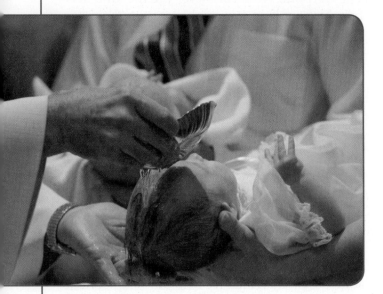

The Mystery of Faith Made Present

The Church was revealed to the world with the coming of the Spirit on Pentecost. This gift of the Spirit ushered in a new era in the history of salvation. This era is the age of the Church in which Christ makes present and communicates his work of salvation through the liturgy. The Church, as Christ's Body, is the first sacrament, the sign and instrument through which the Holy Spirit dispenses the mystery of salvation. In this age of the Church, Christ lives and acts through the sacraments.

The Seven Sacraments

Jesus touches our lives through the sacraments. In the sacraments, physical objects such as water, bread and wine, and oil are the signs of Jesus' presence.

Sacraments of Initiation

These sacraments lay the foundation of Christian life.

Baptism
In Baptism, we are born into new life in Christ. Baptism takes away Original Sin and makes us members of the Church. Its sign is the pouring of water.

Confirmation
Confirmation seals our life of faith in Jesus. The signs of Confirmation are the laying on of hands and the anointing with oil on a person's head, most often done by a bishop. Confirmation and Baptism are received only once.

Eucharist
The Eucharist nourishes our life of faith. We receive the Body and Blood of Christ under the appearances of bread and wine.

Sacraments of Healing

These sacraments celebrate the healing power of Jesus.

Reconciliation
Through Reconciliation we receive God's forgiveness. Forgiveness requires being sorry for our sins. In Reconciliation we receive Jesus' healing grace through absolution by the priest. The signs of this sacrament are the confession of sins, repentance and satisfaction, and the words of absolution.

Anointing of the Sick
This sacrament unites a sick person's sufferings with those of Jesus. Oil, a symbol of strength, is the sign of this sacrament. A person is anointed with the oil of the sick and receives the laying on of hands by a priest.

Sacraments at the Service of Communion

These sacraments help members serve the community.

Matrimony

In Matrimony a baptized man and woman are united with each other as a sign of the unity between Jesus and his Church. Matrimony requires the consent of the husband and the wife as expressed in the marriage promises. The husband and wife and their wedding rings are signs of this sacrament.

Holy Orders

In Holy Orders, men are ordained priests to serve as leaders of the community or as deacons to be reminders of our baptismal call to serve others. The signs of this sacrament are the laying on of hands and the prayer by the bishop asking God for the outpouring of the Holy Spirit.

Holy Days of Obligation

The holy days of obligation are the days other than Sundays on which we celebrate the great things God has done for us through Jesus and the saints. On holy days of obligation, Catholics attend Mass.

Six holy days of obligation are celebrated in the United States.

January 1—Mary, Mother of God

40 days after Easter—Ascension (in many U.S. dioceses the Seventh Sunday of Easter)

August 15—Assumption of the Blessed Virgin Mary

November 1—All Saints

December 8—Immaculate Conception

December 25—Nativity of Our Lord Jesus Christ

The Order of Mass

The Sabbath, the day on which God rested after creating the world, represents the completion of creation. Saturday has been replaced by Sunday as the Sabbath for Christians because it recalls the beginning of the new creation through the Resurrection of Christ. Since it is the day of the Resurrection, Sunday is called the Lord's Day. The Sunday celebration of the Lord's Day is at the heart of the Church's life. That is why we are required to participate in the Mass on Sundays and other holy days of obligation. We also rest from work, take time to enjoy our families, enrich our cultural and social lives, and perform works of mercy. On Sunday, people from all over the world gather at God's eucharistic table.

The Mass is the high point of Christian life, and it follows a set order.

Introductory Rites

We prepare to celebrate the Eucharist.

Entrance Chant

We gather as a community, praising God in song.

Greeting

We pray the Sign of the Cross, recognizing the presence of Christ in the community.

Penitential Act

We remember our sins and ask God for mercy.

Gloria

We praise God in song.

Collect Prayer

We pray for the grace to celebrate this Mass.

Liturgy of the Word
We hear the story of God's plan for salvation.

First Reading
We listen to God's Word, usually from the Old Testament.

Responsorial Psalm
We respond to God's Word in song.

Second Reading
We listen to God's Word from the New Testament.

Gospel Acclamation
We sing "Alleluia!" to praise God for the Good News. During Lent, we sing an alternate acclamation.

Gospel Reading
We stand to acclaim Christ present in the Gospel.

Homily
The priest or deacon explains God's Word.

Profession of Faith
We proclaim our faith through the Creed.

Prayer of the Faithful
We pray for our needs and the needs of others.

Liturgy of the Eucharist
We celebrate the meal Jesus instituted at the Last Supper and remember the sacrifice he made for us.

Presentation and Preparation of the Gifts
We bring gifts of bread and wine to the altar.

Prayer over the Offerings
The priest prays that God will accept our sacrifice.

Eucharistic Prayer
This prayer of thanksgiving is the center and high point of the entire celebration.

- *Preface Dialogue*—We give thanks and praise to God.

- *Holy, Holy, Holy (Preface Acclamation)*—We sing an acclamation of praise.

- *Institution Narrative*—The prayer over the bread and wine whereby, through the power of the Holy Spirit and the ministry of the priest, the bread and wine are transformed into the Body and Blood of Jesus Christ.

- *The Mystery of Faith*—We proclaim Jesus' Death and Resurrection.

- *Amen*—We affirm the words and actions of the Eucharistic prayer.

Communion Rite
We prepare to receive the Body and Blood of Jesus.

- *The Lord's Prayer*—We pray the Lord's Prayer.

- *Sign of Peace*—We offer one another Christ's peace.

- *Lamb of God*—We pray for forgiveness, mercy, and peace.

- *Communion*—We receive the Body and Blood of Jesus Christ.

- *Prayer after Communion*—We pray that the Eucharist will strengthen us to live as Jesus did.

Concluding Rites
We go forth to serve the Lord and one another.

Final Blessing
We receive God's blessing.

Dismissal
We go forth in peace to glorify the Lord by our lives.

Making Good Choices

Our conscience is the inner voice that helps us know the law God has placed in our hearts. Our conscience helps us judge the moral qualities of our actions. It guides us to do good and avoid evil.

The Holy Spirit can help us form our conscience. We form our conscience by studying the teachings of the Church and following the guidance of our parents and pastoral leaders.

God has given every human being freedom of choice. This does not mean that we have the right to do whatever we please. We can live in true freedom if we cooperate with the Holy Spirit, who gives us the virtue of prudence. This virtue helps us recognize what is good in every situation and make the correct choice. The Holy Spirit gives us the gifts of wisdom and understanding to help us make the right choices in life in relationship to God and others. The gift of counsel helps us reflect on making correct choices in life.

The Ten Commandments, the Beatitudes, and the two Great Commandments help us make moral choices. We also have the grace of the sacraments, the teachings of the Church, and the good example of saints and fellow Christians.

Making moral choices involves the following steps:

1. Ask the Holy Spirit for help.

2. Think about God's law and the teachings of the Church.

3. Think about what will happen as a result of your choice. Ask yourself, will the consequences be pleasing to God? Will my choice hurt someone else?

4. Seek advice from someone you respect, and remember that Jesus is with you.

5. Ask yourself how your choice will affect your relationships with God and others.

In making moral choices, we must take into consideration the object of the choice, our intention in making the choice, and the circumstances in which the choice is made. It is never right to make an evil choice in the hope of gaining something good.

The Morality of Human Acts

Human beings are able to act morally only because we are free. If we were not free to decide what to do, our acts could not be good or evil. Human acts that are freely chosen after a judgment of conscience can be morally evaluated. They are either good or evil.

The morality of human acts depends on

- the object chosen;
- the end in view or the intention;
- the circumstances of the action.

For an act to be good, what you choose to do must be good in itself. If the choice is not good, the intention or the circumstances cannot make it good. You cannot steal a digital camera because it is your father's birthday and it would make him happy to have one. But a good act done with a bad intention is not necessarily good either. Participating in a hunger walk, not out of concern for the poor but to impress a teacher from whom you want a good grade, is not necessarily a good act. Circumstances can affect the morality of an

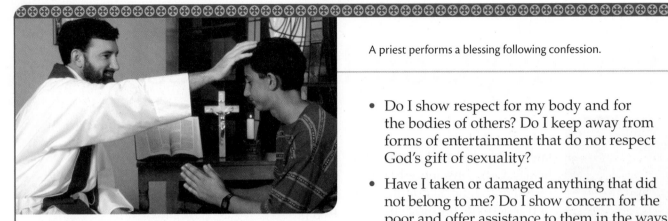

A priest performs a blessing following confession.

act. They can increase or lessen the goodness of an act. Acting out of fear of harm lessens a person's responsibility for an act.

An Examination of Conscience

An examination of conscience is the act of looking prayerfully into our hearts to ask how we have hurt our relationships with God and with other people through our thoughts, words, and actions. We reflect on the Ten Commandments and the teachings of the Church.

My Relationship with God

- What steps am I taking to help me grow closer to God and to others? Do I turn to God often during the day, especially when I am tempted?

- Do I participate at Mass with attention and devotion on Sundays and holy days? Do I pray often and read the Bible?

- Do I use God's name and the names of Jesus, Mary, and the saints with love and reverence?

My Relationships with Family, Friends, and Neighbors

- Have I set a bad example through my words or actions? Do I treat others fairly? Do I spread stories that hurt other people?

- Am I loving toward those in my family? Am I respectful of my neighbors, my friends, and those in authority?

- Do I value human life? Do I do what I can to promote peace and to end violence? Do I avoid talking about others in ways that could harm them?

- Do I show respect for my body and for the bodies of others? Do I keep away from forms of entertainment that do not respect God's gift of sexuality?

- Have I taken or damaged anything that did not belong to me? Do I show concern for the poor and offer assistance to them in the ways I am able? Do I show concern for the environment and care for it as God has asked?

- Have I cheated or copied homework? Have I told the truth even when it was difficult?

- Do I quarrel with others just so I can get my own way? Do I insult others to try to make them think they are less than I am? Do I hold grudges and try to hurt people who I think have hurt me?

How to Make a Good Confession

An examination of conscience is an important part of preparing for the Sacrament of Reconciliation. The Sacrament of Reconciliation includes the following steps:

- The priest greets us, and we pray the Sign of the Cross. He invites us to trust in God. He may read God's Word with us.

- We confess our sins. The priest may help and counsel us.

- The priest gives us a penance to perform. Penance is an act of kindness, prayers to pray, or both.

- The priest asks us to express our sorrow, usually by reciting the Act of Contrition.

- We receive absolution. The priest says, "I absolve you from your sins in the name of the Father, and of the Son, and of the Holy Spirit." We respond, "Amen."

- The priest dismisses us by saying, "Go in peace." We go forth to perform the act of penance he has given us.

The Bible

God speaks to us in many ways. One way God speaks to us is through the Bible. The Bible is the most important book in Christian life because it is God's message, or Revelation. The Bible is the story of God's promise to care for us, especially through his Son, Jesus. At Mass, we hear stories from the Bible. We can also read the Bible on our own.

The Bible is not just one book; it is a collection of many books. The writings in the Bible were inspired by the Holy Spirit and written by different authors using different styles.

The Bible is made up of two parts: the Old Testament and the New Testament. The Old Testament contains 46 books that tell stories about the Jewish people and their faith in God before Jesus was born.

The first five books of the Old Testament—Genesis, Exodus, Leviticus, Numbers, and Deuteronomy—are referred to as the *Torah,* meaning "instruction" or "law." The central story in the Torah is the Exodus, the liberation of the Hebrew slaves as Moses led them out of Egypt and to the Promised Land. During the journey, God gave the Ten Commandments to Moses and the people.

A beautiful part of the Old Testament is the Book of Psalms. A psalm is a prayer in the form of a poem. Each psalm expresses an aspect or feature of the depth of human emotion. Over several centuries, 150 psalms were gathered to form the Book of Psalms. They were once sung at the Temple in Jerusalem, and they have been used in the public worship of the Church since its beginning. Catholics also pray the psalms as part of their private prayer and reflection.

The prophets were called by God to speak for him and to urge the Jewish people to be faithful to the Covenant. A large part of the Old Testament (18 books) presents the messages and actions of the prophets.

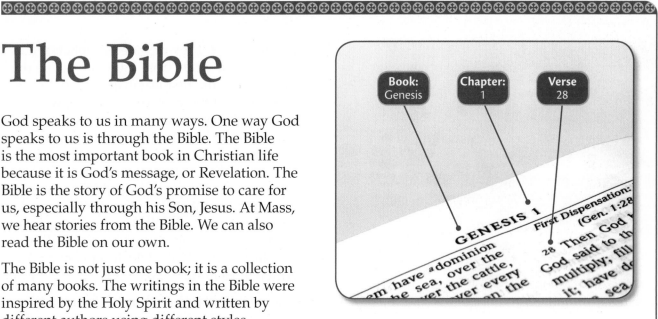

The New Testament contains 27 books that tell the story of Jesus' life, Death, and Resurrection, and the experience of the early Christians. For Christians, the most important books of the New Testament are the four Gospels—Matthew, Mark, Luke, and John. Many of the 27 books are letters written by leaders such as Paul.

How can you find a passage in the Bible? Bible passages are identified by book, chapter, and verse—for example, Genesis 1:28. The name of the book comes first. Sometimes it is abbreviated. Your Bible's table of contents will help you determine what the abbreviation means. For example, *Gn* stands for *Genesis.* After the name of the book, there are two numbers. The first one identifies the chapter, which in our example is chapter 1; it is followed by a colon. The second number identifies the verse or verses. Our example shows verse 28.

How the Old Testament and the New Testament Were Put Together

The Old and New Testaments developed in oral cultures, and much of the material was passed on by word of mouth before ever being written down. Stories from the prehistory of Israel were probably the first part of the Old Testament to be written down. These can be

King David.

found in parts of the 2nd through 11th chapters of Genesis. They would have been written by the court historian of King David around 1000 B.C. This writer always referred to God as Yahweh and spoke of God in human terms. It was this writer who wrote the story of God walking in the garden with Adam and Eve. Other stories developed in the northern kingdom of Israel and favor the religious sites of that region, such as Bethel.

The Old Testament as we know it today did not begin to take shape until the Babylonian Exile (587–537 B.C.). There members of the priestly class took many of the oral and written accounts of God's saving work and put them together in what we know as the Torah, the first five books of the bible—Genesis, Exodus, Leviticus, Numbers, and Deuteronomy.

The writers in Babylon also wrote the opening chapter of Genesis that tells of God's orderly creation of the world in six days and his rest on the seventh day.

The historical books were put together from the court accounts of various kings of Israel and Judah. The psalms were gathered from collections of prayers, and new psalms were written for the temple that was rebuilt after 537 B.C. Other Wisdom Literature was also gathered. Finally, the writings of the prophets were gathered together and collected by

their followers. They included prophets who preached and wrote from 150 years before the exile, such as the first Isaiah and Amos, to the second part of the book of Zechariah, which was probably written after 330 B.C. In the middle of the third century B.C., these books were translated from Hebrew into Greek in Alexandria, Egypt. In time a number of other books, such as First and Second Maccabees, were added to the Bible in Greek. By the end of the first century A.D., religious leaders in Israel decided which books would be in their Bible. They included only the Old Testament books written in Hebrew.

In about year 50, Paul wrote his first letter to the Thessalonians, followed by a second one later that year. This was more than 20 years after the Death and Resurrection of Jesus. Over the next 13 years, Paul wrote letters to other Christian communities as well as to the Christians of Rome, a city he hoped to visit. Meanwhile, Christians were passing on stories about Jesus—his message, his miracles, and others things he did. Probably the first stories to come together centered on his final days— his passion, Death, and Resurrection. This is why all four Gospels tell similar stories about Jesus' last days.

Mark.

The first Gospel to be written was the Gospel of Mark. It was written in Rome during and after Nero's persecution in the second half of the 60s. In the 80s, the authors of the Gospels of Matthew and Luke, using Mark's Gospel as a starting point, wrote their own Gospels for their specific Christian communities. Matthew, Mark, and Luke, though writing about Jesus in different ways, tell stories that are similar enough to be read side by side. Because of their similarities, we call them the *Synoptic Gospels.* They also made use of a collection of Jesus' sayings. The Gospel of John was written in the mid-to-late 90s. It is very different in tone and theology. The last book of the New Testament to be written was Second Peter, shortly after the year 100.

Showing Our Love for the World

The Catholic Church has developed a large body of teaching on social justice issues, because action on behalf of justice and work to create a more just world are essential parts of preaching the Gospel. In the story of the Good Samaritan (Luke 10:29–37), Jesus makes clear our responsibility to care for those in need.

The major development of the social doctrine of the Church began in the 19th century, when the Gospel encountered the modern industrial society. There were new structures for the production of consumer goods, new concepts of society, new types of states and authorities, and new forms of labor and ownership.

Since that time the Church has been making judgments about economic and social matters that relate to the basic rights of individuals and communities. The Church's social teaching is a rich treasure of wisdom about how to build a just society and how to live holy lives amid the challenges of the modern world. The Catholic Church teaches this responsibility in the following themes of Catholic Social Teaching.

Life and Dignity of the Human Person

All human life is sacred, and all people must be respected and valued over material goods. We are called to ask whether our actions as a society respect or threaten the life and dignity of the human person.

Call to Family, Community, and Participation

Participation in family and community is central to our faith and to a healthy society. Families must be supported so that people can participate in society, build a community spirit, and promote the well-being of all, especially the poor and vulnerable.

Volunteers distribute free bottled water to survivors of Hurricane Jeanne, Florida.

Rights and Responsibilities

Every person has a right to life as well as a right to those things required for human decency. As Catholics, we have a responsibility to protect these basic human rights in order to achieve a healthy society.

Option for the Poor and Vulnerable

In our world, many people are rich while others are poor. As Catholics, we are called to pay special attention to the needs of the poor by defending and promoting their dignity and meeting their immediate material needs.

The Dignity of Work and the Rights of Workers

The basic rights of workers must be respected: the right to productive work, fair wages, and private property; the right to organize, join unions, and pursue economic opportunity. Catholics believe that the economy is meant to serve people and that work is not merely a way to make a living, but an important way in which we participate in God's creation.

Solidarity

Because God is our Father, we are all brothers and sisters with the responsibility to care for one another. Solidarity is the attitude that leads Christians to share spiritual and material goods. Solidarity unites rich and poor, weak and strong, and helps create a society that recognizes that we depend on one another.

Care for God's Creation

God is the Creator of all people and all things, and he wants us to enjoy his creation. The responsibility to care for everything God has made is a requirement of our faith.

A teen weeds a native habitat restoration site, California.

Glossary

A

Abba an informal word for *father* in Aramaic, the language Jesus spoke. It is like "dad" in English. When Jesus spoke to God the Father, he called him "Abba."

abortion the deliberate ending of a pregnancy that results in the death of the unborn child. The Church teaches that since life begins at conception, abortion is a serious crime against life and is gravely against the moral law.

Abraham the model of faith in God in the Old Testament. Because of his faith, he left his home and traveled to Canaan, where God made a covenant with him that promised him land and many descendants. He became the father of the Chosen People.

absolution the forgiveness we receive from God through the priest in the Sacrament of Penance and Reconciliation

abstain the practice of denying oneself food, drink, or other pleasures. Catholics over age 14 abstain from eating meat on Ash Wednesday and on the Fridays of Lent.

actual grace the gift of God, freely given, that unites us with the life of the Trinity. Actual grace helps us make the choices that conform our lives to God's will.

adore to worship God above all else because he is our Creator. The First Commandment requires us to adore God alone.

adultery an injury to the marriage bond covenant. It occurs when a man or a woman who are married to each other has sexual relations with another person. The Sixth Commandment forbids adultery because it undermines the institution of marriage and is harmful to children, who need the stability of their parents' marriage commitment.

Advocate Jesus' name for the Holy Spirit. The Holy Spirit comforts us, speaks for us in difficult times, and makes Jesus present to us.

Alleluia an acclamation meaning "praise God." Alleluia is sung before the Gospel except during Lent.

altar the table in the church on which the priest celebrates Mass, where the sacrifice of Christ on the Cross is made present in the Sacrament of the Eucharist. The altar represents two aspects of the mystery of the Eucharist. It is the place where Jesus Christ offers himself for our sins and where he gives us himself as our food for eternal life.

ambo a raised stand from which a person reads the Word of God during Mass

Amen a Hebrew word meaning "it is so" or "let it be done." It signifies agreement with what has been said. Prayers in the New Testament, in the Church's liturgies, and the Creed end with *Amen*. In the Gospels, Jesus uses *Amen* to reinforce the seriousness of what he is about to say.

angel a spiritual creature who worships God in heaven. Angels serve God as messengers. They tell us of his plans for our salvation.

Angelus a prayer honoring the Incarnation of Jesus. The *Angelus* is prayed in the morning, at noon, and in the evening.

annulment a finding by a Church tribunal that at least one essential element for a real marriage was not present on the day of the wedding. The Church can declare that the Sacrament of Marriage did not take place if at least one of the parties was not freely choosing to marry, had been married before and that marriage was not annulled, or was not open to having children. An annulment cannot be considered until after a person is divorced. Catholics who receive an annulment are free to marry in the Church and can receive Communion.

Annunciation the announcement to Mary by the angel Gabriel that God had chosen her to be the mother of Jesus. When Mary agreed, the Son of God became human in her. The feast of the Annunciation is celebrated on March 25, nine months before Christmas.

anoint to put oil on things or people to dedicate them to the service of God. The anointing of the kings of Israel was a sign that they were chosen to rule God's people.

Anointing of the Sick one of the seven sacraments. In this sacrament, a sick person has the oil of the sick applied and receives the strength, peace, and courage to overcome the difficulties associated with illness. Through this sacrament, Jesus brings the sick person spiritual healing and forgiveness of sins. If it is God's will, healing of the body is given as well.

apostle one of twelve special men who accompanied Jesus in his ministry and were witnesses to the Resurrection. Apostle means "one sent." These were the people sent to preach the Gospel to the whole world.

Apostles' Creed a statement of Christian belief that developed out of a creed used in Baptism in Rome. The Apostles' Creed lists simple statements of belief in God the Father, Jesus Christ the Son, and the Holy Spirit. The profession of faith used in Baptism today is based on the Apostles' Creed.

apostolic one of the four Marks of the Church. The Church is apostolic because it continues to hand on the teaching of the apostles through their successors, the bishops, in union with the successor of Saint Peter, the pope.

Ark of the Covenant a portable box that held the tablets of the Ten Commandments. The Ark was the most important item in the shrine that was carried through the desert and then placed in the holiest part of the Temple in Jerusalem. Two angels are depicted on the cover of the Ark of the Covenant. The wings of the angels curve upward, representing the place where God came close to Israel and revealed his will.

Ascension the entry of Jesus into God's presence in heaven. In the Acts of the Apostles, it is written that Jesus, after his Resurrection, spent 40 days on earth, instructing his followers. He then returned to his Father in heaven.

Assumption Mary's being taken, body and soul, into heaven. Mary had a special relationship with her Son, Jesus, from the very beginning, when she conceived him. Because of this relationship, she enjoys a special participation in Jesus' Resurrection and has been taken into heaven where she now lives with him. We celebrate this event in the feast of the Assumption on August 15.

B

Baptism the first of the seven sacraments. Baptism frees us from Original Sin and is necessary for salvation. Baptism gives us new life in Jesus Christ through the Holy Spirit. The celebration of Baptism consists of immersing in water or pouring water upon a person while declaring that the person is baptized in the name of the Father, the Son, and the Holy Spirit.

Beatitudes the teachings of Jesus in the Sermon on the Mount in Matthew's Gospel. The Beatitudes are eight ways of living the Christian life. They are the fulfillment of the commandments given to Moses. These teachings present the way to true happiness.

benediction a prayer service in which we honor Jesus in the Blessed Sacrament and receive his blessing

Bible the collection of books containing the truths of God's Revelation to us. These writings were inspired by the Holy Spirit and written by human beings. The Bible is made up of the 46 books in the Old Testament and 27 books in the New Testament.

bishop a man who has received the fullness of Holy Orders. As a successor to the original apostles, he takes care of the Church and is a principal teacher in it.

blasphemy speaking or thinking words of hatred or defiance against God. It extends to language that disrespects the Church, the saints, or holy things. It is also blasphemy to use God's name as an excuse to enslave people, to torture them, or to put them to death. Using God's name to do these things can cause others to reject religion.

Blessed Sacrament the hosts, which are the Body of Christ, that have been consecrated at Mass. They are kept in the tabernacle to adore and to be taken to those who are sick.

blessing a prayer that calls for God's power and care upon some person, place, thing, or special activity

Body and Blood of Christ consecrated by the priest at Mass. In the Sacrament of the Eucharist, all of the risen Lord Jesus Christ—body, blood, soul, and divinity—is present under the appearances of bread and wine.

Buddhism a philosophy based on the teaching of Siddhartha Gautama, who was known as the Buddha, which means "Enlightened One." The Buddha was born to a royal family in northern India about five and a half centuries before Jesus. At age 29 he became disillusioned with life and left his comfortable home to find an answer to the question of why humans suffer.

C

calumny (slander) a false statement about the reputation of someone that makes other people think badly of that person. Calumny, also called *slander,* is a sin against the Eighth Commandment.

canon law the official laws that guide all aspects of Church life. Canon law assists the Church in its task of revealing and communicating God's saving power to the world.

capital sins those sins that can lead us to more serious sin. They are pride, avarice (greed), envy, wrath (anger), gluttony, lust, and sloth.

cardinal virtues the four main virtues that direct right living: prudence, justice, temperance, and fortitude. Cardinal comes from the Latin word *cardo,* which means "hinge."

catechumen a person being formed in the Christian life through instruction and by the example of the parish community. Through conversion and maturity of faith, a catechumen is preparing to be welcomed into the Church at Easter through the Sacraments of Baptism, Confirmation, and the Eucharist.

catechumenate the process of becoming a Christian through the Rite of Christian Initiation for Adults (RCIA). In the early Church, the process took several years.

catholic one of the four Marks of the Church. The Church is catholic because Jesus is fully present in it, because it proclaims the fullness of faith, and because Jesus has given the Church to the whole world. The Church is universal.

Catholic Social Teaching the body of teaching on social justice issues, action on behalf of justice, and work to create a more just world. The Church makes judgments about economic and social matters that relate to the basic rights of individuals and communities. The Church's social teaching is a rich treasure of wisdom about how to build a just society.

charity a virtue given to us by God that helps us love God above all things and love our neighbor as ourselves

chastity the integration of our physical sexuality with our spiritual nature. Chastity helps us be completely human, able to give to others our whole life and love. All people, married or single, are called to practice chastity.

chrism a perfumed oil, consecrated by a bishop, that is used in the Sacraments of Baptism, Confirmation, and Holy Orders. Anointing with chrism signifies the call of the baptized to the threefold ministry of priest, prophet, and king.

Christ a title that means "anointed one." It is from a Greek word that means the same thing as the Hebrew word *Messiah*, or "anointed." It is the name given to Jesus as priest, prophet, and king.

Christian the name given to all those who have been anointed through the gift of the Holy Spirit in Baptism and have become followers of Jesus Christ

Christmas the feast of the birth of Jesus (December 25)

Church the People of God throughout the whole world, or diocese (the local Church), or the assembly of those called together to worship God. The Church is one, holy, catholic, and apostolic.

clergy those men who are set apart as sacred ministers to serve the Church through Holy Orders

collegiality shared decision making between the pope and the bishops

commandment a standard, or rule, for living as God wants us to live. Jesus summarized all of the commandments into two: love God and love your neighbor.

Communion of Saints the unity of all, dead or living, who have been saved in Jesus Christ. The Communion of Saints is based on our one faith, and it is nourished by our participation in the Eucharist.

confession the act of telling our sins to a priest in the Sacrament of Penance and Reconciliation. The sacrament itself is sometimes referred to as "confession."

Confirmation the sacrament that completes the grace we receive in Baptism. It seals, or confirms, this grace through the seven Gifts of the Holy Spirit that we receive as part of Confirmation. This sacrament also makes us better able to participate in the worship and apostolic life of the Church.

conscience the inner voice that helps each of us judge the morality of our own actions. It guides us to follow God's law by doing good and avoiding evil.

consecration the making of a thing or a person to be special to God through a prayer or blessing. At Mass, the words of the priest are a consecration that transforms the bread and wine into the Body and Blood of Jesus Christ. People or objects set apart for God in a special way are also consecrated. For example, churches and altars are consecrated for use in liturgy, and bishops are consecrated as they receive the fullness of the Sacrament of Holy Orders.

contrition the sorrow we feel when we know that we have sinned, followed by the decision not to sin again. Perfect contrition arises from a love that loves God above all else. Imperfect contrition arises from other motives. Contrition is the most important act of the penitent preparing to celebrate the Sacrament of Penance and Reconciliation.

Corporal Works of Mercy kind acts by which we help our neighbors with their everyday material needs. Corporal Works of Mercy include feeding the hungry, giving drink to the thirsty, clothing the naked, sheltering the homeless, visiting the sick and the imprisoned, and burying the dead.

Council of Jerusalem the name of the meeting that happened about A.D. 50 that is described in chapter 15 of the Acts of the Apostles. The meeting was the result of a disagreement between Paul and his followers and the Jewish Christian followers of James, the leader of the Jerusalem Church. James felt that those who became Christians should also observe the rules of traditional Judaism and that the men should be circumcised. Paul said that there should be no such necessity. It was finally agreed that circumcision was not necessary for Gentiles who became Christians.

counsel one of the seven Gifts of the Holy Spirit. Counsel helps us make correct choices in life through reflection, discernment, consulting, and the advising of others.

covenant a solemn agreement between people or between people and God. God made covenants with humanity through agreements with Noah, Abraham, and Moses. These covenants offered salvation. God's new and final covenant was established through Jesus' life, Death, and Resurrection. *Testament* is another word for covenant.

covet to want to take what belongs to someone else. The Ninth and Tenth Commandments tell us it is sinful to covet.

creation God's act of making everything that exists outside himself. Creation is everything that exists. God said that all creation is good.

Creator God, who made everything that is and whom we can come to know through everything he created

creed a brief summary of what people believe. The word *creed* comes from the Latin *credo,* which means "I believe." The Nicene Creed is the most important summary of Christian beliefs.

culture the activity of a group of people that includes their music, art, language, and celebrations. Culture is one of the ways people experience God in their lives.

D

deacon a man ordained through the Sacrament of Holy Orders to the ministry of service in the Church. Deacons help the bishop and priests by serving in the various charitable ministries of the Church. They also help by proclaiming the Gospel, preaching, and assisting at the Liturgy of the Eucharist. Deacons can celebrate Baptisms, witness marriages, and preside at funerals.

detraction the act of talking about the faults and sins of another person to someone who has no reason to hear this and cannot help the person. Detraction damages the reputation of another person without any intent to help that person.

devil a spirit created good by God who became evil through disobedience. The devil tempted Adam and Eve to sin and still tempts us today. But God's grace is stronger than the works of the devil.

dignity of the human person a basic principle at the center of Catholic Social Teaching. It is the starting point of a moral vision for society because human life is sacred and should be treated with great respect. The human person is the clearest reflection of God among us.

dignity of work a basic principle at the center of Catholic Social Teaching. Since work is done by people created in the image of God, it is not only a way to make a living but an important way we participate in God's creation. In work, people fulfill part of their potential given to them by God. All workers have a right to productive work, to decent and fair wages, and to safe working conditions.

diocese the members of the Church in a particular area, united in faith and the sacraments, and gathered under the leadership of a bishop

disciple a person who has accepted Jesus' message and tries to live as he did, sharing his mission, his suffering, and his joys

discrimination the act of mistreating other people because of how they look or act, or just because they are different

Divine Providence the guidance of God over all he has created. Divine Providence exercises care for all creation and guides it toward its final perfection.

Doctor of the Church a man or a woman recognized as a model teacher of the Christian faith

doctrine the revealed teaching of Christ, which the Magisterium of the Church has declared Catholics are obliged to believe. Growth in the understanding of doctrine continues in the Church through the prayer and study of the faithful and theologians and through the teaching of the Magisterium.

E

Easter the celebration of the bodily raising of Jesus Christ from the dead. Easter is the festival of our redemption and the central Christian feast, the one from which other feasts arise.

Eastern Catholic Church a group of churches that developed in the East (in countries such as Lebanon) that are in union with the Roman Catholic Church, but have their own liturgical, theological, and administrative traditions. They show the truly catholic nature of the Church, which takes root in many cultures.

ecumenical council a gathering of Catholic bishops from the entire world, meeting under the leadership of the pope or his delegates. Ecumenical councils discuss pastoral, legal, and doctrinal issues. There have been 21 ecumenical councils recognized by the Catholic Church. The first was the First Council of Nicaea in 325. The most recent was the Second Vatican Council, which took place between 1962 and 1965.

ecumenism the movement for unity among Christians. Christ gave the Church the gift of unity from the beginning, but over the centuries that unity has been broken. All Christians are called by their common Baptism to pray and work to maintain, reinforce, and perfect the unity Christ wants for the Church.

Emmanuel a Hebrew name from the Old Testament that means "God with us." In Matthew's Gospel, Jesus is called Emmanuel.

encyclical a letter written by the pope and sent to the whole Church and sometimes to the whole world. It expresses Church teaching on specific and important issues.

epistle a letter written by Saint Paul or another leader to a group of Christians in the early Church. Of the 27 books of the New Testament, 21 are epistles. The second reading at Mass on Sundays and holy days is always from one of these books.

eternal life the never-ending life after death with God, granted to those who die as God's friends, with the grace of God alive in them

Eucharist the sacrament in which we give thanks to God for giving us Jesus Christ. The Body and Blood of Christ, which we receive at Mass, brings us into union with Jesus' saving Death and Resurrection.

Eucharistic Liturgy the public worship, held by the Church, in which bread and wine are transformed into the Body and Blood of Jesus Christ which we receive in Holy Communion. The Sunday celebration of the Eucharistic Liturgy is at the heart of Church life.

euthanasia an act with the intent to cause the death of a handicapped, sick, or dying person. Euthanasia is considered murder and is gravely contrary to the dignity of the human person and to the respect due to the living God, our Creator.

evangelist anyone engaged in spreading the gospel. Letters in the New Testament, along with the Acts of the Apostles, list evangelists along with apostles and prophets as ministers in the Church. The term is principally used to describe the writers of the four Gospels: Matthew, Mark, Luke, and John.

evangelization the sharing of the good news, by word or example, of the salvation we have received in Jesus Christ. Jesus commissioned his disciples to go forth into the world and tell the good news. Evangelization is the responsibility of every Christian. The New Evangelization calls believers to a deeper faith and invites those who have heard the Gospel but not been transformed by it to have a true encounter with Christ.

examination of conscience the act of prayerfully thinking about what we have said or done in light of what the Gospel asks of us. We also think about how our actions may have hurt our relationship with God or others. An examination of conscience is an important part of our preparing to celebrate the Sacrament of Penance and Reconciliation.

excommunication a severe penalty that is imposed by Church authorities for serious crimes against the Catholic religion. A person who is excommunicated is excluded from participating in the Eucharist and the other sacraments and from ministry in the Church.

Exile the period in the history of Israel between the destruction of Jerusalem in 587 B.C. and the return to Jerusalem in 537 B.C. During this time, many of the Jewish people were forced to live in Babylon, far from home.

Exodus God's liberation of the Hebrew people from slavery in Egypt and his leading them to the Promised Land

F

faith a gift of God that helps us believe in him. We profess our faith in the Creed, celebrate it in the sacraments, live by it through our good conduct of loving God and our neighbor, and express it in prayer. It is a personal adherence of the whole person to God, who has revealed himself to us through words and actions throughout history.

fasting limiting the amount we eat for a period of time to express sorrow for sin and to make ourselves more aware of God's action in our lives. Adults 18 years old and older fast on Ash Wednesday and Good Friday. The practice is also encouraged as a private devotion at other times of penitence.

fear of the Lord one of the seven Gifts of the Holy Spirit. This gift leads us to a sense of wonder and awe in the presence of God because we recognize his greatness.

fortitude the strength to choose to do the right thing, even when it is difficult. Fortitude is one of the four central human virtues, called the cardinal virtues, by which we guide our conduct through faith and the use of reason. It is also one of the Gifts of the Holy Spirit.

free will the ability to choose to do good because God has made us like him. Our free will is what makes us truly human. Our exercise of free will to do good increases our freedom. Using free will to choose sin makes us slaves to sin.

G

Gentiles the name given to foreign people by the Jews after the Exile. They were nonbelievers who worshiped false gods. They stand in contrast to the Jewish people, who received God's law.

Gifts of the Holy Spirit the permanent willingness, given to us by the Holy Spirit, that makes it possible for us to do what God asks of us. The Gifts of the Holy Spirit are wisdom, understanding, counsel, fortitude, knowledge, piety, and fear of the Lord.

Gospel the good news of God's mercy and love that we experience by hearing the story of Jesus' life, Death, and Resurrection. The story is passed on in the teaching ministry of the Church as the source of all truth and right living. It is presented to us in four books in the New Testament—the Gospels of Matthew, Mark, Luke, and John.

grace the gift of God, given to us without our meriting it. Sanctifying grace fills us with God's life and makes it possible for us always to be his friends. Grace is the Holy Spirit alive in us, helping us live out our Christian vocation. Grace helps us live as God wants us to.

Great Commandment Jesus' commandment that we are to love God and to love our neighbor as we love ourselves. Jesus tells us that this commandment sums up everything taught in the Old Testament.

greed too great a desire for wealth, material possessions, or power. It is also called *avarice* and is one of the seven deadly, or capital, sins.

H

heaven union with God the Father, Son, and Holy Spirit in life and love that never ends. Heaven is a state of complete happiness and the goal of the deepest wishes of the human heart.

Hebrews the descendants of Abraham, Isaac, and Jacob, who were enslaved in Egypt. God helped Moses lead these people out of slavery.

hell a life of total separation from God forever. In his infinite love for us, God can only desire our salvation. Hell is the result of the free choice of a person to reject God's love and forgiveness once and for all.

heresy a religious belief that opposes or denies any divinely revealed truth of the Catholic faith

holiness the fullness of Christian life and love. All people are called to holiness, which is made possible by cooperating with God's grace to do his will. As we do God's will, we are transformed more and more into the image of the Son, Jesus Christ.

holy one of the four Marks of the Church. It is the kind of life we live when we share in the life of God, who is all holiness. The Church is holy because it is united with Jesus Christ.

Holy Communion the reception of the Body and Blood of Christ during holy Mass. It brings us into union with Jesus Christ and his saving death and Resurrection.

holy days of obligation the principal feast days, other than Sundays, of the Church. On holy days of obligation, we celebrate the great things that God has done for us through Jesus and the saints. Catholics are obliged to participate in the Eucharist on these days, just as we are on Sundays.

Holy Family the family of Jesus as he grew up in Nazareth. It included Jesus; his mother, Mary; and his foster father, Joseph.

Holy of Holies the holiest part of the Temple in Jerusalem. The high priest entered this part of the Temple once a year to address God and to ask God's forgiveness for the sins of the people.

Holy Orders the sacrament through which the mission given by Jesus to his apostles continues in the Church. The sacrament has three degrees: deacon, priest, and bishop. Through the laying on of hands in the Sacrament of Holy Orders, men receive a permanent, sacramental mark that calls them to minister to the Church.

Holy Spirit the third Person of the Trinity, who is sent to us as our helper and, through Baptism and Confirmation, fills us with God's life. Together with the Father and the Son, the Holy Spirit brings the divine plan of salvation to completion.

homily the explanation by a bishop, a priest, or a deacon of the Word of God in the liturgy. The homily relates the Word of God to our life as Christians today.

hope the confidence that God will always be with us, make us happy now and forever, and help us live so that we will be with him forever

I

idolatry The worship of false gods, either a person or a thing, in place of worshiping God. Idolatry is worshiping a creature, which could be power, pleasure, or money, in place of the Creator. Idolatry is a sin against the First Commandment.

Immaculate Conception the Church teaching that Mary was free from Original Sin from the first moment of her life. She was preserved through the merits of her Son, Jesus, the Savior of the human race. It was declared a belief of the Catholic Church by Pope Pius IX in 1854 and is celebrated on December 8.

Incarnation the Son of God, Jesus, becoming human without the loss of his divinity in order to save us. The Son of God, the second Person of the Trinity, is both true God and true man.

indulgence a lessening of the punishment due for sins that have been forgiven. Indulgences move us toward our final purification, when we will live with God forever.

inerrancy the teaching of the Church that the Bible teaches the truths of the faith necessary for our salvation without error. Because God inspired the human authors, he is the author of the Sacred Scriptures. This gives us the assurance that they teach his saving truth without error, even though certain historical and scientific information may not be accurate. With the help of the Holy Spirit and the Church, we interpret what God wants to reveal to us about our salvation through the sacred authors.

infallibility the gift the Holy Spirit has given to the Church that assures that the pope and the bishops in union with the pope can proclaim as true the doctrines that involve faith or morals. It is an extension of the fact that the whole body of believers cannot be in error when it comes to questions of faith and morals.

Infancy Narrative accounts of the infancy and childhood of Jesus that appear in the first two chapters of Matthew's and Luke's Gospels. Each Gospel contains a different series of events. They have in common that Jesus was born in Bethlehem through the virginal conception of Mary. The intention of these stories is to proclaim Jesus as Messiah and Savior.

inspired influenced by the Holy Spirit. The human authors of Scripture were inspired by the Holy Spirit. The creative inspiration of the Holy Spirit makes sure that the Scripture is taught according to the truth God wants us to know for our salvation.

intercession prayer or petition on behalf of another or others. Intercession for others in prayer knows no boundaries and includes even those who might wish to do us harm.

interpretation explanation of the words of Scripture, combining human knowledge and the teaching office of the Church, under the guidance of the Holy Spirit

interreligious dialogue the work to build a relationship of openness with the followers of non-Christian religions. The Church's bond with non-Christian religions comes from our common bond as children of God. The purpose of this dialogue is to increase understanding of one another, to work for the common good of humanity, and to establish peace.

Islam the third great religion, along with Judaism and Christianity, professing belief in one God. *Islam* means "submission" to that one God.

Israelites the descendants of Abraham, Isaac, and Jacob. God changed Jacob's name to "Israel," and Jacob's 12 sons and their children became the leaders of the 12 tribes of Israel. (*See* Hebrews.)

J

Jesus the Son of God, who was born of the Virgin Mary and who died and was raised from the dead for our salvation. He returned to God and will come again to judge the living and the dead. His name means "God saves."

Jews the name given to the Hebrew people, from the time of the Exile to the present. The name means "the people who live in the territory of Judah," the area of Palestine surrounding Jerusalem.

Joseph the foster father of Jesus, who was engaged to Mary when the angel announced that Mary would have a child through the power of the Holy Spirit. In the Old Testament, Joseph was the son of Jacob who was sold into slavery in Egypt by his brothers and then saved them from starvation when famine came.

Judaism the name of the religion of Jesus and all the people of Israel after they returned from exile in Babylon and built the second Temple

justice the virtue that guides us to give to God and others what is due them. Justice is one of the four central human virtues, called the cardinal virtues, by which we guide our Christian life.

justification being in a right relationship with God through moral conduct and observance of the Law. We have merit in God's sight and are able to do this because of the work of God's grace in us. Paul speaks of justification in a new way that is no longer dependent on observance of the Law. It comes through faith in Jesus and in his saving Death and Resurrection. To be justified or made righteous in Jesus is to be saved, vindicated, and put right with God through his grace.

K

Kingdom of God God's rule over us, announced in the Gospel and present in the Eucharist. The beginning of the kingdom here on earth is mysteriously present in the Church, and it will come in completeness at the end of time.

knowledge one of the seven Gifts of the Holy Spirit. This gift helps us know what God asks of us and how we should respond.

L

laity those who have been made members of Christ in Baptism and who participate in the priestly, prophetic, and kingly functions of Christ in his mission to the whole world. The laity is distinct from the clergy, whose members are set apart as ministers to serve the Church.

Last Judgment the final judgment of all human beings that will occur when Christ returns in glory and all appear in their own bodies before him to give an account of all their deeds in life. In the presence of Christ, the truth of each person's relationship with God will be laid bare, as will the good each person has done or failed to do during his or her earthly life. At that time God's kingdom will come in its fullness.

Last Supper the last meal Jesus ate with his disciples on the night before he died. At the Last Supper, Jesus took bread and wine, blessed them, and they became his Body and Blood, Soul and Divinity. Jesus' Death and Resurrection, his sacrifice that we celebrate in the Eucharist, were anticipated in this meal.

Law the first five books of the Old Testament. The Hebrew word for *law* is *Torah*. The ancient law is summarized in the Ten Commandments.

Lectionary the official book that contains all the Scripture readings used in the Liturgy of the Word

Lent the 40 days before Easter (not counting Sundays) during which we prepare, through prayer, fasting, and giving aid to the poor, to change our lives and to live the Gospel more completely

liturgical year the celebrations throughout the year of all the mysteries of Jesus' birth, life, Death, and Resurrection. The celebration of Easter is at the heart of the liturgical year. The other feasts celebrated throughout the year make up the basic rhythm of the Christian's life of prayer.

liturgy the public prayer of the Church that celebrates the wonderful things God has done for us in Jesus Christ, our high priest, and the way in which he continues the work of our salvation. The original meaning of *liturgy* was "a public work or service done for the people."

Liturgy of the Eucharist the second half of the Mass, in which the bread and wine are transformed into the Body and Blood of Jesus Christ, which we then receive in Holy Communion

Liturgy of the Hours the public prayer of the Church to praise God and to sanctify the day. It includes an office of readings before sunrise, morning prayer at dawn, evening prayer at sunset, and prayer before going to bed. The chanting of psalms makes up the major portion of each of these services.

Liturgy of the Word the first half of the Mass, in which we listen to God's Word from the Bible and consider what it means for us today. The Liturgy of the Word can also be a public prayer and proclamation of God's Word that is not followed by the Liturgy of the Eucharist.

Lord the name used for God to replace *Yahweh*, the name he revealed to Moses, which was considered too sacred to pronounce. It indicates the divinity of Israel's God. The New Testament uses the title *Lord* for both the Father and for Jesus, recognizing him as God himself. (*See* Yahweh.)

Lord's Day Sunday is the day Christians set aside for special worship of God. Each Sunday Mass commemorates the Resurrection of Jesus on Easter Sunday. Besides requiring us to offer God the worship owed him, the Third Commandment tells us Sunday is a day to relax the mind and body and to perform works of mercy.

M

Magisterium the living, teaching office of the Church. This office, through the bishops and with the pope, provides an authentic interpretation of the Word of God. It ensures faithfulness to the teaching of the apostles in matters of faith and morals.

Magnificat Mary's song of praise to God for the great things he has done for her and planned for us through Jesus

Marks of the Church the four most important aspects of the Church found in the Nicene Creed. According to the Nicene Creed, the Church is one, holy, catholic, and apostolic.

martyrs those who have given their lives for the faith. *Martyr* comes from the Greek word for "witness." A martyr is the supreme witness to the truth of the faith and to Christ to whom he or she is united. The seventh chapter of the Acts of the Apostles recounts the death of the first martyr, the deacon Stephen.

Mary the mother of Jesus. She is called blessed and "full of grace" because God chose her to be the mother of the Son of God, the second Person of the Trinity.

Mass the most important sacramental celebration of the Church, established by Jesus at the Last Supper as a remembrance of his Death and Resurrection. At Mass, we listen to God's Word from the Bible and receive the Body and Blood of Jesus Christ in Holy Communion.

Matrimony a solemn agreement between a woman and a man to be partners for life, both for their own good and for bringing up children. Marriage is a sacrament when the agreement is properly made between baptized Christians.

meditation a form of prayer using silence and listening that seeks through imagination, emotion, and desire to understand how to adhere and respond to what God is asking. By concentrating on a word or an image, we move beyond thoughts, empty the mind of contents that get in the way of our experience of God, and rest in simple awareness of God. It is one of the three major expressions of the life of prayer.

Mendicant Order a unique variety of religious order that developed in the 13th century. Unlike monks who remain inside a monastery, members of Mendicant Orders have ministries of preaching, teaching, and witnessing within cities. They are called *mendicant* from the Latin word for "begging," which is their main means of supporting themselves. The two main Mendicant Orders are the Dominicans, founded by Saint Dominic de Guzman, and the Franciscans, founded by Saint Francis of Assisi.

Messiah a title that means "anointed one." It is from a Hebrew word that means the same thing as the Greek word *Christ*. Messiah is the title that was given to Jesus as priest, prophet, and king.

miracles signs or acts of wonder that cannot be explained by natural causes but are works of God. In the Gospels, Jesus works miracles as a sign that the Kingdom of God is present in his ministry.

mission the work of Jesus Christ that is continued in the Church through the Holy Spirit. The mission of the Church is to proclaim salvation in Jesus' life, Death, and Resurrection.

missionary one who proclaims the Gospel to others and leads them to know Christ. Missionaries are lay, ordained, and religious people engaged in mission.

monasticism a form of religious life in which men and women live out their vows of poverty, chastity, and obedience in a stable community life in a monastery. The goal of monasticism is to pursue, under the guidance of a rule, a life of public prayer, work, and meditation for the glory of God. Saint Benedict of Nursia, who died around A.D. 550, is considered the father of Western monasticism.

moral choice a choice to do what is right or not do what is wrong. We make moral choices because they are what we believe God wants and because we have the freedom to choose what is right and avoid what is wrong.

moral law a rule for living that has been established by God and people in authority who are concerned about the good of all. Moral laws are based on God's direction to us to do what is right and avoid what is wrong. Some moral laws are "written" in the human heart and can be known through our own reasoning. Other moral laws have been revealed to us by God in the Old Testament and in the new law given by Jesus.

mortal sin a serious decision to turn away from God by doing something that we know is wrong. For a sin to be mortal it must be a very serious offense, and the person must know how serious the sin is and freely choose to do it anyway.

Mother of God the title for Mary proclaimed at the Council of Ephesus in 431. The council declared that Mary was not just the mother of Jesus, the man. She became the Mother of God by the conception of the Son of God in her womb. Because Jesus' humanity is one with his divinity, Mary is the mother of the eternal Son of God made man, who is God himself.

Muslim a follower of the religion of Islam. *Muslim* means "one who submits to God."

mystagogy the last stage of the Rite of Christian Initiation of Adults, in which the newly initiated reflect on the deep meaning of the sacraments they have celebrated and on living the Christian life fully

mystery a religious truth that we can know only through God's Revelation and that we cannot fully understand. Our faith is a mystery that we profess in the Creed and celebrate in the liturgy and sacraments.

Mystical Body of Christ the members of the Church formed into a spiritual body and bound together by the life communicated by Jesus Christ through the sacraments. Christ is the center and source of the life of this body. In it, we are all united. Each member of the body receives from Christ gifts fitting for him or her.

N

natural law the moral law that is "written" in the human heart. We can know natural law through our own reason because the Creator has placed the knowledge of it in our hearts. It can provide the solid foundation on which we can make rules to guide our choices in life. Natural law forms the basis of our fundamental rights and duties and is the foundation for the work of the Holy Spirit in guiding our moral choices.

New Testament the 27 books of the second part of the Bible, which tell of the teaching, ministry, and saving events of the life of Jesus. The four Gospels present Jesus' life, Death, and Resurrection. The Acts of the Apostles tells the story of the message of salvation as it spread through the growth of the Church. Various letters instruct us in how to live as followers of Jesus Christ. The Book of Revelation offers encouragement to Christians living through persecution.

Nicene Creed the summary of Christian beliefs developed by the bishops at the first two councils of the Church, held in A.D. 325 and 381. It is the Creed shared by most Christians in the East and in the West.

O

obedience the act of willingly following what God asks us to do for our salvation. The Fourth Commandment requires children to obey their parents, and all people are required to obey civil authority when it acts for the good of all. To imitate the obedience of Jesus, members of religious communities make a special vow of obedience.

Old Testament the first 46 books of the Bible, which tell of God's Covenant with the people of Israel and his plan for the salvation of all people. The first five books are known as the Torah. The Old Testament is fulfilled in the New Testament, but God's covenant presented in the Old Testament has permanent value and has never been revoked.

one one of the four Marks of the Church. The Church is one because of its source in the one God and because of its founder, Jesus Christ. Jesus, through his Death on the Cross, united all to God in one body. Within the unity of the Church, there is great diversity because of the variety of the gifts given to its members.

Ordinary Time the part of the liturgical year outside of the seasons and feasts and the preparation for them. *Ordinary* means not common but counted time, as in ordinal numbers. It is devoted to growth in understanding the mystery of Christ in its fullness. The color of Ordinary Time is green to symbolize growth.

ordination the rite of the Sacrament of Holy Orders, by which a bishop gives to men, through the laying on of hands, the ability to minister to the Church as bishops, priests, and deacons

Original Sin the consequence of the disobedience of the first human beings. They disobeyed God and chose to follow their own will rather than God's will. As a result, human beings lost the original blessing God had intended and became subject to sin and death. In Baptism, we are restored to life with God through Jesus Christ, although we still experience the effects of Original Sin.

P

parable one of the simple stories that Jesus told to show us what the Kingdom of God is like. Parables present images drawn from everyday life. These images show us the radical choice we make when we respond to the invitation to enter the Kingdom of God.

parish a stable community of believers in Jesus Christ, who meet regularly in a specific area to worship God under the leadership of a pastor

particular judgment a judgment made by Christ received by every person at the moment of death that offers either entrance into heaven (after a period of purification, if needed) or immediate and eternal separation from God in hell. At the moment of death, each person is rewarded by Christ in accordance with his or her works and faith.

Paschal Mystery the work of salvation accomplished by Jesus Christ through his passion, Death, Resurrection, and Ascension. The Paschal Mystery is celebrated in the liturgy of the Church, and we experience its saving effects in the sacraments. In every liturgy of the Church, God the Father is blessed and adored as the source of all blessings we have received through his Son in order to make us his children through the Holy Spirit.

Passover the Jewish festival that commemorates the delivery of the Hebrew people from slavery in Egypt. In the Eucharist, we celebrate our passover from death to life through Jesus' Death and Resurrection.

penance the turning away from sin with a desire to change our life and more closely live the way God wants us to live. We express our penance externally by praying, fasting, and helping the poor. This is also the name of the action that the priest asks us to take or the prayers that he asks us to pray after he absolves us in the Sacrament of Penance and Reconciliation. (*See* Sacrament of Penance and Reconciliation.)

Penitential Act that part of the Mass before the Liturgy of the Word in which we ask God's forgiveness for our sins. The Penitential Act prepares us to celebrate the Eucharist.

Pentateuch Greek for "five books." It refers to the first five books of the Bible: Genesis, Exodus, Leviticus, Numbers, and Deuteronomy. The Pentateuch tells of Creation, the beginning of God's special people, and the Covenant. In Hebrew it is called *Torah*, which means "law."

Pentecost the 50th day after Jesus was raised from the dead. On this day, the Holy Spirit was sent from heaven, and the Church was born. It is also the Jewish feast that celebrated the giving of the Ten Commandments on Mount Sinai 50 days after the Exodus.

perjury lying while under oath or making a promise under oath without planning to keep it. Perjury is both a sin and a crime. Perjury is a violation of the Second and Eighth Commandments.

personal sin a sin we choose to commit, whether serious (mortal) or less serious (venial). Although the consequences of Original Sin leave us with a tendency to sin, God's grace, especially through the sacraments, helps us choose good over sin.

Pharisees a party or sect in Judaism that began more than 100 years before Jesus. They saw Judaism as a religion centered on the observance of the Law. The Gospels present a picture of mutual hostility between Jesus and the Pharisees. Pharisees were later found in the Christian community in Jerusalem. (Acts of the Apostles 15:5) Paul was proud to call himself a Pharisee.

piety one of the seven Gifts of the Holy Spirit. It calls us to be faithful in our relationships, both with God and with others. Piety helps us love God and behave responsibly and with generosity and affection toward others.

pope the Bishop of Rome, successor of Saint Peter, and leader of the Roman Catholic Church. Because he has the authority to act in the name of Christ, the pope is called the Vicar of Christ. The pope and all the bishops together make up the living, teaching office of the Church, the Magisterium.

poverty a vow taken by religious men and women to live a simple lifestyle and to give up control of material possessions

prayer the raising of our hearts and minds to God. We are able to speak to and listen to God in prayer because he teaches us how to pray.

prayer of petition a request to God asking him to fulfill a need. When we share in God's saving love, we understand that every need is one that we can ask God to help us with through petition.

precepts of the Church those positive requirements that the pastoral authority of the Church has determined are necessary to provide a minimum effort in prayer and the moral life. The precepts of the Church ensure that all Catholics move beyond the minimum by growing in love of God and love of neighbor.

pride a false image of ourselves that goes beyond what we deserve as God's creation. Pride puts us in competition with God. It is one of the seven capital sins.

priest a man who has accepted God's special call to serve the Church by guiding it and building it up through the ministry of the Word and the celebration of the sacraments

priesthood all the people of God who have been given a share of the one mission of Christ through the Sacraments of Baptism and Confirmation. The ministerial priesthood, which is made up of those men who have been ordained bishops and priests in Holy Orders, is essentially different from the priesthood of the faithful because its work is to build up and to guide the Church in the name of Christ.

prophet one called to speak for God and to call the people to be faithful to the Covenant. A major section of the Old Testament presents the messages and actions of the prophets.

Protestant Reformation a religious, political, and economic movement that swept Europe in the 16th and 17th centuries and separated Protestants from the Catholic Church. The Catholic Reformation, or Counter-Reformation, was an attempt to respond to the major concerns of the Reformers by a sincere reform within the Catholic Church.

prudence the virtue that directs us toward the good and helps us choose the correct means to achieve that good. When we act with prudence, we carefully and thoughtfully consider our actions. Prudence is one of the cardinal moral virtues that guide our conscience and influence us to live according to the law of Christ.

psalm a prayer in the form of a poem, written to be sung in public worship. Each psalm expresses an aspect of the depth of human prayer. Over several centuries, 150 psalms were assembled into the Book of Psalms in the Old Testament. Psalms were used in worship in the Temple in Jerusalem, and they have been used in the public worship of the Church since its beginning.

purgatory a state of final cleansing after death of all our human imperfections to prepare us to enter into the joy of God's presence in heaven

R

racism the opinion that race determines human traits and capacities and that a particular race has an inherent, or inborn, superiority. Discrimination based on a person's race is a violation of human dignity and a sin against justice.

rationalism an approach to philosophy developed by René Descartes. It dominated European thought in the 17th and 18th centuries. The main belief of rationalism was that human reason is the principal source of all knowledge. It stresses confidence in the orderly character of the world and in the mind's ability to make sense of this order. Rationalism recognizes as true only those religious beliefs that can be rationally explained.

real presence the way in which the risen Jesus Christ is present in the Eucharist under the appearances of bread and wine. Jesus Christ's presence is called real because in the Eucharist, his Body and Blood, soul and divinity, are wholly and entirely present.

reconciliation the renewal of friendship after that friendship has been broken by some action or lack of action. In the Sacrament of Penance and Reconciliation, through God's mercy and forgiveness, we are reconciled with God, the Church, and others.

Redeemer Jesus Christ, whose life, sacrificial Death on the Cross, and Resurrection from the dead set us free from the slavery of sin and bring us redemption

redemption our being set free from the slavery of sin through the life, sacrificial Death on the Cross, and Resurrection from the dead of Jesus Christ

religious life a state of life recognized by the Church. In the religious life, men and women freely respond to a call to follow Jesus by living the vows of poverty, chastity, and obedience in community with others.

Resurrection the bodily raising of Jesus Christ from the dead on the third day after his Death on the Cross. The Resurrection is the crowning truth of our faith.

Revelation God's communication of himself to us through the words and deeds he has used throughout history to show us the mystery of his plan for our salvation. This Revelation reaches its completion in his sending of his Son, Jesus Christ.

rite one of the many forms followed in celebrating liturgy in the Church. A rite may differ according to the culture or country where it is celebrated. A *rite* is the special form for celebrating each sacrament.

Rite of Christian Initiation of Adults (RCIA) a series of rituals, accompanied by religious instruction, through which a person is formed in the Christian life through instruction and by the example of the parish community. Through conversion and maturity of faith, a catechumen is preparing to be welcomed into the Church at Easter through the Sacraments of Baptism, Confirmation, and Eucharist. Baptized Christians who are preparing to be received into full communion with the Roman Catholic Church may also take part in the Rite of Christian Initiation of Adults.

Roman Missal the book containing the prayers used for the celebration of the Eucharist. It is placed on the altar for the celebrant to use during Mass.

Rosary a prayer in honor of the Blessed Virgin Mary. When we pray the Rosary, we meditate on the mysteries of Jesus Christ's life while praying the Hail Mary on 5 sets of 10 beads and the Lord's Prayer on the beads in between. In the Latin Church, praying the Rosary became a way for ordinary people to reflect on the mysteries of Christ's life.

S

Sabbath the seventh day, when God rested after finishing the work of creation. The Third Commandment requires us to keep the Sabbath holy. For Christians, Sunday became the Sabbath because it was the day Jesus rose from the dead and the new creation in Jesus Christ began.

sacrament one of seven official rites through which God's life enters our lives in the liturgy through the work of the Holy Spirit. Christ's work in the liturgy is sacramental because his mystery is made present there by the power of the Holy Spirit. Jesus gave us three sacraments that bring us into the Church: Baptism, Confirmation, and the Eucharist. He gave us two sacraments that bring us healing: Penance and Reconciliation and Anointing of the Sick. He also gave us two sacraments that help members serve the community: Matrimony and Holy Orders. (*See also* sacramental.)

Sacrament of Penance and Reconciliation the sacrament in which we celebrate God's forgiveness of sin and our reconciliation with God and the Church. Penance and Reconciliation includes sorrow for the sins we have committed, confession of sins, absolution by the priest, and doing the penance that shows our willingness to amend our ways.

sacramental an object, a prayer, or a blessing given by the Church to help us grow in our spiritual life

Sacraments at the Service of Communion the Sacraments of Holy Orders and Matrimony. These two sacraments contribute to the personal salvation of individuals by giving them a way to serve others.

Sacraments of Healing the Sacraments of Penance and Reconciliation and Anointing of the Sick, by which the Church continues the healing ministry of Jesus for soul and body

Sacraments of Initiation the sacraments that are the foundation of our Christian life. We are born anew in Baptism, strengthened by Confirmation, and receive in the Eucharist the food of eternal life. By means of these sacraments, we receive an increasing measure of divine life and advance toward the perfection of charity.

sacrifice a ritual offering of animals or produce made to God by the priest in the Temple in Jerusalem. Sacrifice was a sign of the people's adoration of God, giving thanks to God, or asking for his forgiveness. Sacrifice also showed union with God. The great high priest, Christ, accomplished our redemption through the perfect sacrifice of his Death on the Cross.

Sacrifice of the Mass the sacrifice of Jesus on the Cross, which is remembered and mysteriously made present in the Eucharist. It is offered in reparation for the sins of the living and of the dead and to obtain spiritual or temporal blessings from God.

sacrilege deliberate damage or harm to a sacred person, place, or thing. A sacrilege can be a mortal or venial sin, depending on the seriousness of the evil done.

saint a holy person who has died united with God. The Church has said that this person is now with God forever in heaven.

salvation the gift, which God alone can give, of forgiveness of sin and the restoration of friendship with him

salvation history the story of God's loving relationship with his people, which tells how God carries out his plan to save all people

sanctify to make holy, to separate from sin, to set aside for sacred use, to consecrate

sanctifying grace the gift of God, given to us without our earning it, that introduces us to the intimacy of the Trinity, unites us with its life, and heals our human nature that has been wounded by sin. Sanctifying grace helps us respond to our vocation as God's adopted children, and it continues the work of making us holy that began at our Baptism.

Satan the enemy of anyone attempting to follow God's will. Satan tempts Jesus in the Gospels and opposes his ministry. In Jewish, Christian, and Muslim thought, Satan is associated with those angels who refused to bow down before human beings and serve them as God commanded. They were thrown out of heaven as a punishment. Satan and the other demons tempt human beings to join them in their revolt against God.

Savior Jesus, the Son of God, who became human to forgive our sins and to restore our friendship with God. *Jesus* means "God saves."

scandal leading another person to sin by bad example

schism a willful split or separation in the Church, stemming from a refusal to obey lawful authority

Scripture the holy writings of Jews and Christians collected in the Old and New Testaments of the Bible

Second Vatican Council the 21st and most recent ecumenical council of the Catholic Church. It met from October 11, 1962 to December 8, 1965. Its purpose, according to Pope Saint John XXIII, was to renew the Church and to help it promote peace and unity among Christians and all humanity.

Sermon on the Mount the words of Jesus, written in chapters 5 through 7 of the Gospel of Matthew, in which Jesus reveals how he has fulfilled God's law given to Moses. The Sermon on the Mount begins with the eight Beatitudes and includes the Lord's Prayer.

sexism a prejudice or discrimination based on sex, especially discrimination against women. Sexism leads to behaviors and attitudes that foster a view of social roles based only on sex.

sin a deliberate thought, word, deed, or failure to act that offends God and hurts our relationships with other people. Some sin is mortal and needs to be confessed in the Sacrament of Penance and Reconciliation. Other sin is venial, or less serious.

social justice the fair and equal treatment of every member of society. It is required by the dignity and freedom of every person. The Catholic Church has developed a body of social principles and moral teachings described in papal and other official documents issued since the late 19th century. This teaching deals with the economic, political, and social order of the world. It is rooted in the Bible as well as in the traditional theological teachings of the Church.

social sin social situations and institutions that are against the will of God. Because of the personal sins of individuals, entire societies can develop structures that are sinful in and of themselves. Social sins include racism, sexism, structures that deny people access to adequate health care, and the destruction of the environment for the benefit of a few.

Son of God the title revealed by Jesus that indicates his unique relationship to God the Father. The revelation of Jesus' divine sonship is the main dramatic development of the story of Jesus of Nazareth as it unfolds in the Gospels.

soul the part of us that makes us human and an image of God. Body and soul together form one unique human nature. The soul is responsible for our consciousness and for our freedom. The soul does not die and is reunited with the body in the final resurrection.

Spiritual Works of Mercy the kind acts through which we help our neighbors meet the needs that are more than material. The Spiritual Works of Mercy include counseling the doubtful, instructing the ignorant, admonishing sinners, comforting the afflicted, forgiving offenses, bearing wrongs patiently, and praying for the living and the dead.

spirituality our growing, loving relationship with God. Spirituality is our way of expressing our experience of God in both the way we pray and the way we love our neighbor. There are many different schools of spirituality. Some examples of these schools are the monastic, Franciscan, Jesuit, and lay. These are guides for the spiritual life and have enriched the traditions of prayer, worship, and living in Christianity.

suicide the act of deliberately and intentionally taking one's own life. Because we are stewards, not owners, of the life God has given us, suicide is a sin against the Fifth Commandment. But serious psychological disturbances, fears, and suffering can lessen the responsibility of the person committing suicide. By ways known to him alone, God can offer salvation to people who have taken their own life. The Church encourages us to pray for such people.

Summa Theologiae the major work of Saint Thomas Aquinas that organized and clarified thinking on many religious topics in the 13th century. In it Thomas addressed topics such as proof for the existence of God, the nature of the human soul, making moral decisions, the Incarnation, and transubstantiation.

synagogue the Jewish place of assembly for prayer, instruction, and study of the Law. After the destruction of the Temple in 587 B.C., synagogues were organized as places to maintain Jewish faith and worship. Jesus attended the synagogue regularly to pray and to teach. Paul went to the synagogue first in every city he visited. The synagogue played an important role in the development of Christian worship and in the structure of Christian communities.

Synoptic from the Greek word meaning to "see together," it describes the Gospels of Matthew, Mark, and Luke. These are called the Synoptic Gospels because although they are different from one another, there are similarities that can be seen by looking at them together. Most Scripture scholars agree that Mark was the first Gospel written and that Matthew and Luke used Mark as the pattern for their Gospels.

T

tabernacle the container in which the Blessed Sacrament is kept so that Holy Communion can be taken to the sick and the dying. *Tabernacle* is also the name of the tent sanctuary in which the Israelites kept the Ark of the Covenant from the time of the Exodus to the construction of Solomon's Temple.

temperance the cardinal virtue that helps us control our attraction to pleasure so that our natural desires are kept within proper limits. This moral virtue helps us choose to use created goods in moderation.

Temple the house of worship of God, first built by Solomon. The Temple provided a place for the priests to offer sacrifice, to adore and give thanks to God, and to ask for forgiveness. It was destroyed and rebuilt. The second Temple was also destroyed, this time by the Romans in A.D. 70, and was never rebuilt. Part of the outer wall of the Temple mount remains to this day in Jerusalem.

temptation an attraction, from outside us or inside us, that can lead us to disobey God's commands. Everyone is tempted, but the Holy Spirit helps us resist temptation and choose to do good.

Ten Commandments the 10 rules given by God to Moses on Mount Sinai that sum up God's law and show us what is required to love God and our neighbor. By following the Ten Commandments, the Hebrews accepted their Covenant with God.

Theological Virtues those virtues given us by God and not by human effort. They are faith, hope, and charity.

Torah the Hebrew word for "instruction" or "law." It is also the name of the first five books of the Old Testament: Genesis, Exodus, Leviticus, Numbers, and Deuteronomy.

Tradition the beliefs and practices of the Church that are passed down from one generation to the next under the guidance of the Holy Spirit. What Christ entrusted to the apostles was handed on to others both orally and in writing. Tradition and Scripture together make up the single deposit of the Word of God, which remains present and active in the Church.

transubstantiation the unique transformation of the bread and wine in the Eucharist into the Body and Blood of the risen Jesus Christ, while retaining its physical appearance as bread and wine

Trinity the mystery of the existence of God in three Persons—the Father, the Son, and the Holy Spirit. Each Person is God, whole and entire. Each is distinct only in the relationship of each to the others.

U

understanding one of the seven Gifts of the Holy Spirit. This gift helps us make the right choices in life and in our relationships with God and others.

V

venial sin a choice we make that weakens our relationship with God or with other people. Venial sin wounds and lessens the divine life in us. If we make no effort to do better, venial sin can lead to more serious sin. Through our participation in the Eucharist, venial sin is forgiven when we are repentant, strengthening our relationship with God and with others.

viaticum the Eucharist that a dying person receives. It is spiritual food for the last journey we make as Christians, the journey through death to eternal life.

virtue an attitude or way of acting that enables us do good

vocation the call each of us has in life to be the person God wants each to be and the way we each serve the Church and the Kingdom of God. Each of us can live out his or her vocation as a layperson, as a member of a religious community, or as a member of the clergy.

vow a deliberate and free promise made to God by people who want especially to dedicate their lives to God. The vows give witness now to the kingdom that is to come.

W

wisdom one of the seven Gifts of the Holy Spirit. Wisdom helps us understand the purpose and plan of God and live in a way that helps bring about this plan. It begins in wonder and awe at God's greatness.

witness the passing on to others, by our words and by our actions, the faith that we have been given. Every Christian has the duty to give witness to the good news about Jesus Christ that he or she has come to know.

worship the adoration and honor given to God in public prayer

Y

Yahweh the name of God in Hebrew, which God told Moses from the burning bush. *Yahweh* means "I am who am" or "I cause to be all that is."

Index

A

Abba, 5, 253
abortion, 105–6, 253
Abraham, 253
absolution, 96, 99, 101, 253
abstain, 253
Act of Contrition, 101, 233, 248
Acts of the Apostles, 25
actual grace, 253
adore, 253
adultery, 131, 253
Advent, 217–18
Advocate, 227, 253
ageism, 107
Agnes, Saint, 136
Agnus Dei, 235
All Saints Day, 215
Alleluia, 253
altar, 253
ambo, 253
Ambrose, Saint, 6
Amen, 253
André Bessette, Saint, 94
Andrew of Crete, Saint, 6
Andrew Dũng-Lạc, Saint, 178
Andrew the Apostle, Saint, 53, 60
angel, 253
Angelus, 253
anger, 105
Annas, 28
annulment, 253
Annunciation, 35, 37, 253
anoint, 253
Anointing of the Sick, Sacrament of the, 101, 253
  anointing, 98
  healing power, 95, 244
  laying on of hands, 98
Anthony Claret, Saint, 120
apostle, 11, 52, 57, 179, 253. *See also* disciple; *specific apostles*
  twelve, chosen, 52
Apostles' Creed, 236, 253
apostolic, 254. *See also* Marks of the Church
Aramaic, 30
Archelaus, 28
Ark of the Covenant, 254
Ascension, 5, 9, 183, 185, 209, 254
Assumption, 37, 38, 254
Augustine, Saint, 6, 125
Ave Maria, 235. *See also* Hail Mary

B

Baptism, Sacrament of, 67, 209, 244, 254
  gifts received through, 63, 193
  God calls us through, 195
  marked forever by, 63
  risen Jesus encountered through, 181
  symbols used during, 64
Bartholomew, Saint, 53
Beatitudes, 113–16, 119, 215, 241, 254
benediction, 254
Bernadette, Saint, 38
Bethlehem, 27
Bible, 249–50, 254. *See also* New Testament; Old Testament
bishops, 254
  mission, 199
  ordination, 197
  successors of apostles, 55
blasphemy, 254
Blessed Sacrament, 254
blessing, 254
Body and Blood of Christ, 163, 254. *See also* Eucharist, Sacrament of the
Book of Revelation, 25
Bread of Life, 163, 164. *See also* Eucharist, Sacrament of the
Buddhism, 254

C

Caesar, Augustus, 28
Caesar, Tiberius, 28
calumny (slander), 254
Cana wedding feast, 88
canon law, 254
capital punishment, 107
capital sins, 254
cardinal virtues, 149, 150, 151, 243, 254, 153
catechumen, 254
catholic, 255. *See also* Marks of the Church
Catholic Social Teaching, 121, 125, 251–2, 255
charity, 150, 153, 243, 255
chastity, 132, 133, 198, 243, 255. *See also* self-control
choices, right
  freedom of choice, 247
  guides to help us, 247
  Ten Commandments as model for, 247
chrism, 255
Christ, 5, 255. *See also* Jesus; Messiah
  name, meaning of, 43
  roles of, 47
Christian, 255
Christmas, 219–20, 255
Church, 255
  birth, at Pentecost, 189, 190
  community, 189–191
  early growth of, 189
  vision of, 189
Clement of Alexandria, 6
clergy, 255
Collect Prayer of the Common of Holy Men and Women, 216
collegiality, 255
commandment, 255
Commandment, Great, 241
Commandment, New, 164, 167, 241
Commandments, Ten, 242, 266
  Eighth, 125, 126, 127, 254
  Fifth, 105, 111, 143
  model for living, 247
  Ninth, 131–32, 135, 143
  Seventh, 121–24
  Sixth, 131–32, 135, 143
  Tenth, 121–24, 121
communion. *See also* Holy Communion
Communion of Saints, 166, 255
Communion Rite of the Mass, 166, 246
compassion, 90
Concluding Rite of the Mass, 246
confession, 96, 255. *See also* Penance and Reconciliation, Sacrament of
confidences, 124
Confirmation, Sacrament of, 64, 67, 244, 255
conscience, 255. *See also* examination of conscience
consecration, 255
contemplation, 236. *See also* prayer
contrition, 96, 255
Corporal Works of Mercy, 107, 243, 255
Council of Jerusalem, 255
counsel, 193, 243, 255
courage, 188, 189
covenant, 255
covet, 255
creation, 256
Creator, 256
creed, 256. *See also* Apostles' Creed; Nicene Creed
crisis, 106
Crucifix, 177
Crucifixion, 13
culture, 256

D

Day, Dorothy, 78
deacon, 197, 199, 256
Dead Sea, 27
deadly sins. *See* capital sins
death
  Christian perspective on, 158, 159
  particular judgment following, 173
  views regarding, 158
detraction, 256
devil, 256
dignity
  human person, of the, 256
  work, of, 256
diocese, 256

symbols of, 218
   temptations, 45
   tested in the desert, 45
Jews, 33, 259
John, Saint, 25, 53
John Bosco, Saint, 154
John of Capistrano, Saint, 128
John the Evangelist, Saint, 210
John Leonardi, Saint, 202
John Paul II (Saint, Pope), 163
John the Baptist, 44
Jordan River, 27
Joseph, 259
Joyful Mysteries, 238
Juan Diego, Saint, 38, 42
Judaism, 33, 259
Judas Iscariot, 54, 172
Jude, Saint, 54
Judea, 27
Judith, 19
Julian of Norwich, 2
Julie Billiart, Saint, 112
justice, 150, 153, 243, 259
justification, 259

K

Keller, Helen, 187
king, 197
Kingdom of God, 49, 259
Kingdom of Heaven, 177
Knights of Columbus, 142
knowledge, 193, 243, 259
Koenig, Rosemary, 37

L

laity, 260
Lake Gennesareth, 27
Lamb of God, 166, 235. *See also* Jesus
Last Judgment, 174, 177, 260
Last Supper, 169, 260
Law, 260
Law, Jewish, 29
Lazarus, 13, 114, 157, 158, 180
Lectio divina, 75
Lectionary, 219, 260
Lent, 221-22, 260
Letters, 25
Levi, 53–54. *See also* Matthew, Saint
life
   gift of, 103
   respecting, 105–7
Light of the World, 75, 79, 85. *See also*
   Jesus
liturgical calendar, 214
liturgical year, 260
liturgy, 260

Liturgy of the Eucharist, 165, 169, 246,
   260. *See also* Eucharist, Sacrament
   of the; Mass
Liturgy of the Hours, 75, 260
Liturgy of the Word, 164, 169, 246, 260.
   See also Mass
Lord, 260
Lord's Day, 29, 260. *See also* Sabbath
Lord's Prayer, 17, 166, 236, 237, 246
Lucy, Saint, 10
Luke, Saint, 22, 25
Lumen Christi Award, 70
Luminous Mysteries, 238

M

magi, 35
Magisterium, 79, 260
Magnificat, 260
manna, 163
Maria Goretti, Saint, 144
Mark, Saint, 19, 25, 26
Marks of the Church, 260. *See also*
   apostolic; catholic; holy; one
marriage, 135. *See also* Matrimony,
   Sacrament of
   call for most people, 196
   created in heaven, 129
   friendship, importance of, 129
   preparing for, 130
Martha, 13, 14
Martin of Tours, Saint, 18
martyrs, 53, 260. *See also specific*
   martyrs
Mary, 260
   disciple, first, 56
   faith of, 37
   faithfulness, 56
   honoring, 38, 41
   Mother of God, 37, 41, 59
   Mother of the Church, 56, 59
   privileges of, 39
   Queen of Heaven, 38
Mary Magdalene, 13, 34
Mary, sister of Martha, p. 13, 14
Mass, 17, 260. *See also*
Matrimony, Sacrament of, 129, 135, 201,
   245, 260. *See also* marriage
   children, gift of, 196
   fidelity, 196
   vows, 196
Matthew, Saint, 25, 53–54
Matthias, Saint, 55
meditation, 232, 261. *See also* prayer
Mediterranean Sea, 27
meek, 114
Mendicant Order, 261
mercy. *See* Corporal Works of Mercy;
   Spiritual Works of Mercy
Messiah, 20, 261. *See also* Christ; Jesus

Jewish expectations vs. Christ's
   reality, 43
mezuzah, 29
miracles, 93, 261
   Cana wedding feast, 88
   definition, 87
   heals paralysis, 89
   Jesus', 87–88
   Lazarus rises, 157, 158
   storm, stills, 89
mission, 261
missionary, 261
modesty, 132, 243
monasticism, 261
moral choices, 261
moral law, 261
Morning Offering, 119
mortal sin, 173, 261. *See also* sin
Mother of God, 261. *See also* Mary
Mother of the Church, 56. *See also* Mary
Mount Hermon, 27
Muslim, 261
mystagogy, 63, 261
Mysteries of the Rosary, 238. *See also*
   specific Mysteries of the Rosary
mystery, 261
Mystery of Faith, 9, 169, 244
Mystical Body of Christ, 61, 189, 261

N

Nativity, the, 35, 41
natural law, 261
Nazareth, 27
New Commandment. *See*
   Commandment, New
New Evangelization, 9–10, 17–18, 25–26,
   33–34, 41–42, 49–50, 59–60,67–68,
   75–76, 85–86, 93–94, 101–2,
   111–12, 119–20, 127–28, 135–36,
   143–44,153–54, 161–62, 169–70,177–
   78, 185–86, 193–94, 201–2, 209–10
New Testament, 20, 22, 23, 25, 249–50,
   261
Newman, Cardinal, 114
Nicene Creed, 220, 262
Nicodemus, 148

O

obedience, 198, 262
Old Testament, 249–50, 262
one, 262. *See also* Marks of the Church
Ordinary Time, 262
ordination, 262
Original Sin, 46, 149, 262. *See also* sin
   results of, 87
Our Father, *See* Lord's Prayer
Our Lady of Guadalupe, 38

P

Palestine, 27
  daily life in time of Jesus, 30
  division of, 28
parable, 85
  definition, 262
  Good Samaritan, the, 104
  Hidden Treasure, the, 81
  Lost Coin, the, 96
  Lost Sheep, the, 81, 96
  Lost Son, the, 96
  Mustard Seed, the, 81, 91
  Net, the, 81
  Pearl of Great Price, the, 81
  Persistent friend, the, p. 81
  Pharisee and the Tax Collector, the, 81
  Rich Fool, the, 80
  Sower, the, 82
  Wedding Feast, the, 81
  Weeds, the, 81
  Yeast, the, 81
parish, 262
particular judgment, 173, 262
paschal candles, 161
Paschal Mystery, 5, 7, 9, 167, 262
Passover, 29, 262
Pater Noster, 235. *See also* Our Father
Paul, Saint, 68, 228
  1 Corinthians (writings on love), 150
  persecutor of early Church, 22, 68
Paul Miki, Saint, 162
peace, 115, 243
penance, 96, 153, 262
Penance and Reconciliation, Sacrament of, 262
  absolution, 96
  confession, 96
  contrition, 96
  forgiveness, 96, 244
  healing offered through, 95
  penance, 96
  preparing for, 248
Penitential Act, 262
Pentateuch, 262
Pentecost, 29, 193, 194, 227–228, 262
  feast of, 193
  significance of, 191
  transformation of the disciples, 187–188
perjury, 263
personal sin, 263. *See also* sin
Peter, Saint, 19, 22, 52, 55, 194
Peter Claver, Saint, 50
Pharisees, 28, 263
Philip, 28
Philip, Saint, 53
phylacteries, 29
piety, 193, 243, 263

Pilate, Pontius, 28, 172
Pius II, Pope, 128
poor people, 114, 119
pope, 59, 263
  successor of Peter, 55, 59
poverty, vow of religious life, 198, 263
prayer. *See also* prayers
  communion with God, 231
  definition, 263
  instructions for how to pray, 231–32
  preparing for, 232
  types of, 231–32
prayer of petition, 263
prayers. *See also* prayer
  Agnus Dei, 235
  Angelus, 253
  Apostles' Creed, 236, 253
  Ave Maria, 235
  Collect Prayer of the Common of Holy Men and Women, 216
  Eucharistic Prayers, 165–166
  Gloria Patri, 235
  Glory Be to the Father, 49, 235, 236, 237
  Hail, Holy Queen (*see* Hail, Holy Queen)
  Hail Mary (*see* Hail Mary)
  Holy, Holy (*see* Holy, Holy)
  Magnificat, 260
  Nicene Creed (*see* Nicene Creed)
  Our Father (*see* Our Father)
  Pater Noster, 235
  Rosary, 236–37
  Sanctus, 235
Precepts of the Church, 242, 263
Presentation, the, 35
pride, 263
priests
  call, 197
  definition, 263
  duties, 197
  mission, 199
priesthood, 263
Prince of Peace, 107. *See also* Jesus
prophets, 197, 263
Protestant Reformation, 263
prudence, 143, 150, 153, 243, 263
psalm, 263
purgatory, 173, 177, 263

R

racism, 107, 263
Rameses the Great, 4
rationalism, 263
RCIA. *See* Rite of Christian Initiation of Adults (RCIA)
real presence, 263

reconciliation, 101, 244, 263. *See also* Penance and Reconciliation, Sacrament of
Redeemer, 263
redemption, 263
reflection notebook, 14, 69, 175
religious life, 263
  vows, 198, 199
Resurrection, 5, 9, 185, 263
  empty tomb, 179
  risen Christ appears to disciples, 180, 181
  significance of, 183
Revelation, 5, 263
rite, 263
Rite of Christian Initiation of Adults (RCIA), 61–62, 65, 67, 264
Roman Missal, 165, 264
Rosary, 153, 236–37, 264. *See also* Mysteries of the Rosary

S

Sabbath, 29, 33, 264. *See also* Lord's Day
sacramentals, 181, 185, 264
sacraments, 264. *See also specific sacraments*
  grace offered through, 61
  healing, 99
  seven, 244-45
  signs Jesus is with us, 181, 185
Sacraments at the Service of Communion, 201, 212, 264
Sacraments of Healing, 101, 212, 264
Sacraments of Initiation, 62–64, 67, 211, 264
sacrifice, 264
Sacrifice of the Mass, 265. *See also* Mass
sacrilege, 265
Sadducees, 28
saints, 216, 265. *See also specific saints*
salvation, 265
salvation history, 265
Samaria, 27
sanctify, 265
sanctifying grace, 153, 265
Sanctus, 235
Sanhedrin, the, 28, 148, 172
Satan, 265
  power of evil, 46
  tempts Jesus in the desert, 45
Savior, 5, 265. *See also* Jesus
  personal, 6
scandal, 105, 265
schism, 265
scribes, 28
Scriptures, 15, 17, 85, 265. *See also* Bible; New Testament; Old Testament
  living Word, 22
  origin of, 19

Scripture Index

Art Credits

Page positions are abbreviated as follows: (t) top, (c) center, (b) bottom, (l) left, (r) right.

188(t) AgnusImages.com; (b) © iStockphoto.com/sebastianiov. 189 Phil Martin Photography. 190(bl) The Crosiers/Gene Plaisted, OSC; (br) 191 © iStockphoto.com/EdChambers. 192 Ralph Orlowski/Getty Images News/Getty Images. 194 The Crosiers/Gene Plaisted, OSC. 195 Franco Origlia/Getty Images News/Getty Images. 196(t) © iStockphoto.com/tarinoel; (b) © iStockphoto.com/video1. 197 Con Tanasiuk/Design Pics/Corbis. 198(b) © iStockphoto.com/MsSponge. 199 © marco iacobucci/Alamy. 200 The Crosiers/Gene Plaisted, OSC. 202 Courtesy of the Clerks Regular of the Mother of God. 205(l) © iStockphoto.com/JohnArcher; (r) The Bridgeman Art Library Ltd./Alamy. 207(t) Photos.com; (b) Carsten Koall/StringerGetty Images News/Getty Images. 210 The Crosiers/Gene Plaisted, OSC.

SACRAMENT CHART:

211 The Crosiers/Gene Plaisted, OSC; © iStockphoto.com/dem10; Phil Martin Photography; The Crosiers/Gene Plaisted, OSC; AgnusImages.com. 212 Elio Ciol/Corbis; Greg Kuepfer; Barbara Penoyar/Photodisc/Getty Images; © iStockphoto.com/duncan1890.

SPECIAL SEASONS AND LESSONS:

213(t) Siede Preis/Photodisc/Getty Images; (c) The Crosiers/Gene Plaisted, OSC; (bl) Stockbyte/Getty Images; (br) Photos.com. 214 Julie Lonneman/www.thespiritsource.com. 215(t) Phil Martin Photography; (bc) Leif Skoogfors/Corbis; (br) © Office Central de Lisieux. 216(b) Stockbyte/Getty Images. 217 Thomas Northcut/Photodisc/Getty Images; The Crosiers/Gene Plaisted, OSC. 218 (*Left to right, top to bottom*) Royalty-free image; The Crosiers/Gene Plaisted, OSC; Art Directors & TRIP/Alamy; The Crosiers/Gene Plaisted, OSC; Ablestock.com/Photos.com; C Squared Studios/Photodisc/Getty Images. The Crosiers/Gene Plaisted, OSC; Scala/Art Resource, NY; Royalty-free image; Royalty-free image; © iStockphoto.com/RainforestAustralia; © iStockphoto.com/Pixlmaker; Royalty-free image; © iStockphoto.com/philberndt; Royalty-free image; Jupiterimages; Photos.com; The Crosiers/Gene Plaisted, OSC. 219(t) Stockbyte/Getty Images; (b) © iStockphoto.com/Hogie. 220(t) Steve Skjold/Alamy; (c) Siede Preis/Photodisc/Getty Images. (b) The Crosiers/Gene Plaisted, OSC. 221(t) © iStockphoto.com/jrsower. 222(t) © iStockphoto.com/morrismedia; (b) Operation Rice Bowl, Catholic Relief Services. 224(t) © iStockphoto.com/akaplummer. 225(t) The

Crosiers/Gene Plaisted, OSC; (b) The Bridgeman Art Library Ltd./Alamy. 226(t) Steven Miric/Alamy; (b) Photos.com. 227(t) The Crosiers/Gene Plaisted, OSC; (b) The Crosiers/Gene Plaisted, OSC. 228(t) The Crosiers/Gene Plaisted, OSC; (b) © iStockphoto.com/mikdam.

WHAT CATHOLICS SHOULD KNOW:

229 © iStockphoto.com/abalcazar. 230(t) © iStockphoto.com/colevineyard; (b) Rob Melnychuk/Digital Vision/Getty Images. 231 Jack Hollingsworth/Photodisc/Getty Images. 235(b) The Crosiers/Gene Plaisted, OSC. 236 AgnusImages.com. 237 Greg Kuepfer. 238 Design Pics/Fotosearch. 240 From Fourteen Mosaic Stations of the Cross © Our Lady of the Angels Monastery Inc., Hanceville, Alabama. All Rights Reserved. 241(b) Digital Vision/Getty Images. 242 Stock Montage, Inc./Alamy. 243 © iStockphoto.com/Lightguard. 244 © iStockphoto.com/TerryHealy. 245 Bob Daemmrich/PhotoEdit. 247(t) © iStockphoto.com/hidesy. 248 Myrleen Pearson/PhotoEdit. 250(t) SuperStock/SuperStock. 251(t) The Crosiers/Gene Plaisted, OSC; (b) Jeff Greenberg/Alamy. 252 © iStockphoto.com/Nnehring.

LESSON PULLOUTS:

277(t) Stockbyte/Getty Images; (c) Design Pics/Fotosearch; (br) Bill Wood.
Map of Palestine: Bill Wood.
Making Sunday Special: (c) © iStockphoto.com/kreci.
Reconciliation Booklet, p. 3: Photos.com.
Reconciliation Booklet, p. 8: The Crosiers/Gene Plaisted, OSC.
Scripture Booklet Cover: Design Pics/Fotosearch.
Scripture Booklet, p. 11: Craft Alan King/Alamy.
Scripture Booklet, p. 2: Stockbyte/Getty Images.
Scripture Booklet, p. 10: © iStockphoto.com/Gordo25.
Scripture Booklet, p. 8: The Crosiers/Gene Plaisted, OSC.
Scripture Booklet, p. 5: (t) © iStockphoto.com/kalistenna.
Scripture Booklet, p. 7: © iStockphoto.com/winterling.

Loyola Press has made every effort to locate the copyright holders for the cited works used in this publication and to make full acknowledgment for their use. In the case of any omissions, the Publisher will be pleased to make suitable acknowledgments in future editions.

Lesson Pullouts

- **Map of Palestine**

- **Making Sunday Special**

- **Reconciliation Booklet**

- **Scripture Booklet**

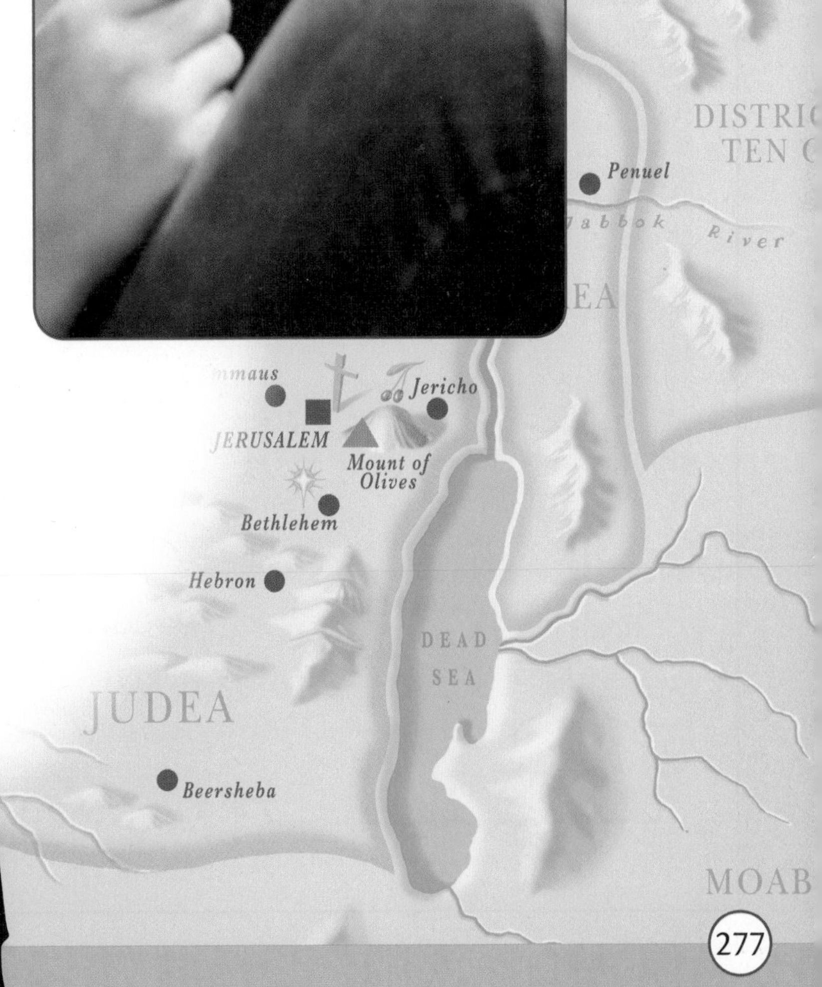

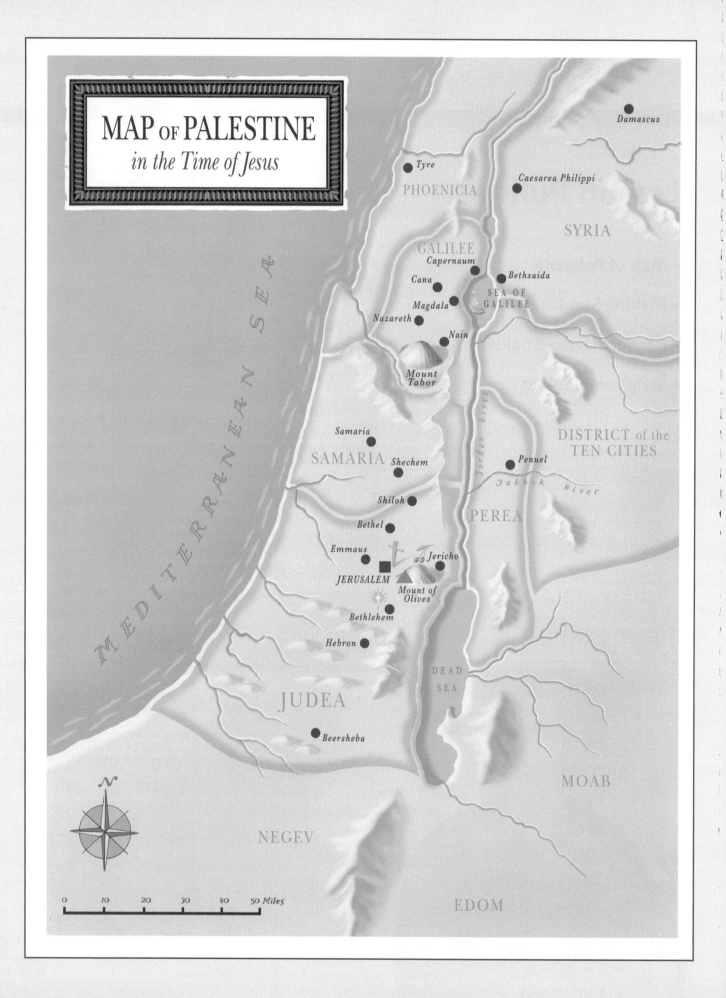

Making Sunday Special

My Family

> Place a photo of
> your family here.

My Family Activities on Sunday

Make a list of what your family does on a Sunday.

_____

_____

Family Activities

Make a list of five additional activities you want your family to do on a Sunday.

_Making Sunday special in the
_____ family,_

this year, :

1. _____

2. _____

3. _____

4. _____

5. _____

Our Family Prayer

Compose a prayer for your family, or choose one that your family will pray together.

_____

_____

_____

_____

_____

_____

My Family Promise

Make the following promise to help make Sunday special for your family.

I, _____, promise to make Sunday special for my family by

_____

_____

(Invite other members of your family to make the same promise.)

- Have I taken anything that is not mine? Have I returned things I borrowed? Have I damaged anything that belongs to someone else? Did I pay for or repair the damage?

- Have I been speaking the truth? Have I been kind in talking about other people? Have I guarded the good reputation of others?

- Am I willing to be friendly to everyone, or do I belong to a closed group of friends?

- Do I do what I can to help those who are poor? Have I omitted doing good things?

- Is anything else I did or did not do bothering me? Do I think that Jesus would be pleased with my behavior? Am I the person he is calling me to be?

Examine Your Conscience

The Lord says: "You shall love the Lord your God with your whole heart."

- Have I made other things more important than God? Am I paying attention to my relationship with God through prayer?

- Do I show respect for God's name and for all that is holy in my words and actions?

- Have I faithfully attended Mass on Sundays and holy days? Do I participate fully at Mass?

- Do I remember to thank God for his goodness to me?

How to Go to Confession

- Greet the priest.
- Make the Sign of the Cross.
- Listen as the priest prays.
- Read or listen to the Word of God (optional).
- Confess your sins. (Mention how long it has been since your last confession.)
- Speak about anything that is troubling you.
- Listen to the priest's advice.
- Accept your penance.
- Pray an Act of Contrition.
- Receive absolution, silently making the Sign of the Cross. Respond "Amen."
- Proclamation of praise and dismissal:
  Priest: Give thanks to the Lord for he is good.
  Response: His mercy endures forever.
- Say, "Thank you, Father."
- Spend some time in quiet reflection.
- Do your penance.

Reconciliation Booklet

Have mercy on me, God, in your goodness; in your abundant compassion blot out my offense.   PSALM 51:3

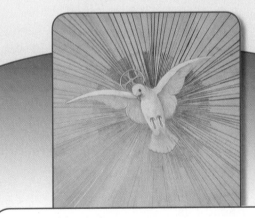

This booklet belongs to

The Lord says: "You shall love your neighbor as yourself."

- Have I shown respect for my parents or guardians and those who care for me?

- Do I keep the peace in my family or have I been causing conflict? Have I been doing my fair share of work around the house?

- Have I been a responsible student? Do I show respect for other students, for my teachers, and for others in authority?

- Am I taking care of my physical health? Have I hurt myself with the use of drugs or alcohol or risky behavior?

- Have I shown disrespect for the lives of others by hurting them, by using violence, by calling them names, by using unkind words, by making fun of others, or by putting them down?

- If I became angry or jealous, did I handle my feelings in a positive way?

- Have I shown respect for my body and the bodies of others? Have I spoken in such a way or viewed images that disrespect the human body?

- Do I respect the act of sex as a part of God's beautiful plan of life, which is to be protected by the love of married people? Am I open to learning God's plan for sex, or do I think it is all right to do whatever I feel like doing?

- Am I grateful for my possessions, or am I envious of others' possessions? Do I show respect for the possessions of others? Do I show respect for God's creation and for the earth's resources?

Prayer to the Holy Spirit

Breathe in me, O Holy Spirit,
That my thoughts may all be holy;
Act in me, O Holy Spirit,
That my work, too, may be holy;
Draw my heart, O Holy Spirit,
That I love but what is holy;
Strengthen me, O Holy Spirit,
To defend all that is holy;
Guard me, then, O Holy Spirit,
That I always may be holy.

St. Augustine

Read the Word of God

Be imitators of God, as beloved children, and live in love, as Christ loved us and handed himself over for us as a sacrificial offering to God for a fragrant aroma. (Ephesians 5:1–2)

Other Readings:
Matthew 9:9–13   Luke 15:11–32
Matthew 26:69–75   John 20:19–23

Pray an Act of Contrition

My God,
I am sorry for my sins with all my heart.
In choosing to do wrong
and failing to do good,
I have sinned against you
whom I should love above all things.
I firmly intend, with your help,
to do penance,
to sin no more,
and to avoid whatever leads me to sin.
Our Savior Jesus Christ
suffered and died for us.
In his name, my God, have mercy.

Plan for the Future

What is something I will do to follow Jesus more faithfully?

The Book of Revelation

Jesus continues to invite you to a deeper relationship with him. The Book of Revelation tells how God will triumph over any evil. Read the following sections thoughtfully. Write your prayer response in the space provided.

Reference	Prayer Response
Revelation 3:20	
Revelation 4:11	
Revelation 22:17	

COME, LORD JESUS!
Rev. 22:20

12

Scripture Booklet

This booklet belongs to

Acts of the Apostles

The Acts of the Apostles describes the first Christian communities. It has many stories about how the Church grew and spread. Read the passages below. Write a headline for each story that proclaims the wonders of the Lord.

Reference	Headline
Acts 3:1–10	
Acts 4:32–35	
Acts 9:1–19	
Acts 14:8–18	

Other sections to read:

Acts 1:15–26   Acts 12:1–19
Acts 4:1–12   Acts 16:16–34
Acts 9:32–43   Acts 22:1–21

God loves you and asks you to believe and to trust. God invites you to follow the way Jesus his Son has shown, the way to life.

It takes time to form deep friendships. If you want to come to know Jesus better, spend a few minutes with him each day reading, thinking, and praying with the Scriptures. Help yourself form the habit of using the Scriptures for prayer. Begin, starting today.

Before you begin your reading and praying of Scripture, place yourself in the presence of Jesus and pray:

> Jesus, I believe you are the Savior
> of the world.
> I praise and thank you for calling me
> to live in your love.
> Send your Spirit to enlighten my mind.
> Give me the strength I need to follow
> your way of love.
> I love you, Lord, above all things!

Then, follow these steps:

1. Select a brief passage from the Scriptures.
2. Read the passage slowly.
3. Pause and then read the passage again slowly and prayerfully.
4. If the passage describes a story or an event, use your imagination to place yourself within the scene.
5. Reflect on any words or phrases that jump out at you.
6. Pause in silence and let the Word of God speak to your heart.
7. Pray in your own words, thanking God for speaking to you and asking him for the grace to follow his Word.

Words for Life

Write God's message to you at the following times:

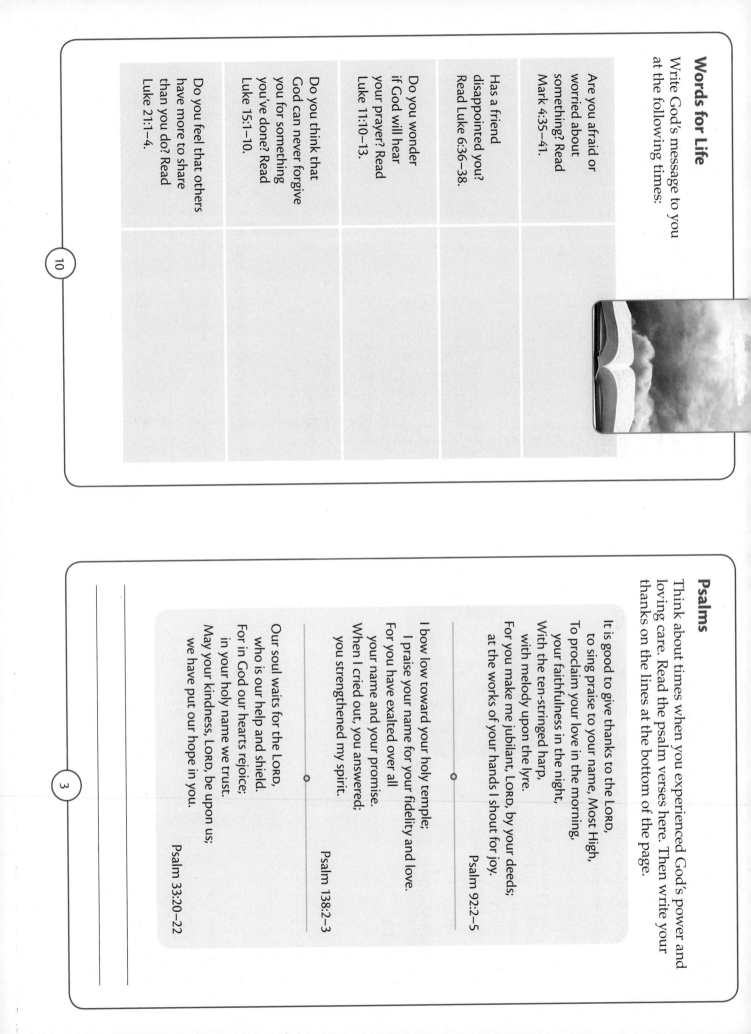

Are you afraid or worried about something? Read Mark 4:35–41.	
Has a friend disappointed you? Read Luke 6:36–38.	
Do you wonder if God will hear your prayer? Read Luke 11:10–13.	
Do you think that God can never forgive you for something you've done? Read Luke 15:1–10.	
Do you feel that others have more to share than you do? Read Luke 21:1–4.	

Psalms

Think about times when you experienced God's power and loving care. Read the psalm verses here. Then write your thanks on the lines at the bottom of the page.

It is good to give thanks to the LORD,
to sing praise to your name, Most High,
To proclaim your love in the morning,
your faithfulness in the night,
With the ten-stringed harp,
with melody upon the lyre.
For you make me jubilant, LORD, by your deeds;
at the works of your hands I shout for joy.

Psalm 92:2–5

I bow low toward your holy temple;
I praise your name for your fidelity and love.
For you have exalted over all
your name and your promise.
When I cried out, you answered;
you strengthened my spirit.

Psalm 138:2–3

Our soul waits for the LORD,
who is our help and shield.
For in God our hearts rejoice;
in your holy name we trust.
May your kindness, LORD, be upon us;
we have put our hope in you.

Psalm 33:20–22

Gospels

Read the following sections when you are in the situation described, and write your prayer response.

When you've hurt someone, read Matthew 5:23–24.	
When someone has hurt you, read Matthew 18:21–35.	
When you feel troubled or confused, read John 14:27.	
When you're in trouble, read Matthew 11:28–30.	
When you think of death, read John 11:21–26.	

Write your favorite Scripture text here:

Sayings of Jesus

Select a saying of Jesus from one of the Gospels. Read it slowly and prayerfully, conscious that Jesus is speaking to you. As you read, ask yourself:

- What is Jesus saying?
- What is he asking me to do?
- How can I respond to Jesus?

Then pray, thanking Jesus for his message. Tell him how you want to respond, what difficulties you see, and how you'd like him to help you.

Mark.

Scripture Saying	Your Prayer Response
John 6:37	
Luke 6:37	
Matthew 5:16	

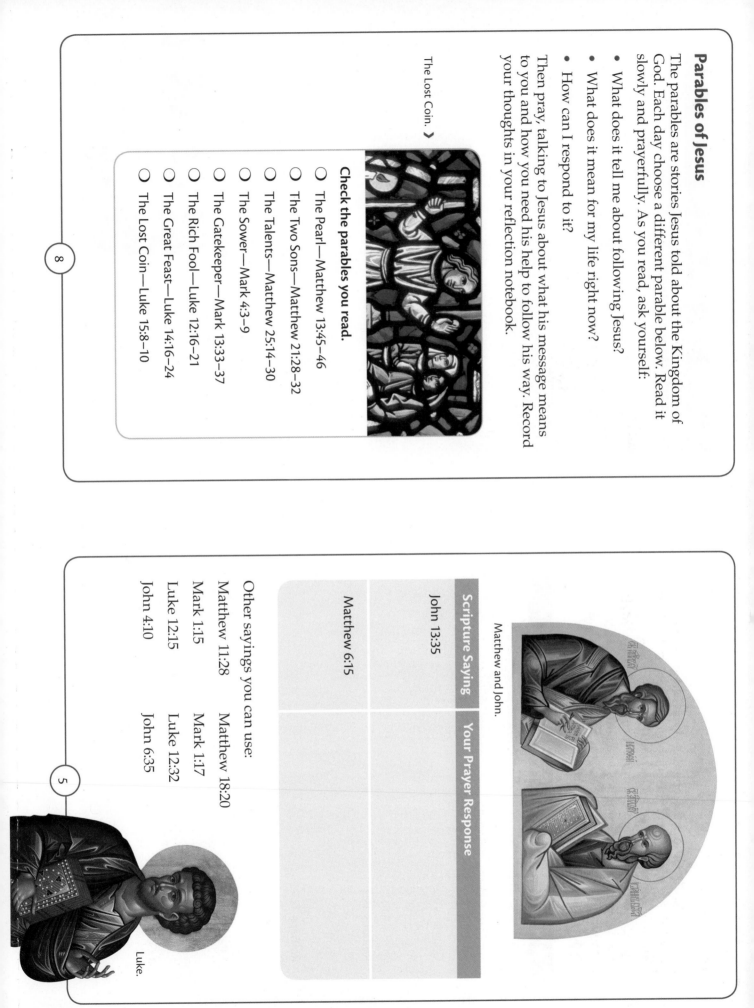

Parables of Jesus

The parables are stories Jesus told about the Kingdom of God. Each day choose a different parable below. Read it slowly and prayerfully. As you read, ask yourself:

- What does it tell me about following Jesus?
- What does it mean for my life right now?
- How can I respond to it?

Then pray, talking to Jesus about what his message means to you and how you need his help to follow his way. Record your thoughts in your reflection notebook.

The Lost Coin. ❯

Check the parables you read.

- ○ The Pearl—Matthew 13:45–46
- ○ The Two Sons—Matthew 21:28–32
- ○ The Talents—Matthew 25:14–30
- ○ The Sower—Mark 4:3–9
- ○ The Gatekeeper—Mark 13:33–37
- ○ The Rich Fool—Luke 12:16–21
- ○ The Great Feast—Luke 14:16–24
- ○ The Lost Coin—Luke 15:8–10

Matthew and John.

Scripture Saying	Your Prayer Response
John 13:35	
Matthew 6:15	

Other sayings you can use:

Matthew 11:28	Matthew 18:20	
Mark 1:15	Mark 1:17	
Luke 12:15	Luke 12:32	
John 4:10	John 6:35	

Luke.

The Letters

The Letters, also known as epistles, apply the message of Jesus to daily life. Each of the Scripture verses on the next two pages contains a maxim, or words to live by. As often as possible, read one verse of Scripture listed here, and think how the message applies to a situation in your life. Then write your maxim and ask the Lord to help you do it! Memorize and pray each day's maxim.

Reference	Maxim
Colossians 3:13	
Galatians 6:2	
Romans 15:2	
Romans 12:21	
1 Peter 2:1	
1 Corinthians 13:6	

Reference	Maxim
Romans 15:17	
2 Thessalonians 3:13	
James 4:8	
1 Peter 4:8	
1 Thessalonians 5:14	
1 Timothy 6:10	

Other Scripture passages to read:
1 Corinthians 6:20
1 Thessalonians 5:11
2 Timothy 3:12
James 4:17
1 Peter 5:7
1 John 4:16